This book belongs to

D. JORGENSON

The Jewish Word Book

The Jewish Word Book

Sidney J. Jacobs

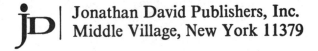 Jonathan David Publishers, Inc.
Middle Village, New York 11379

THE JEWISH
WORD BOOK

Jonathan David Publishers, Inc.
68-22 Eliot Avenue
Middle Village, New York 11379

This is a reprint edition distributed by Bookthrift, New York. Bookthrift is a registered trademark of Simon & Schuster, Inc.

ISBN 0-671-07538-1

Library of Congress Cataloging in Publication Data

Jacobs, Sidney J.
    The Jewish word book.

    1. Hebrew language—Dictionaries—English.
2. English language—Foreign terms and phrases—Hebrew.
3. Yiddish language—Dictionaries—English.   4. English
language—Foreign words and phrases—Yiddish.   I. Title.
PJ4833.J25   492.4'321   81-12641
                    AACR2

Printed in the United States of America

To
BETTY JANE LAZAROFF JACOBS,
who has enriched the vocabulary
of my life and my love

Preface

Jews have been more preoccupied from the inception of their identity with the flowing rhythm of prose and poesy and less with the "frozen" rhythm of form, line, and dimension. The classic evidence is the Hebrew Bible, more especially the Book of Psalms.

The words Jews have lived by have been, first, those of Hebrew, the tongue of sacred writ and liturgy and, later, the "mother tongue" of Yiddish among Ashkenazic (European) Jews and Ladino in Sephardic (Iberian) Jewry.

There is no "Jewish" language, no "Jewish" newspaper, no "Jewish" theater. There *is* a Jewish people, Jewish civilization, and culture; and when language and vocabulary are to be denoted, the proper adjectives are Hebrew, Yiddish, Ladino.

As a glossary of the vocabulary of Jewish living, *The Jewish Word Book* contains the most familiar articulations of these languages, more precisely Hebrew and Yiddish words, phrases, and idioms that the reader whose primary language is English has often heard but may not understand or be able to define with any degree of precision.

Because there are endless varieties of and distortions in pronunciation, we have attempted to list words and phrases in such a manner that they may be most easily tracked. The reader more familiar with variations and pronunciation eccentricities need only search a bit to trace the term he or she seeks.

* * *

Hebrew, the Semitic language of the Bible and post-biblical Mishna and Midrash, has remained the classic language of Jews throughout the centuries. It was the medium of discourse of the Jewish people until about 100 B.C.E., when it was supplanted as the language of daily use by Aramaic, which was originally brought to the Holy Land by the returnees from the Babylonian Exile.

Revived as a popular tongue with Jewish settlement in Palestine beginning in the last decade of the nineteenth century, Hebrew is the *lingua franca* of the State of Israel with its polyglot population.

Yiddish had its origins in the ninth century in the Rhine Valley, where it was known as *Ivri/Teutsch*, then *Juden/Teutsch*, and still later *Judisch*. From the thirteenth through the seventeenth centuries, it was extended into the kingdom of Poland-Lithuania, where it became the language of the Jewish masses.

Written in Hebrew characters, Yiddish is an amalgam of Hebrew, High German, and Slavic, plus an infusion of words adapted from the vocabulary of each country where it was commonly employed—for example, Polish, Lithuanian, and (from the 1880s) English.

Ladino, also variously called Judezmo, Spaniolish, Haketia, and Jidyo, is the Judeo-Spanish language spoken by Jewry of the Iberian peninsula and the Middle East. (Some scholars distinguish between Ladino as a "translation language" and Judezmo, the spoken language.)

Ladino became especially popular following the expulsion of Jews from Spain in 1492. It rests upon a Spanish linguistic base with the addition of Hebrew, Arabic, Greek, Turkish, French, Italian, and Portugese words, and with Turkish as the most influential.

* * *

The renaissance of the Hebrew language is a miracle of modern Jewish history. For centuries, the language was associated solely with sacred scripture, liturgy, and formal correspondence of primarily religious content.

Its revival began to take shape in the latter decades of the nineteenth century with the emergence both of the Haskalah movement of Jewish Enlightenment in its East European phase and of political and cultural Zionism. From the period of the earliest settlements of Jewish pioneers in the Land of Israel, it came into daily usage. Modernized, it has flourished as the dominant language of science, government, the arts and *belles-lettres* of the State of Israel.

Yiddish is the tongue that will not be silenced. Its obsequies have been legion in the contemporary era, especially since its nourishment in Eastern European Jewry was cut off in the Holocaust, which destroyed the millions and thus strangled their voices.

Nevertheless, Yiddish is living proof that pratfalls should not be confused with rigor mortis. True, the period which witnessed the zenith of Yiddish literature, theater, and press is past. However, four Yiddish theaters were playing simultaneously in New York City as late as the winter of 1980. The YIVO Institute for Yiddish Research reports that Yiddish is being taught in sixty-five institutions of higher learning (and accredited in thirty-five courses) in the United States and Canada as well as in universities in Bergen, Norway; Melbourne, Australia; Ule, Finland; Paris; Frankfurt; Jerusalem, Tel Aviv, and Haifa.

Amazing as is the refusal of this language to accept the funereal fate decreed for it by a legion of pundits, its osmotic effect on American English is only slightly less astounding. Examples proliferate of the infiltration of *mame lawshn* into the vocabulary of Americans of varying creeds and ethnic origins: *shlep, shlemil, oi vei, yentuh, mihsh-mash, chootzpuh (chutzpa), shmaltz, ganef, nash (nosh), nebihsh, gelt, shtihk, blihntz, tuhchuhs (tuches), megihluh (megilla), klawtz (klutz), kihbetz (kibbitz), l'chayihm, meivihn (mayven)*—as well as a host of vulgarisms.

Yiddish is rich in oaths and curses, a circumstance which the editor of *Maledicta: the International Journal of Verbal Aggression* attributes to historic anti-Semitism against which no physical, retaliatory relief was available.

My preference for an example of malediction, which has not lost its vividness over the forty-five years since I first read it, was splashed in a four-column headline in the *Chicago Yiddish Courier* (1887-1944) over a photograph of Nazi Field Marshal Herman Goering, head of Hitler's *Luftwaffe,* beaming at his wife as she held their newborn son.

Characteristic of the personal quality of Yiddish journalism, the headline read, *A Ruach Ihn Zain Taten Arain! Awmein!* ("May an Evil Wind Enter His Father! Amen!"). The concluding word was in keeping with the Yiddish wish, "From your mouth into God's ear!"

I am eternally grateful to the *melamuhd,* my private Hebrew tutor who, on his own initiative, introduced me to the Yiddish word more than a half-century ago. As I moved into adolescence and young adulthood, I heard the language used at meetings, conferences, and conventions of the Zionist movement, especially the Labor Zionists with whom I identified ideologically. *"Ains, tsvai, drai, fir; Poylei Tziyon zainen mir!"*

At one time reviled as the *jargon* of the Jewish masses of Eastern Europe, Yiddish has revealed a capacity for dimension and adaptation that never ceases to astonish: *yentuh* traces her roots to the sultry Spanish *Juanita,* possibly to the French *Gentille; bobe-maise* derives from *Buovo d'Antona,* the Italian version of *Sir Bevis of Hampton!*

In sum, Yiddish is a language of infinite variety. The late and sorely-missed folk humorist Sam Levenson used to compare the English paucity of "ugly . . . uglier . . . ugliest" with the rich Yiddish sequence of *mies . . . nihsht duh gedacht . . . chaluhshes* ("ugly . . . it shouldn't happen here . . . one may faint!").

I shudder when I consider how close I came as a child to the precipice of life without intimacy with Yiddish, once described by a West Coast theater critic as "that peculiar mixture of German and Hebrew designed to maximize the expression of pain and joy at once."

* * *

I am indebted to Rabbi Alfred J. Kolatch, editor-in-chief of Jonathan David Publishers, Inc., both for his suggestion which led to the writing of this book and for his invaluable counsel in the process of its compilation.

SIDNEY J. JACOBS

Culver City, CA
January 16, 1981

Erev Shabbat
12 Shevat 5741 (the 38th *Yahrtzeit* of my father)

How to Use
The Jewish Word Book

Most of the Yiddish and Hebrew words and phrases chosen for inclusion in this book can be "correctly" pronounced in more than one way (varying with local custom and usage). And over the years many different systems have been employed to transliterate these various pronunciations using English characters. All this has been taken into account when planning this book, and every effort has been made to render it as easy as possible for the reader to find the word or phrase in question.

All entries are listed alphabetically. The main entry is printed in boldface type, and is divided syllabically. This is followed by one or more alternate pronunciations, alternate spellings, and as many definitions as apply. The main entry represents the pronunciation of the word as it is most commonly heard. This is not necessarily the spelling most often used in the print media or the pronunciation and spelling as accepted by the scholarly community. The modern Israeli (Sephardic) pronunciation of a given term is indicated by an asterisk (*) placed after the term.

The transliteration system created for *The Jewish Word Book* is a combination of several of the most popular in current use. So that the reader does not have to continually refer to the front matter to recall the basic elements in the system, a complete Key to Transliteration appears at the bottom of each two-page spread of text.

The Jewish Word Book

Key to Transliteration / Pronunciation

a as in f*a*ther
aw as in l*aw*
ai as in *ai*sle
ei as in n*ei*ghbor
e as in b*e*t
i as in vacc*i*ne
ih as in t*i*n
o as in s*o*lar
oi as in v*oi*d
oo as in f*oo*d
u as in p*u*t
uh as in b*u*t
ch as in *ch*utzpa
zh as in *Zh*ivago

* (asterisk) after an entry indicates modern Israeli (Sephardic) pronunciation

A

Ab see *Av*

a-ba*

> Also *a-baw, a-buh.*
> Also spelled *abba.*
> Aramaic form of the Hebrew *av,* * meaning "father, dad."

Ab Beth Din see *Av Bet Dihn*

a-bi ge-zoont

> Also *a-bi ge-zunt.*
> So long as you are (one is) healthy, implying that nothing else matters, nothing else is important.

a-cha-ro-nihm*

> Also *ach-ro-nihm, ach-roi-nihm.*
> Also spelled *ahronim.*
> 1. Literally, "the latter ones," referring to post-talmudic rabbinic authorities in contrast with *rishonihm,* "earlier ones."
> 2. Occasionally refers to the Latter Prophets.

achraiyes see *achrayoot*

ach-rai-yoot*

> Also *ach-rai-us, ach-rai-yuhs, ach-rai-yes.*
> Also spelled *achrayut.*
> 1. Responsibility.
> 2. To assume responsibility.

achronihm see *acharonihm*

a-da-fi-na

> The Spanish-Judeo (Ladino) designation for *cholent.* See *cholent.*

a-da-ma*

> Also *a-du-muh, a-daw-muh.*
> Earth, ground. See also *erd.*

---

a as in father; aw as in law; ai as in aisle; ei as in neighbor; e as in bet; i as in vaccine; ih as in tin; o as in solar; oi as in void; oo as in food; u as in put; uh as in but; ch as in chutzpa; zh as in Zhivago.

a-dam ha-ri-shon*
Also *aw-dawm haw-ri-shon, aw-duhm huh-rishoin*
The first man (Adam) mentioned in the Book of Genesis.

A-dar*
Also *Oo-duhr.*
Twelfth and final month of the Jewish religious calendar, the sixth of the Civil calendar, corresponding to February-March. The Purim holiday occurs on the fourteenth of the month. When a leap year occurs in the Jewish calendar, an extra month is added to the year. This is called *Ve-Adar,* meaning "and Adar." The formal Hebrew designation for the First Adar is *Adar Rishon** and for the Second Adar, *Adar Sheini (Sheni*).*

Adar Rishon see *Adar*

Adar Sheini see *Adar*

adawmuh see *adama*

Ad-lo-ya-da*
Also *Ad-lo-yaw-da.*
A combination of three Hebrew words: *ad, d'lo, yada.* Literally, "until one cannot know (tell) the difference." The annual Purim carnival held in Tel Aviv and other cities in Israel. The name is derived from the talmudic dictum that on Purim one should imbibe until no longer able to distinguish between the words "blessed is Mordecai" and "cursed is Haman," that is, between the hero and villain of the biblical Book of Esther.

A-do-nai*
Also *A-do-noi.*
Also spelled *Adonei.*
1. Literally, "my Lord."
3. Commonly used in the Bible when referring to God.
2. Used as a substitute for the taboo name Yahweh (Jehovah), considered too sacred for commonplace use. Pronounced by traditional Jews

---

a as in father: **aw** as in law; **ai** as in aisle; **ei** as in neighbor; **e** as in bet; **i** as in vaccine; **ih** as in tin; **o** as in solar; **oi** as in void; **oo** as in food; **u** as in put; **uh** as in but; **ch** as in chutzpa; **zh** as in Zhivago.

only during prayer and with heads covered. *Adoshem* and *Hashem* are used as substitutes.

A-don O-lam*
Also *A-don O-lawm*.
1. Literally, "Lord of the universe."
2. The title and opening words of a popular hymn praising the unity and the providence of God and attributed to Solomon ibn Gabirol.

A-do-shem
A combination of two words, *Adonai* and *Hashem* (the Name), used as a substitute for *Adonai* in a nonsacred context. See *Adonai* and *Hashem*.

a-duh-ra-buh
Also *a-de-ra-ba,** *a-de-ra-be*.
Also spelled *aderabbuh*.
An Aramaic word occurring in the Talmud.
1. Not at all.
2. On the contrary.
3. In point of fact.
4. By all means. For special emphasis the word is repeated, as in the phrase *aduhrabuh v'aduhrabuh*, signifying "absolutely," "by all means," or "with the greatest of pleasure."

adumuh see *adama*

af al pi
1. Nevertheless.
2. Despite all.

a-fi-ko-man*
Also *a-fi-ko-muhn*.
Also spelled *afikomen, afikomon*.
From the Greek, meaning "dessert." A piece of *matza* set aside during the early part of the Passover *Seder* to be distributed and eaten at the end of the meal.

a-fi-loo
Also spelled *afilu*.
Even, even if.

---

a as in father; aw as in law; ai as in aisle; ei as in neighbor; e as in bet; i as in vaccine; ih as in tin; o as in solar; oi as in void; oo as in food; u as in put; uh as in but; ch as in chutzpa; zh as in Zhivago.

a-ga-da*
Also *a-gaw-duh.*
Also spelled *aggada.*
1. The narrative and homiletical portions of the Talmud and Midrash as contrasted with *halacha,* the legalistic portions.
2. A legend, tale, fable.

ag-mat ne-fesh*
Also *ag-mas ne-fesh; ag-muhs ne-fesh.*
Grief, sadness, depression.

agmuhs nefesh see *agmat nefesh*

a-goo-na*
Also *a-goo-nuh.*
Also spelled *aguna, agunah.*
From the Aramaic, meaning "tied." A woman uncertain of her husband's whereabouts who may not remarry because she was never divorced according to rabbinic law *(halacha).*

a guten Shabes see *gut Shabuhs*

a-ha!
The expletive "so!" signifying comprehension, surprise, delight, vindication, triumph.

a-hihn awdr a-her
Also spelled *ahin awder aher.*
1. Literally, "here or there."
2. Make up your mind!

aidelkeit see *eidlkait*

ai-er kihchl
Also *ei-er kihchl.*
Also spelled *aier kichel.*
Egg cookies.

ailt zihch
Also *hailt zihch.*
Also spelled *eilt zich.*
Hurry up! Rush!

ain-bren
A roux, a thickener for sauces and stews.

---

a as in father; aw as in law; ai as in aisle; ei as in neighbor; e as in bet; i as in vaccine; ih as in tin; o as in solar; oi as in void; oo as in food; u as in put; uh as in but; ch as in chutzpa; zh as in Zhivago.

ain-fal
Also spelled *einfahl.*
An idea.

ain-ge-fal-en
1. Literally, "fell in."
2. Duped.

ain-ge-machtz
Also spelled *eingemachts.*
Preserves, jam, jelly.

ain-ge-shpart
Also spelled *eingeshpart.*
Obstinate, stubborn, headstrong.

ain-ge-toonkn
Also spelled *aingetunken, eingetunken.*
Dipped in, dunked.

ain haw-re
Also *a-yihn haw-raw, a-yihn ha-ra.**
Also spelled *einhore.*
Literally, "evil eye."

ain-lauf
A soup mix made of egg plus potato or *matza* meal.

ain-red-e-nihsh
Also spelled *einredenish.*
1. Literally, "self-suggestion."
2. Delusion, misconception.
3. Fantasy.

ains, tsvai, drai, fir
Also *eins, tsvei, drai, fir.*
One, two three, four.

Ak-da-moot*
Also *Ak-du-mes, Ak-duh-mes.*
Also spelled *Akdamut.*
An Aramaic prayer recited on Shavuot praising the greatness of God and emphasizing the importance of Torah and the rewards of righteous living.

A-kei-duh
Also *A-kei-da.**
Also spelled *Akeda.*

---

a as in father; aw as in law; ai as in aisle: ei as in neighbor; e as in bet; i as in vaccine; ih as in tin; o as in solar; oi as in void; oo as in food; u as in put; uh as in but; ch as in chutzpa; zh as in Zhivago.

1. Literally, "the binding."
2. The name given to the biblical episode (Genesis 22) of Abraham's intended offering of his son Isaac as a sacrifice to God.

alaichem shoolem see *aleichem shalom*

a-lav ha-sha-lom see *awlawv hashawlom*

Al Cheit
Also spelled *Al Het, Al Chet.*
Literally, "for the sin of. . . ." A Yom Kippur penitential prayer.

alef see *aluhf*

alef baiz see *aluhf beis*

aleha hashalom see *awlehaw hashawlom*

a-lei-chem sha-lom*
Also *a-lai-chem shoo-lem, a-lei-chem shaw-lem.*
1. Literally, "Upon you be peace."
2. A response to the popular greeting *shalom aleichem,* "peace be unto you."

a-le mai-les huht zi
Also spelled *alle meiles hot zi.*
1. She has every good quality.
2. Refers to a woman who is a suitable mate because she possesses everything a man would want: character, beauty, intelligence, etc.

aleph see *aluhf*

aleph beis see *aluhf beis*

ale shoos-ters gei-en bawr-ves
1. Literally, "All shoemakers go barefoot."
2. Refers to a person who doesn't have things you would expect him or her to have.

alevai see *haluhvai*

Al Ha-ni-sihm*
Also spelled *Al Hanisim.*
1. Literally, "for the miracles."
2. The opening words and title of a hymn that is part of the liturgies of Chanukah and Purim, two holidays in which miracles occurred.

---

a as in father; aw as in law; ai as in aisle; ei as in neighbor; e as in bet; i as in vaccine; ih as in tin; o as in solar; oi as in void; oo as in food; u as in put; uh as in but; ch as in chutzpa; zh as in Zhivago.

a-li-ya*
> Also *a-li-yuh.*
> Also spelled *aliyah.*
> 1. Literally, "going up" or "ascending."
> 2. A Torah honor in which one is called to ascend to the reading table to recite the blessings over the Torah.
> 3. To "go up" to live in Israel, that is, to immigrate to Israel.

alle meiles hot zi see *ale mailes huht zi*

alman see *almuhn*

almana see *almuhne*

al-muhn
> Also *al-man.**
> Also spelled *almon.*
> A widower.

al-muhn-e
> Also *al-maw-naw, al-ma-na.**
> Also spelled *almoona, almoone.*
> A widow.

Al-pha Be-ta
> Psalms recited in Sephardic congregations on Saturday afternoons.

al-rait-nihk
> Also spelled *alrightnik, alritnik.*
> 1. An "all right" person, referring to a "greenhorn" who rapidly Americanized. A term popular among Jewish immigrants from Europe.
> 2. A boastful, ostentatious person; a nouveau riche, parvenu.

alte see *altuh*

alter see *altr*

al-tihsh-kuh
> A pet form of *alte.* See *altuh.*

altr
> Also spelled *alter.*
> Old man. *Altuh* is the feminine form.

---

a as in father; aw as in law; ai as in aisle; ei as in neighbor; e as in bet; i as in vaccine; ih as in tin; o as in solar; oi as in void; oo as in food; u as in put; uh as in but; ch as in chutzpa; zh as in Zhivago.

altr ba-kantr
Also spelled *alter bakanter.*
An old acquaintance.

altr bawchr
Also *al-ter buchr.*
1. Literally, "old boy."
2. A bachelor.

altr kakr
Also spelled *alter kaker.*
1. Literally, "old defecator."
2. Contentious, lecherous.
3. A harmless old man.
Often abbreviated "a.k."

altr truhm-buh-nihk
Also spelled *alter trombenihk.*
1. An old derelict.
2. A bum.

al-tuh
Also spelled *alte.*
1. Literally, "old one."
2. Old woman.

al-tuh buh-be
Also spelled *alte bobe, alte bube.*
1. Literally, "old grandmother."
2. Old woman.

al-tuh ma-cha-shei-fuh
Also spelled *alte machshayfeh.*
Old witch.

alt-varg
1. Old clothing.
2. Something stale, outdated.
3. A decrepit person.

altz ihz gut
1. Literally, "all is good."
2. Everything is fine.

altz vaws (ihz) ihn der kawrt
1. Literally, "all that is in the (dealing of a) card."
2. Every conceivable bad thing.

---

a as in father; aw as in law; ai as in aisle; ei as in neighbor; e as in bet; i as in vaccine; ih as in tin; o as in
solar; oi as in void; oo as in food; u as in put; uh as in but; ch as in chutzpa; zh as in Zhivago.

a-luhf
Also spelled *alef, aleph.*
First letter of the Hebrew and Yiddish alphabet. Its numerical value is one.

a-luhf beis
Also *a-lef bet.**
Also spelled *aleph bet, aleph beis, aleph bays, alef baiz.*
1. First two consonants of the Hebrew and Yiddish alphabet, therefore
2. Basis or beginning of anything.
3. The ABCs.
4. Cf. Greek *alpha beta* and English "alphabet."

am-cha*
Also *am-chu, am-chaw.*
1. Literally, "your (God's) people."
2. Average Jews.
3. The Jewish masses.

a-men*
Also *aw-mein.*
Also spelled *amain.*
1. Literally, "so be it."
2. A response to a prayer.
3. An acronym from the Hebrew words *Eil Melech Ne'eman,* meaning "the Lord is a trustworthy King."

am ha-a-retz*
Also *am haw-aw-retz.*
1. Literally, "people of the earth, land folk."
2. Farmers.
3. The uneducated.
4. The masses.

am ha-ra-tzut*
Also *am ha-ra-tzus.*
1. Ignorance.
2. Boorishness.

am ha-sei-fer
Also spelled *am hasefer.*
1. Literally, "people of the book."

---

a as in father; aw as in law; ai as in aisle el as in neighbor; e as in bet; i as in vaccine; ih as in tin; o as in solar; oi as in void; oo as in food; u as in put; uh as in but; ch as in chutzpa; zh as in Zhivago.

2. A designation for the Jewish people, attributed
to Muhammed, founder of Islam.

A-mi-da*
Also *A-mi-duh.*
1. Literally, "stand, standing."
2. A major prayer in the Jewish liturgy recited
three times each day in a standing position. Also
referred to as the *Tefila* ("prayer") and as the
Shmone Esrei ("eighteen," the number of benedictions it contains).

a-mood*
Also *aw-mood.*
Also spelled *amud.*
1. A synagogue pulpit.
2. A lectern.
3. One of the posts of the *sukka,* in the Sephardic
tradition.

a-mo-ra*
Also *a-mo-ruh.*
A title for Talmudic scholars of the third to sixth
centuries in the academies of learning in Palestine
and Babylonia.

a-mo-ra-ihm
Plural of *amora.* See *amora.*

a-nav*
Also *aw-nuhv.*
1. A humble person.
2. A poor person.

a nech-tih-ger tawg see *nechtiger tawg*

aninoos see *aninoot*

a-ni-noot*
Also *a-ni-noos, a-ni-nus.*
Also spelled *aninut.*
The period of mourning between the death and
burial of a relative.

a-ni-voot*
Also *a-ni-ves, a-ni-voos, a-ni-vus.*
Also spelled *anivut.**
Humility, modesty, meekness.

---

a as in father; aw as in law; ai as in aisle; ei as in neighbor; e as in bet; i as in vaccine; ih as in tin; o as in
solar; oi as in void; oo as in food; u as in put; uh as in but; ch as in chutzpa; zh as in Zhivago.

a-noo-sihm
Also spelled *anusim.*
1. Jews forced to covert to another religion, particularly in fifteenth-century Spain and Portugal.
2. Marranos.

ant-shool-dihk
Excuse (me) please!

ant-shool-dihk mihr
Also *ant-shool-dihkt mihr.*
Excuse me!

ant-shool-dihkn
Also spelled *antshuldiken.*
Pardon (me)! Excuse (me)!

an-uh-ve-nuh
Also *a nu-ve-ne.*
1. Literally, "a small sin." Diminutive of the Hebrew *avon.*
2. A mild exaggeration.
3. A minor offense.

apikawrsihm*
Also spelled *apikorsim.*
Plural of *apikores.* See *apikores.*

a-pi-ko-res
Also *a-pi-ko-ruhs.*
Also spelled *apikoros.*
Akin to the Greek-based word "epicurean."
1. A religious heretic.
2. A freethinker.
3. A skeptic.

a-rain
Also spelled *arein.*
1. In, into.
2. Enter. Used most often with *koom* ("come"), as in *koom (kum) arain,* "come in."

a-ra-va*
Also *a-raw-vuh.*
1. A willow.

---

a as in father; aw as in law; ai as in aisle; ei as in neighbor; e as in bet; i as in vaccine; ih as in tin; o as in solar; oi as in void; oo as in food; u as in put; uh as in but; ch as in chutzpa; zh as in Zhivago.

2. One of four species of plants used on the Sukkot festival.

a-ra-vot*

Also *a-raw-ves, a-ru-ves.*
Plural of *arava.* See *arava.*

arba kanfot see *arba kanfuhs*

ar-ba kan-fuhs

Also *ar-ba kan-fos, ar-ba kan-fot.**
Also spelled *arba kanfes.*
1. Literally, "four corners."
2. The fringes attached to the four corners of a garment or *talit* (prayer shawl).
3. A garment worn by Orthodox Jews under their shirts; fringes are attached to the four corners of the garment. Also called *talit katan,* "a small *talit.*"

ar-ba ko-sot*

Also *ar-ba ko-sos*
1. Literally, "four cups."
2. The four goblets of wine served at the Passover *Seder.*

ar-ba mi-nihm*

1. Literally, "four kinds."
2. The four species of plants used during the observance of the Sukkot festival: the palm branch, the citron, willow branches, and myrtle branches.

ar-buhs

Also spelled *arbes.*
Peas.

a-rihbr chapn di maws

Also spelled *ariber chapen di maws.*
To overdo, carry to excess.

arn

To matter, to be of concern. Generally used in the third person, *"art,"* as in *es art mihr vi di vant,* "it bothers me (as little) as the wall," that is, "I don't care a bit."

---

a as in father; aw as in law; ai as in aisle; ei as in neighbor; e as in bet; i as in vaccine; ih as in tin; o as in solar; oi as in void; oo as in food; u as in put; uh as in but; ch as in chutzpa; zh as in Zhivago.

a-rois
> Out! Get out!

a-rois ge-fawr-en
> Also *a-rois ge-foor-en.*
> Travelled away, left.

a-rois ge vawr-fen
> Literally, "thrown out."

a-rois ge-vawr-fe-ne gelt
> 1. Literally, "thrown-out money."
> 2. Wasted expenditure.

a-rois ge-vawr-fe-ne yawr-en
> Also spelled *arois gevorfeneh yoren.*
> 1. Literally, "wasted years."
> 2. Wasted time.

a-ron*
> Also *aw-ron.*
> 1. A chest, a box.
> 2. A coffin.
> 3. A short form of *aron hakodesh.* See below.

A-ron Ha-ko-desh*
> 1. Literally, "Holy Ark."
> 2. A cabinet that houses the Torah scrolls in a synagogue.

art see *arn*

art mihch vi di vant
> 1. Literally, "it bothers me as (little as) the wall."
> 2. I don't care a bit.

a-rum
> Around.

a-rum guh-val-guhrt
> Also spelled *aroom gevalgert.*
> Wandered around, loafed.

a-rum loifr
> 1. A street urchin.
> 2. A runaround.
> 3. A philanderer.

aruves see *aravot*

---

a as in father; aw as in law; ai as in aisle· ei as in neighbor; e as in bet; i as in vaccine; ih as in tin; o as in solar; oi as in void; oo as in food; u as in put; uh as in but; ch as in chutzpa; zh as in Zhivago.

ar-viht*
Also *ar-vihs.*
1. Evening.
2. Evening prayers, vespers. Also referred to as *tefilat arviht.**

A-sa-ra b'Tei-veit*
Also *A-saw-raw b'Tei-veis.*
Also spelled *Asara b'Tevet.*
1. The tenth day of the Hebrew month Tevet, a fast day.
2. Anniversary of the start of the siege of Jerusalem in the sixth century B.C.E.

A-se-ret Ha-dihb-rot*
Also *A-se-res Ha-dihb-ros.*
1. Literally, "the ten statements."
2. The Ten Commandments, the Decalogue.

A-se-ret Y'mei T'shoo-va*
Also *A-se-res Y'mei T'shoo-vaw.*
Also spelled *Aseret Yemei Teshuvah.*
1. Literally, "Ten Days of Penitence."
2. The ten-day period in the Jewish calendar beginning with Rosh Hoshana and ending with Yom Kippur.

ashir see *awshir*

Ash-ke-na-zi
1. Literally, "German."
2. A Jew of East European extraction, originally from Germany, in contradistinction to a Sephardi, a Jew of West European extraction, principally from Spain or Portugal. *Ashkenazim* is the plural form. *Ashkenazic* is the adjectival form.

Ashkenazim see *Ashkenazi*

Av
Also spelled *Ab.*
The fifth month of the Jewish religious calendar, corresponding to July-August.

---

a as in father; aw as in law; ai as in aisle; ei as in neighbor; e as in bet; i as in vaccine; ih as in tin; o as in solar; oi as in void; oo as in food; u as in put; uh as in but; ch as in chutzpa; zh as in Zhivago.

Av Bet Dihn*
Also spelled *Av Bet Din, Ab Beth Din.*
1. Vice-president of the *Sanhedrin* in Second Temple days.
2. Chief rabbi of an ecclesiastical court.

av-dut*
Also *av-duhs, av-dus.*
Slavery, enslavement.

aveilus see *aveilut*

a-vei-lut*
Also *a-vei-loos, a-vei-lus, a-vei-luhs.*
Also spelled *aveloot, avelut.*
1. Mourning.
2. A period of mourning.
3. The act of mourning.

a-vei-ra*
Also *a-vei-raw, a-vei-ruh.*
Also spelled *avera.*
1. A sin, a transgression.
2. A pity, in the sense of a waste.
Often mispronounced *"naveira,"* from the two words "an *aveira."*

(an) a-vei-ruh daws gelt
1. Literally, "a sin for the money."
2. A waste of money.

a-vek
Away, as in *gei avek,* meaning "go away."

a-vek fihr-en ihn bawd a-rain
1. Literally, "to lead one into the bathhouse."
2. To lead astray, deceive, dupe.

a-vel*
Also *aw-veil, oovl.*
A mourner, after the funeral.

avelus see *aveilut*

avelut see *aveilut*

avera see *aveira*

a-vihv*
Also *aw-vihv*

---

a as in father; **aw** as in law; **ai** as in aisle; **ei** as in neighbor; **e** as in bet; **i** as in vaccine; **ih** as in tin; **o** as in solar; **oi** as in void; **oo** as in food; **u** as in put; **uh** as in but; **ch** as in chutzpa; **zh** as in Zhivago.

Also spelled *aviv*.
1. Spring.
2. Springtime.

aviv see *avihv*

av-la*
Also *av-luh*.
1. A sin.
2. A crime.
3. A wrong, injustice, injury, grievance.

a-vo-da*
Also *a-vo-daw*.
1. Work.
2. Worship.
3. The main service performed in the Holy of Holies by the High Priest on the Day of Atonement.

a-vo-da za-ra*
Also *a-vo-daw zaw-raw*.
1. Literally, "strange, foreign worship."
2. Idolatry.

Av-ra-ham a-vi-noo*
Also *Av-raw-hawm aw-vi-noo*.
Also spelled *Avraham avinu*.
Literally, "Abraham, our father," referring to the biblical patriarch.

awch un vei
Also spelled *och oon vai*.
1. Alas and alack!
2. Tough luck! Too bad!

awdawm hawrishon see *adam harishon*

aw-duhm na-kuht
Also spelled *odem-naket*.
1. Literally, "as naked as Adam."
2. Stark naked.

awlawv hashawlom see *awluhv hashawluhm*

aw-le-haw ha-shaw-lom
Also *a-le-ha ha-sha-lom*.*
The feminine form of *awlawv hashawlom*.
1. Literally, "Peace be upon her."

---

2. May she rest in peace.

aw-luhv ha-shaw-luhm
Also *aw-lawv ha-shaw-luhm, a-lav ha-sha-lom.**
Also spelled *olav hasholem.*
1. Literally, "Peace be upon him."
2. May he rest in peace.

awmein see *amen*

awmood see *amood*

awn-ge-blaw-zen
Also spelled *ongeblozen.*
1. Literally, "blown up, inflated."
2. Conceited.
3. Peevish, sulky, pouting.

awn-ge-blaw-zen-er man
A conceited man.

awn-ge-patsh-ket
Also spelled *ongepatshket.*
1. Overdone, overdecorated.
2. Cluttered, littered.
3. Disordered, sloppy.

awn-ge-shtawpt
Also spelled *ongeshtopt.*
1. Stuffed, packed.
2. Overeaten, bloated.

awn-ge-shtawpt miht gelt
Also spelled *ongeshtopt mit gelt.*
1. Literally, "stuffed with money."
2. Very wealthy.

awn-ge-vawrfn
Also spelled *ongevorfen.*
Cluttered, disordered.

awn-shihk-uh-nihsh
Also spelled *onshikenish.*
1. A hanger-on.
2. A pest, nuisance.

awp-ge-flihkt
Also spelled *opgeflikt.*

---

a as in father; aw as in law; ai as in aisle; ei as in neighbor; e as in bet; i as in vaccine; ih as in tin; o as in solar; oi as in void; oo as in food; u as in put; uh as in but; ch as in chutzpa; zh as in Zhivago.

1. Literally, "plucked, defeathered."
2. Done in, suckered, taken.

awp-ge-hiht
Also spelled *opgehit.*
Careful, guarded.

awp-ge-hihtn
Also spelled *opgehiten.*
1. Careful, cautious.
2. Pious, observant of the commandments.

awp-ge-kraw-chen-e s'choiruh
Also spelled *opgekrochene s'choireh.*
1. Shoddy merchandise.
2. Wornout merchandise.

awp-ge-krawchn
Also spelled *opgekrochen.*
Shoddy, rotten.

awp-ge-lawzn
Also spelled *opgelozen.*
1. Careless, negligent.
2. Shabby.
3. Slipshod.

awp-ge-nart
Also spelled *opgenart.*
Cheated, fooled.

awp-hihtn
Also spelled *ophiten.*
1. To watch out for, guard against.
2. To take care of, keep.

awp-nar-en zihch
Also spelled *opnaren zich.*
1. Literally, "to fool oneself, to kid oneself."
2. To be disappointed.

awnuhv see *anav*

awn-zaltzn
Also spelled *onzaltzen.*
1. Literally, "to salt."
2. To bribe.
3. To sweet-talk, snow-job.

---

a as in father: aw as in law; ai as in aisle; ei as in neighbor; e as in bet; i as in vaccine; ih as in tin; o as in solar; oi as in void; oo as in food; u as in put; uh as in but; ch as in chutzpa; zh as in Zhivago.

awp-nar-er
   Also spelled *opnarer.*
   1. Trickster.
   2. Shady operator.

awp-tshepn
   Also spelled *optshepen.*
   To get rid of, shake off.

aw-rem
   Also spelled *orem.*
   Poor.

aw-re-man
   Also spelled *oreman.*
   Poor man.

aw-rem-kait
   Also spelled *oremkeit.*
   Poverty.

aw-rem-uh-lait
   Also spelled *oremeleit, oremalit.*
   Poor people. Plural of *awreman.*

awron see *aron*

aw-shir
   Also *a-shir.**
   1. A wealthy person.
   2. Wealth, riches.

awveil see *avel*

aw-vent
   Also spelled *ovent.*
   1. Evening.
   2. Night.

awvihv see *avihv*

Aw-vi-noo Mal-kei-noo
   Also *A-vi-noo Mal-kei-noo.**
   Also spelled *Avinu Malkenu.*
   1. Literally "our Father, our King."
   2. A popular prayer in the High Holiday liturgy.

aydem see *eidm*

---

a as in father; aw as in law; ai as in aisle; ei as in neighbor; e as in bet; i as in vaccine; ih as in tin; o as in solar; oi as in void; oo as in food; u as in put; uh as in but; ch as in chutzpa; zh as in Zhivago.

a-yihn
> Also spelled *ayin.*
> Sixteenth letter of the Hebrew alphabet; an un-sounded letter with a numerical value of seventy.

ayihn hara see *ain hawre*

az awch un vei
> Also spelled *az och oon vai.*
> 1. Alas and alack!
> 2. Tough luck! Too bad!

az a yawr oif mir
> 1. Literally, "May I have such a year."
> 2. I swear it!
> 3. May I have no luck if what I say is not true!

a-za-zel*
> Also *a-zaw-zeil.*
> 1. The evil spirit thought to live in the wilderness of Judea, to which the scapegoat was sent during the Temple ceremonies on the Day of Atonement.
> 2. Hell.

az drai zawgn m'shu-guh, darf der fer-ter zawgn "bihm bam"
> 1. Literally, "When three say something crazy, the fourth must go along by uttering a nonsensical phrase (like *bihm bam*)."
> 2. Majority rules.

az es klingt, iz mihs-ta-muh choo-ge
> 1. Literally, "When there is a ringing (of bells), it's probably a festival."
> 2. Where there's smoke, there's fire.

a-zes paw-nihm see *azoot panim*

Az-ha-rot*
> 1. Literally, "warnings."
> 2. Special prayers for Shavuot in the Sephardic liturgy.

a-zoi
> 1. So really!
> 2. Is that so?

---

a as in father; aw as in law; ai as in aisle; ei as in neighbor; e as in bet; i as in vaccine; ih as in tin; o as in solar; oi as in void; oo as in food; u as in put; uh as in but; ch as in chutzpa; zh as in Zhivago.

3. So!
4. That's how it is!

a-zoi geit es
So it goes; that's the way things are.

a-zoi gihch?
So soon? So fast?

a-zoi ret men tzoo a tatn?
Is that how you talk to your father?

a-zoi vert daws kihchl tze-brawchn
That's how the cookie crumbles.

a-zoi zawgst doo!
1. That's what you say!
2. Really! You don't say!

a-zoot pa-nim*
Also *a-zoos pawnim, a-zes paw-nihm.*
Also spelled *azut panim.*
An impudent, insolent person.

B

ba-al*
Also *bal*.
1. Master, owner.
2. Husband.

ba-al a-ga-la*
Also *ba-al a-goo-luh, ba-al a-gaw-law*.
Also spelled *balagoleh*.
1. A teamster, a wagon driver.
2. Occasionally, an uncouth person.
3. An ignoramus.

ba-al ga-a-va*
Also *bal gai-vuh*.
1. A haughty or arrogant person.
2. A showoff, braggart.

ba-al ha-ba-yiht*
Also *ba-al ha-ba-yihs*.
Also spelled *baal habayit*.
1. Literally, "master of the house."
2. The owner, landlord.
3. The male head of the household.
4. A male employer.

ba-al ko-rei*
Also spelled baal *koray*.
A Torah reader in the synagogue.

ba-al m'law-chaw
Also *ba-al m'la-cha,* ba-al me-luh-chuh*.
Also spelled *bal maluchah*.
1. A laborer, a workman.
2. A craftsman.

ba-al moo-sawf
Also *ba-al moo-saf.**
Also spelled *bal musaf*.
One who leads the second half of the Sabbath and
holiday synagogue services.

---

a as in father; aw as in law; al as in aisle; ei as in neighbor; e as in bet; i as in vaccine; ih as in tin; o as in
solar; oi as in void; oo as in food; u as in put; uh as in but; ch as in chutzpa; zh as in Zhivago.

ba-al shach-riht*
Also *ba-al shach-rihs, ba-al sha-cha-rihs, ba-al sha-cha-rit.**
Also spelled *bal shachrit.*
One who leads the first half of the Sabbath or holiday synagogue services.

Ba-al Shem Tov*
Literally, "master of the good name," referring to Israel ben Eliezer, eighteenth-century founder of the Chasidic movement.

ba-al sihm-chaw
Also *ba-al sihm-cha*, ba-al sihm-chuh.*
Also spelled *bal simcha.*
1. A celebrant at a festivity.
2. An honoree.

ba-al t'fi-la*
Also *bal t'fi-luh, ba-al t'fi-law.*
Also spelled *baal tefillah.*
One who leads a group in prayer.

ba-al To-raw
Also *ba-al To-ra.**
Also spelled *bal Torah.*
1. Literally, "master of Torah," the equivalent of *ben Tora.*
2. A scholar.
3. A student.

ba-al t'shoo-vuh
Also *ba-al t'shoo-va.**
Also spelled *bal t'shuva.*
A returnee to the practice of Judaism.

ba-al tz'da-ka*
Also *ba-al tz'daw-kaw.*
Also spelled *bal tzedaka, baal tsedakah.*
A philanthropist, charitable person.

bab-kuh
Also spelled *bobke.*
A sweet cake, a coffeecake.

ba-choor*
Also *baw-choor.*

---

a as in father; aw as in law; ai as in aisle· ei as in neighbor; e as in bet; i as in vaccine; ih as in tin; o as in solar; oi as in void; oo as in food; u as in put; uh as in but; ch as in chutzpa; zh as in Zhivago.

Also spelled *bachur.*
1. A young man.
2. A *yeshiva* student.
3. An unmarried man.

badchan see *badchn*

bad-chaw-nihm
Also *bad-cha-nihm.**
Also spelled *badchanim.*
Plural of *badchn.* See below.

badchn
Also *bad-chan,** *bad-chawn.*
Also spelled *badchen.*
1. A professional jester or entertainer.
2. A master of ceremonies at Jewish weddings in Eastern Europe from the Middle Ages to modern times.

ba-dekn
Also spelled *badeken.*
1. Literally, "to cover."
2. Covering the bride with a veil before the wedding ceremony.

ba-geg-nen
Also *ba-geig-nen.*
To meet, to encounter.

bagel see *beigl*

ba-grawbn
Also *ba-groobn.*
1. To bury.
2. Buried, interred.

bailik see *beilihk*

bai mir bihst doo shein
Also spelled *bai mir bist du shayn.*
1. Literally, "to me you are beautiful."
2. The name of a popular Yiddish/English song of the 1930s.

bai mir poilst doo
It's agreeable to me; its O.K. with me.

bain in haltz see *bein ihn haltz*

---

bais see *bet*

baitza see *beitza*

ba-kakt
1. Literally, "dirtied with feces."
2. All fouled up.

ba-kan-te
Also *ba-kan-tuh*.
An acquaintance.

ba-ka-sha*
Also *ba-koo-shuh*.
1. A supplication, plea, request.
2. A petitionary prayer that is part of the Sephardic High Holiday liturgy.

ba-kvem
Convenient, handy, comfortable.

bal see *baal*

bal-a-ba-tihsh
Also spelled *balebatish*.
Respectable, refined, well-mannered, decent.

bal-a-ba-tih-she Yihdn
1. Respectable Jews.
2. Sometimes, Jews of means.

balagoleh see *baal agala*

balebatihm see *balebaws*

balebatish see *balabatihsh*

bal-e-baws
Also *bal-e-boos*.
Also spelled *balebos*.
Derived from the Hebrew *baal habayiht*.*
1. Literally, "head of the household, master of the house."
2. A landlord.
3. A male employer.
Balebawstuh (baleboostuh) is the feminine form.
Balebatihm is the plural form.

balebooste see *balebaws*

baleboste see *balebaws*

---

a as in father; aw as in law; ai as in aisle; ei as in neighbor; e as in bet; i as in vaccine; ih as in tin; o as in solar; oi as in void; oo as in food; u as in put; uh as in but; ch as in chutzpa; zh as in Zhivago.

bal gaivuh see *baal gaava*
bal maluchah see *baal m'lawchaw*
bal musaf see *baal moosawf*
bal shachrit see *baal shachriht*
bal simcha see *baal sihmchaw*
bal t'filuh see *baal t'fila*
bal Torah see *baal Toraw*
bal tzedaka see *baal tz'daka*
ban-diht
    1. A bandit.
    2. A mischievous child, a rascal.
bang
    1. Pain.
    2. Sorrow.
bang tun
    Regret, be sorry.
ban-kuhs
    Also spelled *bankes, bankis.*
    1. Cupping, in which a cup or glass was used (by
       doctors and also by barbers) in order to draw
       blood to the surface, presumably for remedial
       purposes.
    2. A useless activity, as in the expression, *es vet
       helfen vi a toiten bankuhs,* meaning "it will help
       as much as treating a dead man with *bankuhs*
       (cupping)."
bar
    1. The Aramaic word for the Hebrew *ben,* meaning
       "son."
    2. A contraction of *ben reb,* meaning "son of
       Mr. ———."
bar-a-ban
    A drum.
bar-chuhs
    Also spelled *barches.*
    The German word for *challa,* a Sabbath bread.

---

a as in father; aw as in law; ai as in aisle; ei as in neighbor; e as in bet; i as in vaccine; ih as in tin; o as in
solar; oi as in void; oo as in food; u as in put; uh as in but; ch as in chutzpa; zh as in Zhivago.

ba-redn
Also spelled *vareden;*
1. Gossip.
2. Backbiting.

barg
A mountain.

ba-rihmr
A braggart, a showoff.

Bar Mihtz-va*
Also *Bar Mihtz-vuh, Bar Mihtz-vaw.*
Also spelled *Bar Mitzva, Bar Mitzvah.*
1. Literally, "son of the commandment," referring to a Jewish boy, aged 13, who is obligated to assume his place as an adult member of the Jewish religious community.
2. Name of the ritual induction ceremony of a boy who has attained religious maturity, usually at age 13.

Bar Mitzvah see *Bar Mihtzva*

ba-ruch*
Also *baw-ruch.*
Also spelled *barukh.*
1. Blessed.
2. Praised.

ba-ruch Da-yan E-met*
Also *baw-ruch La-yan T-mes;*
Literally, "blessed is the true Judge (God)," an expression uttered upon hearing of a death. Also pronounced by the immediate family during the service at the funeral parlor or at the graveside.

ba-ruch Ha-Sheim
Also *ba-ruch Ha-Shem,* * *baw-ruch Ha-Shem.*
1. Literally, "blessed is the Name (God)"
2. Thank God!

ba-ruch she-p'ta-ra-ni*
Also *baw-ruch she-p'taw-ra-ni.*
Literally, "blessed is He who freed me of my obligation," a prayer recited by the father of a Bar Mitzvah.

a as in father; aw as in law; ai as in aisle ei as in neighbor; e as in bet; i as in vaccine; ih as in tin; o as in solar; oi as in void; oo as in food; u as in put; uh as in but; ch as in chutzpa; zh as in Zhivago.

barukh see *baruch*

ba-shert
> Preordained, fated, inevitable.

Bas Mihtzva see *Bat Mihtzva*

batlan* see *batln*

bat-lawn-ihm Plural of *batlan*. See above.

batln
> Also *bat-lan*, *bat-lawn*.
> 1. A lazy person, a loafer, a good-for-nothing.
> 2. An alms-seeker in a synagogue.

Bat Mihtz-va*
> Also *Bas Mihtz-va, Bas Mihtz-vuh.*
> Also spelled *Bat Mitzva, Bat Mitzvah.*
> 1. Literally, "daughter of the commandment," the female equivalent of *Bar Mihtzva.*
> 2. The ceremony inducting girls into the Jewish fold.

ba-va
> Literally, "a gate" in Aramaic.

ba-vaibt
> Also spelled *baveibt.*
> A married man.

baw-be see *buhbuh*

bawchoor see *bachoor*

bawd
> Also *buhd.*
> Also spelled *bod.*
> 1. A bath.
> 2. A bathhouse.

bawrd
> Also spelled *bord.*
> A beard.

baw-re-kes
> Also spelled *borekes.*
> Cheese-filled pastries popular among Sephardic Jews.

---

a as in father; aw as in law; ai as in aisle; ei as in neighbor; e as in bet; i as in vaccine; ih as in tin: o as in solar; oi as in void; oo as in food; u as in put; uh as in but; ch as in chutzpa; zh as in Zhivago.

bawrsht
Also spelled *borscht, borsht.*
A variety of soups, usually sweet-sour, the most popular of which are made of beets, cabbage, or spinach.

Bawrsht Belt
Also spelled *Borsht Belt.*
Name given to the Catskill Mountain area in New York State, where hotels cater to a preponderantly Jewish clientele and where many Jewish comedians got their start.

bawruch see *baruch*

bawruch Dayan Emes see *baruch Dayan Emet*

bawruch Ha-shem see *baruch Ha-Sheim*

bawruch shep'tawrani see *baruch shep'tarani*

bawr-vuhs
Also *boor-ves.*
Barefoot.

ba-yiht*
Also *ba-yihs.*
Also spelled *bayit, bayis.*
A house, home.

bayis see *bayiht*

baylick see *beilihk*

bays see *bet*

bays chayim see *bet chayihm*

bays din see *bet dihn*

ba-zuchn
1. To visit.
2. To investigate.

b'chor*
Also spelled *bechor.*
Eldest male child in a family.

b'di-kat cha-metz*
Also *b'di-kas cha-meitz.*
Also spelled *bedikat chametz.*

a as in father; aw as in law; ai as in aisle: ei as in neighbor; e as in bet; i as in vaccine; ih as in tin; o as in solar; oi as in void; oo as in food; u as in put; uh as in but; ch as in chutzpa; zh as in Zhivago.

1. Literally, "searching for the leavened bread."
2. A ceremony held prior to Passover.

B.C.E.
Abbreviation for Before Common Era, used by Jews instead of B.C., "Before Christ." See also C.E.

behema see *b'heima*

beigl
Also spelled *bagel.*
A hard-crusted roll shaped like a doughnut.

bei-lihk
Also *bei-lihg.*
Also spelled *bailik, baylick.*
The white meat of a fowl, usually of a chicken.

bein ihn haltz
Also spelled *bain in haltz.*
1. Literally, "a bone in the throat."
2. An obstruction, a nuisance.

beis see *bet*

beis chayihm see *bet chayihm*

beis din see *bet dihn*

beis hakneses see *bet hakneset*

beis hamedruhsh see *bet hamihdrash*

beis hamihkdawsh see *bet hamihkdash*

beis hatefilaw see *bet hat'fila*

beis medruhsh see *bet hamihdrash*

beis olawm see *bet olam*

bei-tza*
Also *bei-tzaw.*
Also spelled *baitza.*
1. An egg.
2. The name of one of the sixty-three tractates of the Talmud.

beiz
Angry.

bei-zuh cha-yuh
Also spelled *beize chaye.*

---

a as in father; aw as in law; ai as in aisle; ei as in neighbor; e as in bet; i as in vaccine; ih as in tin; o as in solar; oi as in void; oo as in food; u as in put; uh as in but; ch as in chutzpa; zh as in Zhivago.

1. Literally, "angry animal."
2. An angry person.
3. A disagreeable person.

beli naider see *b'li neidr*

ben
1. Son, son of.
2. Used to denote age, as in *ben chamishihm shana,* "50 years of age" (literally, "a son of 50 years").
3. Used to designate affiliation or status, as a person being a *ben Tora.*
Bar is the Aramaic form of *ben.*

ben To-ra*
Also *ben To-raw.*
Also spelled *ben Torah.*
Literally, "son of the Torah," a student of the Bible and Talmud. Synonymous with *baal Tora.*

bentshn
Also spelled *bentshen.*
1. To bless.
2. To pronounce a benediction.
3. Grace After Meals. Often Anglicized as *"bentshing."*

bentshn lihcht
Also spelled *bentshen licht.*
Literally, "blessing the lights," pronouncing a prayer over the candles to usher in Sabbaths and holidays. Also referred to as *lihcht bentshn.*

beracha levatala* see *b'racha l'vatala*

ber-ches
A *chala,* a Sabbath bread.

bereshit see *b'reishiht*

bergl
A small mountain, a hill. A diminutive form of *barg.*

berit see *briht*

ber-yuh
Also spelled *berya.*

---

a as in father; aw as in law; ai as in aisle· ei as in neighbor; e as in bet; i as in vaccine; ih as in tin; o as in solar; oi as in void; oo as in food; u as in put; uh as in but; ch as in chutzpa; zh as in Zhivago.

1. A Yiddish form of the Hebrew *b'ria,* meaning "creature."
2. An efficient, skillful, competent homemaker.

bes medruhsh see *beis medruhsh*

beser see *besr*

besomim see *b'samihm*

besomim biksl see *b'sawmihm biksl*

besr
Also spelled *beser.*
Better.

bet*
Also *beis.*
Also spelled *bais, bays.*
The second letter of the Hebrew alphabet, having the numerical value of two.

bet cha-yihm*
Also *beis cha-yihm.*
Also spelled *bays chayim.*
1. Literally, "house of life."
2. A euphemism for "cemetery."

bet dihn*
Also *beis dihn.*
Also spelled *bays din, beis din, beth din.*
1. Literally, "house of judgment."
2. A court.

bet-guh-vant
Bedding.

bet ha-knes-et*
Also *beis haknes-es.*
1. Literally, "house of assembly."
2. A synagogue.

bet ha-mihd-rash*
Also *beis ha-med-ruhsh, beis ha-mihd-rawsh, beis med-ruhsh.*
Also spelled *bet hamidrash.*
1. Literally, "house of study."
2. A study room, often in the synagogue.
3. A teachers' institute.

---

a as in father; aw as in law; ai as in aisle; ei as in neighbor; e as in bet; i as in vaccine; ih as in tin; o as in solar; oi as in void; oo as in food; u as in put; uh as in but; ch as in chutzpa; zh as in Zhivago.

bet ha-mihk-dash*
Also *beis ha-mihk-dash, beis ha-mihk-dawsh.*
Also spelled *bet hamikdash, beis hamikdash.*
The Holy Temple, referring to the First and Second
Temples in Jerusalem. The First Temple was de-
stroyed in 586 B.C.E. by the Babylonians; the Sec-
ond Temple was destroyed in 70 C.E. by the
Romans.

bet ha-t'fila*
Also *beis ha-te-fi-law.*
Also spelled *bet hatefila, beth hatefila.*
1. Literally, "house of prayer."
2. A synagogue.

beth din see *bet dihn*

bet o-lam*
Also *beis o-lawm.*
1. Literally, "eternal house."
2. A euphemism for "cemetery."

betoola see *b'toola*

betula see *b'toola*

b'ez-rat Ha-shem*
Also *b'ez-ras ha-Shem.*
Literally, "with God's help."

B.H
An abbreviation for *b'ezrat Ha-Shem,* often used
by traditional Jews on legal documents and on
personal or business stationery.

b'hei-ma*
Also *b'hei-maw.*
Also spelled *behema.*
1. A beast.
2. A head of cattle.
3. An uncouth human being.
4. A fool.

bi-a*
Also *bi-aw.*
Sexual intercourse.

bialy see *b'yali*

---

a as in father; aw as in law; ai as in aisle; ei as in neighbor; e as in bet; i as in vaccine; ih as in tin; o as in
solar; oi as in void; oo as in food; u as in put; uh as in but; ch as in chutzpa; zh as in Zhivago.

bih-d'eved
Literally, "after the fact." See also *lechatchilaw.*

bihl-bul
Also spelled *bilbul.*
1. A mixup.
2. Libel.

bihl-bul ha-dam*
Blood libel.

bih-lihg
Also *bih-lihk.*
Also spelled *bilig.*
Cheap, inexpensive.

bih-lihg vi borsht
Also spelled *bilig vi borscht.*
1. Literally, "as cheap as beet soup."
2. Very cheap.

bihmuh see *bima*

bihntl
Also spelled *bintl, bintel.*
A bundle, a batch. See also *bihntl brif.*

bihntl brif
Also spelled *bintel brief.*
1. A pack of letters.
2. The name of a column that appeared in the Yiddish newspaper *Forverts,* in which letters from readers were answered.

bihrkas Ko-ha-nihm see *birkat Kohanihm*

Bihr-kat Ei-roo-sihn*
Also *Bir-kas Ei-roo-sihn.*
Also spelled *Birkat Erusin.*
Betrothal blessings recited during the marriage ceremony.

Bihr-kat Ha-go-meil*
Also *Bir-kas Ha-go-meil.*
Also spelled *Birkat Hagomel.*
Literally, "Prayer of Thanksgiving," recited after recovery from a severe illness or accident or upon the safe return from a journey.

---

a as in father; aw as in law; ai as in aisle; ei as in neighbor; e as in bet; i as in vaccine; ih as in tin; o as in solar; oi as in void; oo as in food; u as in put; uh as in but; ch as in chutzpa; zh as in Zhivago.

Bihr-kat Ha-ma-zon*
Also *Bir-kas Ha-maw-zon.*
Also spelled *Birkat Hamazon.*
Grace After Meals.

Bihr-kat Ko-ha-nihm*
Also *Bir-kas Ko-ha-nihm.*
Also spelled *Birkat Kohanim.*
Priestly blessings uttered in Temple times and later incorporated into the prayerbook.

bihsl
Also spelled *bisl, bisel.*
1. Little bit.
2. Small amount.

bihs-lech-vaiz
A little bit at a time; little by little.
Also expressed as *tzoobihslach.*

bihst m'shu-guh?
Also spelled *bist meshuga?*
Are you crazy?

bihst oif ein fus?
1. Literally, "Are you (standing) on one foot?"
2. What's your hurry?

bih-te-re ge-lechtr
Also spelled *bittere gelechter.*
1. Literally, "bitter laughter."
2. Laughter through tears.

bih-tuh
Also spelled *bitte.*
1. Please.
2. Excuse me.

bihz hun-dert und tzvan-tzihg
Literally, "until one hundred and twenty (years)," said after mentioning a person's age and expressing the hope that one will live a long life.

bi-koor cho-lihm*
Also *bi-kur choi-lihm*
Also spelled *bikur cholim.*

---

a as in father; aw as in law; ai as in aisle; ei as in neighbor; e as in bet; i as in vaccine; ih as in tin; o as in solar; oi as in void; oo as in food; u as in put; uh as in but; ch as in chutzpa; zh as in Zhivago.

1. Literally, "visiting the sick."
2. An organization whose members visit the sick.

bi-koo-rihm
Also spelled *bikurim, bikkurim.*
First fruits brought to the Temple in Jerusalem in Bible times.

bilbul see *bihlbul*
bilig see *bihligh*
bilig vi borscht see *bihlihg vi borsht*
BILU
1. An acronym for the biblical verse, *Beit Yaakov l'choo v'neilcha,* "O House of Jacob, come and let us go" (Isaiah 2:5).
2. The name of a movement organized in 1882 for agricultural settlement and pioneering in Palestine.

bi-ma*
Also *bih-muh, bi-maw.*
Also spelled *bimah.*
1. A platform, a stage.
2. In a synagogue, the pulpit from which services are conducted.

bintel see *bihntl*
bintel brief see *bihntl brif*
Birkas Hamawzon see *Bihrkat Hamazon*
Birkat Erusin see *Bihrkat Eiroosihn*
Birkat Hagomel see *Bihrkat Hagomeil*
Birkat Kohanim see *Bihrkat Kohanihm*
bisel see *bihsl*
bisl see *bihsl*
bist meshuga see *bihst m'shuguh*
bi-taw-chon*
Also *bi-ta-chon.*
1. Hope, faith.
2. Truth.

bitte see *bihtuh*

bittere gelechter see *bihtere gelechtr*

blat
>A sheet (of paper), a page. See also *bletl.*

blech
>1. Tin.
>2. A sheet of tin kept on the stove to keep food warm on the Sabbath.

bletl
>Also spelled *bletel.*
>1. A page, a sheet (a diminutive form of *blat*).
>2. The fine dough wrapping for blintzes or crepes.

blet-lach
>Plural of *blat* and *bletl.* See *blat* and *bletl.*

blihntz
>Also *blihntz-e.*
>Also spelled *blintz, blintzeh.*
>A crepe filled with cheese, potato, or fruit and then baked or fried. *Blihntzes (blintzes)* is the plural form.

b'li neidr
>Also *b'li nedr.**
>Also spelled *beli naider.*
>Without taking a vow. A person makes a promise but excludes it from the category of a vow.

blintz see *blihntz*

blintzes see *blihntz*

blo
>Also *bloi.*
>Blue.

bloom
>Also *bloo-me.*
>Also spelled *blum.*
>A flower.

bloot
>Also spelled *blut.*
>Blood.

blote see *bluhte*

---

a as in father; aw as in law; ai as in aisle· ei as in neighbor; e as in bet; i as in vaccine; ih as in tin; o as in solar; oi as in void; oo ar in food; u as in put; uh as in but; ch as in chutzpa; zh as in Zhivago.

bluhn-jen
>Also spelled *blunjn.*
>1. To ramble, wander.
>2. To be mixed up in one's thinking, as in *ferblunjen.* See *ferblunjen.*

bluhte
>Also spelled *blote.*
>1. Mud, filth.
>2. A mess.

bluhz-en foon zihch
>Also *bluzn fun zihch.*
>1. Literally, "to blow oneself up."
>2. To be haughty.

bluhzn
>Also *bluz-en.*
>Also spelled *bluhzen.*
>1. To blow
>2. To be angry.

blum see *bloom*

blunjn see *bluhnjen*

blut see *bloot*

B'nai B'rith see *B'nei B'rith*
>Preferred spelling by the international organization.

B'nai Yisrael see *B'nei Israel*

B'nei B'rith
>Also *B'nei Brihs, B'nei Briht.**
>*Also spelled B'nai Brith, B'nai Bris, B'nai Brit.*
>1. Literally, "sons of the covenant."
>2. An international Jewish fraternal organization founded in New York in 1843.

B'nei Is-ra-el
>Also *B'nei Yihs-ra-eil, B'nei Yihs-ra-el.**
>Also spelled *B'nai Israel, B'nai Yisrael.*
>1. Literally, "Children of Israel."
>2. The sons of the biblical Jacob, whose offspring became known as the "Children of Israel," also called the "tribes of Israel."

3. The Jewish community in India, sometimes known as "the brown Jews of India."

B'not Is-ra-el
Also *B'nos Yihs-ra-eil, B'not Yihs-ra-el.**
Also spelled *B'not Yisrael, B'nos Yisrael.*
Literally, "Daughters of Israel." Plural of *Bat Mitzva.*

Bo-az
1. Literally, "with strength, strong."
2. Ruth's second husband (Ruth 2:1).
3. The name of one of the two pillars that held up the Temple in Jerusalem (the other was Jachin).

bobe see **buhbuh**

bobe meise see *buhbe maise*

Bobe Yachne see *Bube Yachne*

bobke see *babke* and *buhbkuh*

bobkes see *buhbkes*

bod see *bawd*

boich
Belly, abdomen.

boich vei-tihk
Also *boich vei-tihg.*
Also spelled *boich vaytik.*
Stomachache.

boi-dem
An attic.

boikr see *boker*

boi-tsihk
Also spelled *boitchik.*
A little boy. A Yiddishized diminutive form of "boy."

bo-ker*
Also *boikr.*
Morning.

bo-ker tov*
"Good morning," a greeting.

bokser see *buhkser*

boobe see *buhbuh*

bool-be
Also spelled *bulba, bulbe.*
Potato.

bool-ka-lach
Also spelled *bulkalach.*
Little rolls. Plural of *boolke.*

bool-ke
Also spelled *bulke, bulken.*
A roll.

bool-van
Also spelled *bulvan.*
A rude person, a boor.

boor-e-kes
Also *bur-e-kes, bur-e-kus.*
Beets.

boortsh
1. Complain.
2. Protest.
See also *boortshn.*

boortshn
Also spelled *boortchen, burtchen.*
To grumble, mutter, complain.

boorves see *bawrvuhs*

boosha see *busha*

bord see *bawrd*

borekes see *bawrekes*

borscht see *bawrsht*

Borsht Belt see *Bawrsht Belt*

borves see *bawrves*

bra-cha*
Also *braw-chaw.*
Also spelled *beracha, berakha.*
A blessing, a benediction.

---

bra-cha l'va-ta-la*
  Also *b'raw-chaw l'va-taw-law*.
  Also spelled *beracha levatala*.
  A wasted blessing, an unnecessary blessing.

branfn
  Also *brawnfn*.
  Also spelled *branfen, bronfen*.
  Whiskey, liquor.

brav
  Brave, bold.

(a) brawch
  Also spelled *(a) broch*.
  1. A break, a fracture.
  2. A curse, equivalent to "hell!" or "damn!"

brawchaw see *beracha*

brawchaw l'vatawlaw see *bracha l'vatala*

(a) braw-chaw oif dain kuhp
  1. Literally, "(a) blessing on your head."
  2. God bless you.

(a) brawch tzoo mihr
  Also spelled *(a) broch tzu mir*.
  1. Literally, "a curse to me."
  2. Woe is me!

brawnfn see *branfn*

brech a foos
  Also *brech a fus*.
  Break a foot (leg)!

brechn
  Also spelled *brechen*.
  1. Break.
  2. Vomit.

breingn
  Also spelled *breingen, brengen*.
  To bring, fetch. See also *(a) farbrengung*.

brei-ra*
  Also *brei-raw, brei-ruh*.
  A choice, option, alternative.

---

a as in father; aw as in law; ai as in aisle; ei as in neighbor; e as in bet; i as in vaccine; ih as in tin; o as in solar; oi as in void; oo as in food; u as in put; uh as in but; ch as in chutzpa; zh as in Zhivago.

(a) brei-ruh hawb ihch?
> Do I have a choice?

brei-shiht*
> Also *b'rei-shihs.*
> Also spelled *bereshit.*
> 1. Literally, "in the beginning."
> 2. The first word in the Bible.
> 3. The name of the first *sidra* (section) and of the first book (Genesis) of the Bible.

brei-ter vi lein-ger
> 1. Literally, "wider than longer."
> 2. A fat person.
> 3. A big smile.

bren
> Burn.

(a) bren
> 1. Literally, "a burn."
> 2. An energetic person, one always on the go.

bren-en
> 1. Burn (fire).
> 2. Heartburn.

brengen see *breingn*

brent
> Past tense of *brenen,* as in *es brent a fire,* "a fire is raging," or *es brent mihr oonteren hartzen,* "I have heartburn." See also *brenen.*

brief see *brif*

brif
> Also spelled *brief.*
> A letter.

brihs see *briht*

Brihs Milaw see *Briht Mila*

brihst see *broost*

briht*
> Also *brihs.*
> Also spelled *brit, bris, berit.*
> 1. Covenant.
> 2. Abbreviated form of *Briht Mila.* See *Briht Mila.*

---

a as in father; aw as in law; ai as in aisle; ei as in neighbor; e as in bet; i as in vaccine; ih as in tin; o as in solar; oi as in void; oo as in food; u as in put; uh as in but; ch as in chutzpa; zh as in Zhivago.

Briht Mila*
>Also *Brihs Milaw.*
>Also spelled *Brit Mila.*
>1. Literally, "covenant of circumcision."
>2. A ritual circumcision performed on the eighth day after the birth of a Jewish boy in which the child becomes a part of the Jewish people.

bris see *briht*

brit see *briht*

broch see *brawch*

(a) broch tzu mir see *(a) brawch tzoo mihr*

broi-ges
>1. Angry.
>2. Sullen.
>3. Insulted, offended.

broin
>Brown.

broit
>Bread.

broit-ge-ber
>1. Literally, "breadgiver."
>2. Breadwinner.
>3. Head of the family.

bronfen see *brawnfn*

broodr
>Also *bru-der. Brider* is the plural form.
>1. Brother.
>2. Buddy.

broost
>Also *brihst.*
>Also spelled *brust.*
>1. Breast.
>2. Breast of beef.

broost dekl
>Also spelled *brust dekel.*
>Breast of beef, brisket.

bruder see *broodr*

---

a as in father; aw as in law; ai as in aisle· ei as in neighbor; e as in bet; I as in vaccine; ih as in tin; o as in solar; oi as in void; oo as in food; u as in put; uh as in but; ch as in chutzpa; zh as in Zhivago.

brust see *broost*

brust dekel see *broost dekl*

b'sa-mihm*
Also *b'saw-mihm*.
Also spelled *besomim, besamim*.
Spices, usually those placed in the spicebox used at the *Havdala* ceremony on Saturday night.

b'saw-mihm biksl
Also spelled *besomim biksl*.
Spicebox.

b'sula see *b'toola*

b'too-la*
Also *b'soo-law*.
Also spelled *betula, b'sula, betoola*.
1. A young woman.
2. A girl.
3. A virgin, a maiden.

bub see *buhb*

bubbe see *buhbuh*

bu-be-le
A term of endearment.

bubke see *buhbke*

buch
A book.

buhb
Also *bub*.
A bean. See also *buhbkuh*.

buh-be mai-se
Also *bu-be mai-se*.
Also spelled *bobe meise*.
1. Literally, "a grandmother's story."
2. An old wives' tale.

Buh-be Yach-ne
Also spelled *Bobe Yachne, Bube Yachne*.
The name of a witch in a play by Abraham Gold-faden (1840-1908), father of the Yiddish theater. See *Yachne*.

buhb-kes
Also spelled *bubkes, bobkes.*
Plural of *buhbkuh.*
1. Beans.
2. Something worthless, a trifle.

buhb-kuh
Also spelled *bubke, bobke.*
A bean. See also *buhb.*

buh-buh
Also *baw-be, buh-be, boo-be.*
Also spelled *bobe, bube, bubbe.*
1. Grandmother.
2. Old lady.

buhd see *bawd*

buhksr see *bukser*

buhm-er-ke
Also spelled *bummerkeh.*
1. An evil woman.
2. A prostitute.

buk-ser
Also spelled *bokser.*
Carob, St. John's bread.

bulba see *boolbe*

bulkalach see *boolkalach*

bulkeh see *boolke*

bulvan see *boolvan*

bummerkeh see *buhmerke*

burekes see *boorekes*

burtchen see *boortshn*

burtsh see *boortsh*

bu-sha*
Also *boo-sha, bu-shuh, bu-shaw.*
Shame, disgrace.

b'va-ka-sha*
Also *b'va-kaw-shaw.*
Please; if you please.

---

a as in father; aw as in law; ai as in aisle; ei as in neighbor; e as in bet; i as in vaccine; ih as in tin; o as in solar; oi as in void; oo as in food; u as in put; uh as in but; ch as in chutzpa; zh as in Zhivago.

b'ya-li

Also *bi-a-li.*
Also spelled *bialy.*
A flat hard roll.

C

Cabbalah see *Kabala*

caftan* see *kaftan*

canary
> A popular Anglicized form of *kein ayin hara.*

campote see *kampot*

C.E.
> Abbreviation for Common Era. Used by Jews instead of the Latin A.D., *Anno Domini,* "in the year of the Lord." See also B.C.E.

Cha-bad
> 1. An acronym formed from the initials of *cha-chma* (wisdom), *bina* (understanding), and *dei'a* or *daat* (knowledge).
> 2. A chasidic sect founded in Russia by Shneour Zalman of Ladi (Liady).

chacham see *chawchm*

chag
> Also spelled *hag.*
> A holiday.

chai
> 1. Literally, "life."
> 2. A charm worn on a neckchain, consisting of the two Hebrew letters *chet* and *yad,* considered by some to bring good luck.

chala see *chaluh*

chalav Yisrael see *chawlawv Yihsrawel*

chale see *chaluh*

cha-lef*
> Also *cha-luhf.*
> 1. A knife used by a *shochet* (ritual slaughterer).
> 2. A butcher knife.

---

a as in father; aw as in law; ai as in aisle: ei as in neighbor; e as in bet; i as in vaccine; ih as in tin; o as in solar; oi as in void; oo as in food; u as in put; uh as in but; ch as in chutzpa; zh as in Zhivago.

cha-ler-yuh
Also *cha-ler-ye.*
Also spelled *cholera, cholerya.*
1. Literally, "cholera," a plague.
2. A curse.

(a) cha-ler-yuh zawl dihr chapn
Also spelled *a chalerye zol dir chapen.*
1. May you be struck by cholera!
2. May the plague get you!

chalesh see *chaluhsh*

cha-li-la*
Also *chaw-li-law.*
Also spelled *cholileh.*
God forbid!

chalila v'chas see *chawlilaw v'chas*

cha-li-tzuh
Also *cha-li-tza,* cha-li-tzaw.*
Also spelled *halitza* and *halitzah.*
A religious ceremony by which an unmarried brother is freed from the biblical obligation of marrying his brother's childless widow. The procedure is detailed in Deuteronomy 25:5-10.

cha-lootz*
Also spelled *halutz.*
1. Literally, "pioneer."
2. A pioneer who settled in Palestine between the 1880s and the establishment of the State of Israel in 1948.

cha-loo-tza*
Also spelled *chalutza, halutza, chalootzah.*
Feminine form of *chalootz,* "a pioneer." See *chalootz.*

cha-loo-tzihm*
Also spelled *chalutzihm, halutzim.*
Plural of *chalootz.* See *chalootz.*

cha-lootz-i-yoos
Also *cha-lutz-i-yut.**
Also spelled *halutziyut.*

---

a as in father; aw as in law; ai as in aisle; ei as in neighbor; e as in bet; i as in vaccine; ih as in tin; o as in solar; oi as in void; oo as in food; u as in put; uh as in but; ch as in chutzpa; zh as in Zhivago.

"The pioneer spirit" in the Land of Israel before the creation of the State in 1948.

cha-loo-tzot*
Also *cha-loo-tzos.*
Also spelled *halutzot.*
Plural of *chalootza.* See above.

chaloshes see *chaluhshes*

cha-luh
Also *cha-la,* cha-law, cha-le.*
1. A Sabbath loaf, a braided white bread.
2. The priest's share of the dough in Temple times.
3. A tractate of the Talmud.

chaluhf see *chalef*

cha-luhsh
Also *cha-lesh.*
From the Hebrew *chalash,** meaning "weak, faint."

cha-luh-shes
Also spelled *chaloshes.*
1. Weakness, faintness, feebleness.
2. Something obnoxious.

chalutz see *chalootz*

chalutza see *chalootza*

chalutzihm see *chalootzihm*

chalutziyut see *chalootziyoos*

chalutzot see *chalootzot*

chamalyeh see *chmalye*

chametz see *chawmetz*

chametzdihg see *chawmetzdihg*

cha-mihn
A synonym for *cholent* used by Sephardim. See *cholent.*

cha-mor*
1. Literally, "a jackass, a donkey."
2. A fool.

a as in father; aw as in law; ai as in aisle: ei as in neighbor; e as in bet; i as in vaccine: ih as in tin; o as in solar; oi as in void; oo as in food; u as in put; uh as in but; ch as in chutzpa; zh as in Zhivago.

cha-ni-fuh
> Also *cha-ni-faw* and *cha-ni-fa.**
> Also spelled *chanife.*
> Flattery.

cha-noo-kas ha-ba-yihs
> Also *cha-nu-kat ha-ba-yit.**
> Also spelled *hanukat habayit.*
> 1. Literally, "dedication of the house."
> 2. Housewarming.

cha-noo-ki-yaw
> Also *cha-noo-ki-ya.**
> Also spelled *hanukia.*
> A special nine-branched candelabrum *(menora)*
> equipped with cups to hold oil or candles. Used on
> the eight days of Chanuka. The ninth candle is the
> server *(shamash)* used to light the other candles.

Cha-nu-ka
> Also *Cha-noo-kaw, Cha-noo-ka.**
> Also spelled *Hannuka, Hanuka, Hanukah, Hanuk-*
> *kah, Chanukah.*
> A Jewish holiday that usually falls in the month of
> December, commemorating the victory of the Mac-
> cabees in 165 B.C.E. over the Syrian-Greek rulers of
> Palestine in a struggle for their religious freedom.
> Celebrated for eight days beginning with the twen-
> ty-fifth day of the Hebrew month Kislev.

Cha-nu-ka gelt
> Also *Cha-noo-ka gelt, Cha-noo-kaw gelt.*
> Also spelled *Chanukah gelt, Hanukah gelt, Hanuk-*
> *kah gelt.*
> Literally, "Chanuka money," distributed as gifts
> during the Chanuka festival.

chap
> Also *chapn*
> To catch, to grab.

chap a gang
> 1. Literally, "Catch a walk!"
> 2. Beat it! Go away!

---

a as in father; aw as in law; ai as in aisle; ei as in neighbor; e as in bet; i as in vaccine; ih as in tin; o as in
solar; oi as in void; oo as in food; u as in put; uh as in but; ch as in chutzpa; zh as in Zhivago.

chap a-rain
 1. Literally, "to grab in."
 2. To take advantage of a situation.

chapn see *chap*

chapn a me-tzi-uh
 Also spelled *chapen a metziye.*
 Literally, "to grab a bargain," to get a bargain.

chap niht
 1. Literally, "Don't grab!"
 2. Take it easy! Not so fast!

cha-ro-ses
 Also *cha-roi-ses, cha-ro-set.**
 Also spelled *haroset.*
 A paste –made from wine, nuts, apples, and spices—served at the Passover Seder, symbolic of the mortar used by the Hebrew slaves in Egypt to make bricks for their masters.

chasan see *chawsn*

Cha-san B'rei-shihs
 Also *Cha-tan Be-rei-shiht,* Cha-san B'rei-shit.*
 Also spelled *Chatan B'reshit.*
 1. Literally, "Bridegoom of the Beginning."
 2. Title given to the man awarded the honor of reading the Tora and/or reciting the Tora blessing for the reading of the first chapter of Genesis (Breshit) on Simchat Tora.

Cha-san To-ruh
 Also *Cha-tan To-ra,* Cha-san To-raw.*
 1. Literally, "Bridegroom of the Torah."
 2. Title given to the man chosen to read the concluding section of the Book of Deuteronomy at the Simchat Tora service.

chasene see *chasuhnuh*

chaser deia see *chuhsr deiuh*

chasid see *chuhsihd*

cha-si-dei Ash-ke-naz
 Also spelled *hasidei Ashkenaz.*

---

a as in father; aw as in law; ai as in aisle: ei as in neighbor; e as in bet; i as in vaccine; ih as in tin; o as in solar; oi as in void; oo as in food; u as in put; uh as in but; ch as in chutzpa; zh as in Zhivago.

1. A pietist movement among Jews of medieval Germany.
2. Members of the movement.

cha-si-dei oo-mos haw-o-lawn
Also *cha-si-dei oo-mot ha-o-lam.**
Literally, "the righteous among the nations of the world," used particularly in modern times to describe Gentiles who aided Jews during the Holocaust.

chasihd see *chuhsihd*

cha-sihd-ihzm
Also *ha-sihd-ihzm.*
Also spelled *chasidism, hasidism.*
1. A religious movement revolving around the person of Israel Baal Shem Tov in the first half of the eighteenth century.
2. Popular mysticism.
Often capitalized.

cha-suh-nuh
Also *cha-se-ne, cha-too-na,** *cha-soo-naw.*
A wedding.

chas v'chaw-li-luh
Also *chas v'chaw-li-law, chas v'cha-li-la.**
God forbid! Perish the thought!
The same as *chaw-li-law v'chas,* except in reverse form.

chas v'shaw-luhm
Also *chas v'shaw-lom, chas v'sha-lom.**
God forbid!

chatan see *chawsn*

chatchke see *tzatzke*

chatoona see *chasuhnuh*

chatshke see *tzatzke*

Cha-tzi Ka-dihsh
Also spelled *Hatzi Kaddish, Chatzi Kaddish.*
Literally, "half Kaddish," a short form of the full Kaddish. See *Kadihsh.*

chaver see *chawvr*

---

a as in father; aw as in law; ai as in aisle; ei as in neighbor; e as in bet; i as in vaccine; ih as in tin; o as in solar; oi as in void; oo as in food; u as in put; uh as in but; ch as in chutzpa; zh as in Zhivago.

cha-ve-ra*
Also *cha-vei-raw.*
Also spelled *havera.*
Feminine of *chaver.* See below.

cha-voo-ra*
Also *cha-voo-raw.*
Also spelled *chavura, chavurah, havura.*
1. A friendship cluster.
2. A small group organized to celebrate Jewish holidays and traditions, usually without a rabbi. The first such group organized in Somerville, Massachusetts, in 1968.

chawchm
Also *cha-cham,* *chaw-chawm.*
1. A wise person, a sage.
2. Sarcastically, a "wise guy."
3. The title of the spiritual leader of a Sephardic congregation or community.

chawch-me
Also *chuch-muh, chawch-maw, chawch-muh, chach-ma.**
Also spelled *chochma, hokhma.*
1. Wisdom.
2. A witty saying, a joke.
3. A facetious remark.

chawchm einr
Also spelled *chawchawm einer.*
1. A wise guy.
2. A fool.

chaw-lawv Yihs-raw-el
Also *cha-lav Yis-ra-el.**
1. Literally, "milk of Israel."
2. Milk that has been processed under the scrutiny of a qualified Jewish supervisor.

chaw-lent
Also *cho-lent.*
A Sabbath dish of meat, beans, peas, and other ingredients cooked before sunset on Friday and kept hot until ready to be eaten on Saturday, to avoid violating the Sabbath by cooking.

---

a as in father; aw as in law; ai as in aisle; ei as in neighbor; e as in bet; i as in vaccine; ih as in tin; o as in solar; oi as in void; oo as in food; u as in put; uh as in but; ch as in chutzpa; zh as in Zhivago.

chawlilaw see *chalila*

chaw-li-law v'chas see *chas v'chawliluh*

chaw-metz
> Also *cha-metz,* chaw-meitz.*
> Also spelled *chometz, hametz.*
> 1. Leavened food.
> 2. Food or utensils not kosher for Passover.

chaw-metz-dihk
> Also *chaw-metz-dihg.*
> Also spelled *chometzdig, chometzdik.*
> The adjectival form of *chametz.* See *chametz.*

chawsawn see *chawsn*

chawseir deiaw see *chuhsr deiuh*

chaw-shevr mentsh
> Also spelled *choshever mensh.*
> A prominent person, a celebrity.

chawsihd see *chuhsihd*

chawsn
> Also *cha-san, cha-tan.**
> Also spelled *chawsen.*
> Bridegroom.

chawsn ka-luh
> Also *chaw-sawn ka-law, cha-tan ka-la.**
> Bridegroom and bride.

chawsn ka-luh mazl tuhv
> Also *chaw-sawn ka-law ma-zawl tov, cha-tan ka-la ma-zal tov.**
> Literally, "Bridegroom and bride: congratulations!"

chawvr
> Also *chaw-veir, cha-ver.**
> Also spelled *haver.*
> 1. A friend.
> 2. A comrade, colleague, member of a group.

chaw-zawk see *chazak*

cha-ye
> Also *cha-ya,* cha-yaw, cha-yuh.*

---

1. An animal.
2. A feminine personal name.

cha-yihm
Also spelled *chayim, hayim, hayyim*.
Plural of *chai,* "life." A masculine personal name.

Cha-yihm Yank-kel
Also spelled *Chaim Yankel, Chaim Yonkil*.
1. A combination of two very ordinary names.
2. A non-entity.
3. A nobody.

chayn see *chein*

cha-zak*
Also *chaw-zawk*.
1. Strong.
2. Be strengthened!
3. A strong person.

cha-zak cha-zak v'nihs-cha-zeik
Literally, "Be strong and you will be strengthened!" Repeated by the congregation as the reading of each of the Five Books of Moses is completed in the synagogue.

chazak u'va-ruch*
Also *cha-zak u'ba-ruch*.
Literally, "Be strong and blessed!" Used by Sephardim to express congratulations.

chazan see *chazn*

cha-za-nihm*
Also spelled *chazanim, chazonim*.
Cantors. Plural of *chazan*.

cha-za-niht
Also spelled *chazanit, hazanit*.
A woman cantor. See also *chazntuh*.

cha-zaw-ras ha-shatz
Also *cha-za-rat ha-shatz.**
Literally, "repetition of the *Amida* [by the reader]."

cha-ze-rai
Also *cha-zuh-rai*.

1. Pig-like food, distasteful food, junk food.
2. A mess, filth, anything rotten or unpalatable.

(a) cha-zihr-she tawg
1. Literally, "a piggish day."
2. A miserable day.

chazir see *chazr*

chazn
Also *cha-zan,* cha-zawn.*
Also spelled *hazan, chazzen.*
A male cantor, also referred to as a *shaliach tsibur.*

chazn-tuh
Also *chazn-te.*
1. A cantor's wife.
2. A woman cantor. See also *chazaniht.*

chazr
Also *cha-zir.**
1. A pig.
2. A person who behaves like a pig, a glutton.

(a) chazr blaibt a chazr
1. Literally, "once a pig always a pig."
2. One doesn't change easily.

chazuhrai see *chazerai*

chazzen see *chazn*

cheidr
Also *che-der.**
Also spelled *heder.*
1. A room.
2. An elementary Jewish school.

cheilv
Also *chei-lev, che-lev.**
Fat (of an animal).

chein
Also *chen.**
Also spelled *chayn.*
Grace, charm.

chei-nev-dihk
A person who exudes charm.

---

a as in father; aw as in law; ai as in aisle; ei as in neighbor; e as in bet; i as in vaccine; ih as in tin; o as in solar; oi as in void; oo as in food; u as in put; uh as in but; ch as in chutzpa; zh as in Zhivago.

chei-rem
>Also spelled *cherem, herem.*
>Excommunication, ostracism.

cheit
>Also *chet.**
>Also spelled *het.*
>1. A sin.
>2. A transgression.

chelev see *cheilv*

Chelm
>A fictitious town inhabited by foolish people.

cherem see *cheirem*

ches
>Also *chet.**
>The eighth letter of the Hebrew alphabet.

che-sed
>Also spelled *hesed.*
>Favor, grace, benevolence.

cheshbn
>Also *chesh-bon.**
>Reckoning, computation, accounting.

chesh-bon ha-ne-fesh*
>1. Literally, "inventory of the soul."
>2. Soul-searching, taking spiritual inventory.

Cheshvn
>Also *Chesh-van.**
>Also spelled *Heshvan.*
>The eighth month of the Jewish religious calendar, second of the Civil, corresponding to October-November. Also called *Mar-Cheshvn,* "bitter *Cheshvn,*" because it is a month in which there are no Jewish holidays.

chesron see *chisawroin*

chet see *ches* and *cheit*

chev-ruh
>Also *chev-ra,** *chev-raw.*
>1. A group.
>2. A club, fellowship, association.

Chev-ruh Che-sed V'e-mes
Also *Chev-ra Che-sed V'e-met.**
1. Literally, "Society of Benevolence and Truth," a euphemism for Burial Society. The name of volunteer burial societies among Sephardic Jews (of Iberian and Middle Eastern descent), similar to the Ashkenazic *Chevruh Kadishuh.*

Chev-ruh Ka-di-shuh
Also *Chev-ra Ka-di-sha.**
Also spelled *Hevra Kaddisha.*
Literally, "Sacred Society."
General name for a volunteer burial society in Ashkenazic (European Jewish) communities.

Chev-ruh Shas
Also spelled *Chevra Shas.**
A Talmud study group.

Chev-ruh T'h-lihm
Also spelled *Chevra Tehilim.**
A group devoted to reading or studying the Book of Psalms.

chi-lool ha-Sheim
Also *chi-lul ha-Shem.**
Also spelled *hilul haShem.*
1. Literally, "profanation of the [Divine] Name."
2. Blasphemy.

chi-lool Shab-bes
Also *chi-lul Sha-baws, chi-lul Shabuhs, chi-lul Shabat.**
Also spelled *hilul Shabbat.*
Literally, "desecration of the Sabbath."

chi-saw-roin
Also *chi-sa-ron,** *ches-ron.*
A flaw, defect, deficiency.

(a) chi-saw-roin, di ka-le iz tzoo shein
1. Literally, "The bride's defect is that she is too beautiful," used sarcastically.'
2. An unwarranted complaint.

chlaw-pe
Also spelled *chloppeh.*

---

a as in father; aw as in law; ai as in aisle; ei as in neighbor; e as in bet; i as in vaccine; ih as in tin; o as in solar; oi as in void; oo as in food; u as in put; uh as in but; ch as in chutzpa; zh as in Zhivago.

1. To rain in torrents.
2. A downpour.

Chmel-nihtz-ki's yaw-ren
   1. Literally, "Chmelnitzki's years," a reference to
   the seventeenth-century Ukrainian anti-Semite.
   2. Long ago.

chochma see *chawchme*

cho-desh
   Also spelled *hodesh.*
   Month.

choi-tei
   Also *cho-tei.**
   A sinner.

choi-tei oo-poi-shei
   An outrageous sinner.

choi-zek machn
   Also *choi-zihk ma-chen.*
   To ridicule, to poke fun.

cholent see *chawlent*

cholerya see *chaleryuh*

Chol Ha-mo-eid
   Also spelled *Chol Hamoed,** *Hol Hamoed.*
   The intermediary days of Passover and Sukkot.

cholileh see *chalila*

chometz see *chawmetz*

choo-kas ha-go-yihm
   Also *chu-kat ha-goyim.**
   1. Literally, "the custom (or law) of the nations."
   2. A practice forbidden to Jews (Leviticus 20:23).

choolem see *chulm*

choopa see *chupuh*

choorban see *choorbn*

choor-ban ba-yihs ri-shon
   Also *choor-ban ba-yit ri-shon.**
   Literally, "destruction of the First Temple."

choor-ban ba-yihs shei-ni
> Also *choor-ban ba-yit shei-ni.**
> Literally, "destruction of the Second Temple."

choor-ban beis ha-mihk-dawsh
> Also *chur-ban bet ha-mik-dash*.*
> Literally, "destruction of the Temple."

choorbn
> Also *choor-ban.**
> Also spelled *churban, hurban.*
> 1. Literally, "destruction."
> 2. Specifically, destruction of the First and Second Temples in Jerusalem.

chootz la-a-retz*
> 1. Literally, "outside of the land (of Israel)."
> 2. Countries of exile.
> 3. The Diaspora.

chootz-pe-nihk
> Also spelled *chutzpenik.*
> An impudent person.

chootz-puh
> Also *chootz-pa,** *chootz-paw.*
> Also spelled *chutzpa, hutzpa.*
> Gall, impudence, nerve, impertinence.

choshever mensh see *chawshevr mentsh*

chotei see *choitei*

chrawpe see *chruhpuh*

chrawpn
> To snore.

chrein
> Also spelled *chrain, chrayn.*
> Horseradish.

chremzl
> Also spelled *chremzel, chremsl.*
> A pancake, usually made of potato or matzo meal.

chrupuh
> Also *chraw-pe.*
> Snore.

---

a as in father; aw as in law; ai as in aisle; ei as in neighbor; e as in bet; i as in vaccine; ih as in tin; o as in solar; oi as in void; oo as in food; u as in put; uh as in but; ch as in chutzpa; zh as in Zhivago.

chuchmuh see *chawchem*

chuhn-te
A prostitute.

chuh-sihd
Also *cha-sihd, chaw-sihd, cha-sid.**
Also spelled *hasid.*
1. A pietist, a very pious person.
2. A fan, a buff, a follower of an ideology.
3. In the first and second centuries, one of the militants who were fiercely anti-Roman.
4. A follower of the eighteenth-century Israel Baal Shem Tov in Eastern Europe.
Often capitalized.

chuhsr dei-uh
Also *chaw-seir dei-aw, cha-ser dei-a.**
1. Literally, "deficient of judgment."
2. Insane.
3. Feebleminded.

chukat hagoyim see *chookas hagoyihm*

chulm
Also *choo-lem, cha-lom.**
A dream.

chulmen
Also *choo-lem-en.*
To dream.

Chumash see *Chumuhsh*

Chu-muhsh
Also *Chu-mash.**
Also spelled *Chumesh, Humash.*
The Pentateuch, the Five Books of Moses.

chu-puh
Also *chu-pe, choo-pa,* choo-paw, choo-pe.*
Also spelled *huppa, hupaw.*
1. A bridal canopy.
2. The wedding ceremony.

churban see *choorban*

chutzpa see *chootzpuh*

---

a as in father; aw as in law; ai as in aisle· ei as in neighbor; e as in bet; i as in vaccine; ih as in tin; o as in solar; oi as in void; oo as in food; u as in put; uh as in but; ch as in chutzpa; zh as in Zhivago.

chutz-pe-dihk
 1. An audacious person.
 2. Brazen.

chutzpenik see *chootzpenihk*

cloistr
 Also *clois-ter.*
 A church.

Cohen see *Kohein*

Con-ver-so
 Spanish for Jews and Moors who converted to Christianity under duress during the Inquisition in fifteenth-century Spain and Portugal.

cronkite see *krankhait*

---

a as in father; aw as in law; ai as in aisle; ei as in neighbor; e as in bet; i as in vaccine; ih as in tin; o as in solar; oi as in void; oo as in food; u as in put; uh as in but; ch as in chutzpa; zh as in Zhivago.

D

dai-ge
>Also *da-a-ga**
>1. Worry.
>2. Concern.
>3. Anxiety.

(a) dai-ge hawb ihch
>1. I should worry!
>2. I couldn't care less!

dai-ge nihsht
>Don't worry!

Daitsh
>Yiddish for *Deutsch,* meaning "German."

da-let*
>Also *da-lihd.*
>Fourth letter of the Hebrew alphabet.

dam briht*
>Also *dam brihs.*
>Literally, "blood of the covenant," referring to the rite of circumcision.

Dan
>1. The northermost city of biblical Israel.
>2. A son of Jacob.
>3. One of the twelve tribes.

(a) dank
>Thanks!

(a) dank aich
>Thank you!

dankn
>Also spelled *danken.*
>To thank someone.

dar
>1. Thin, slender.
>2. Dried (fruit).

---

a as in father; aw as in law; ai as in aisle: ei as in neighbor; e as in bet; i as in vaccine: ih as in tin; o as in solar; oi as in void; oo as in food; u as in put; uh as in but; ch as in chutzpa; zh as in Zhivago.

darfn
Also spelled *darfen.*
To need, require.

dar-kei shaw-lom
Also *dar-kei sha-lom.* *
Literally, "ways of peace."
See also *mipnei darkei shalom.*

dar oond kvar
Thin and haggard.

dar-shan*
Also *dar-shawn, dar-shuhn.*
A preacher. *Darshanim* is the plural form.

dar-shan-ihm
Also spelled *darshanim.*
The plural of *darshan.* See above.

darshn
Also spelled *darshenen.*
To preach.

davn
Also *da-ven.*
To pray.

dav-nen
Also *dav-en-en.*
To pray.

Daw-ner-shtihg
Also *Daw-ner-shtihk.*
Thursday.

dawrf
Also spelled *dorf.*
A village.

dawrsh-tig
Also *dawrsh-tik.*
Thirsty.

daws gelt ihz tze-roon-en ge-vawr-en
1. Literally, "the money trickled out."
2. The money went down the drain (wasted).

---

a as in father; aw as in law; ai as in aisle; ei as in neighbor; e as in bet; i as in vaccine; ih as in tin; o as in solar; oi as in void; oo as in food; u as in put; uh as in but; ch as in chutzpa; zh as in Zhivago.

daws hartz hawt mihr ge-zawgt
1. Literally, "my heart told me."
2. I predicted it.

daws ihz altz
That's all.

da-yan*
Also *da-yawn*.
Also spelled *dayyan, dayen*.
A judge. *Dayanim* is the plural form.

dayanim
Plural of *dayan*. See above.

(a) dei-uh hawbn
Also *(a) dei-a ha-ben*.
To have an opinion.

de-rech a-gav
Incidentally, by the way.

de-rech e-retz
1. Literally, "way of the land."
2. Respect, courtesy, politeness, decency, good manners.

der Ei-ber-shter ge-loibt
To praise God, thank God.

der-nihd-er-ihken
To embarrass someone.

der-shtihkt zawlst doo ve-ren
You should only choke!

devar Torah see *d'var Tora*

devekut see *d'veikoot*

d'harg-et
Killed, was killed.

Diaspora
An English word for the Hebrew *gawloos* or *galut*.*
1. The dispersion of Jews to countries outside the Land of Israel.
2. The location of Jews living outside Israel.

dibbuk see *dihbook*

---

a as in father; aw as in law; ai as in aisle: ei as in neighbor; e as in bet; i as in vaccine; ih as in tin; o as in solar; oi as in void; oo as in food; u as in put; uh as in but; ch as in chutzpa; zh as in Zhivago.

di e-me-se s'choi-re
1. Literally, "the true merchandise."
2. The real thing.

di Far-ein-ihg-te Felk-er
The United Nations.

di Far-ein-ihg-te Shtatn
The United States.

dih-book
Also spelled *dybuk, dybbuk, dibbuk.*
1. Literally, "to cleave, to hold to."
2. In Jewish folklore, the spirit of a dead person that enters the body of a living person and assumes control over it.
3. In Jewish mysticism, a soul condemned to wander the world because of its sins.

dihn
Also spelled *din.*
1. Judgment.
2. Law.
3. Jewish religious law.

dihn To-raw
Also *dihn To-ra.**
Also spelled *din Torah.*
1. Literally, "judgment of the Torah."
2. Arbitration of a dispute according to rabbinic law.

dihv-rei To-raw
Also *dihv-rei To-ra.**
Also spelled *divre Torah.*
1. Literally, "words of Torah."
2. A brief Torah-study session.

din see *dihn*

di-na d'mal-choo-ta di-na*
Also *di-naw d'mal-choo-saw di-naw.*
Literally, "the law of the land is the law."

dingn
Also spelled *dingen.*
1. Rent, lease.

---

2. To bargain.
3. Hire, engage.

divre Torah see *dihvrei Toraw*

doochn
Also *du-chan.**
Also spelled *duchen.*
1. The platform in front of the Holy Ark in the synagogue.
2. Ceremony in which Jews of priestly (Aharonic) descent mount the synagogue platform to pronounce the Priestly Benediction at religious services (popularly referred to as *duchening*).

doom kawp
Literally, "dumb head," dunce.
From the German *"Dumkopf."*

doo-nam*
Also *doo-nawm.*
Also spelled *dunam.*
A plot of land approximately one-quarter of an acre.

dorf see *dawrf*

draikop see *dreikawp*

dreidl
Also spelled *draydl, dreidel, dredel.*
A four-sided top used on the Chanuka holiday.

drei-en
To turn, twist.

drei-en a kawp
1. Literally, "to turn one's head."
2. To confuse someone.
3. To annoy someone.

drei-en miht dem tzoong
1. Literally, "twisting with one's tongue."
2. To hem and haw.

drei-en mihtn gruh-ben fihn-ger
1. Literally, "to twist with one's thick finger [thumb]."

2. To force an argument.
3. To infer something unwarranted.

drei-kawp
Also spelled *draikop, dreikop, draykop.*
1. Literally, "twist-head."
2. Scatterbrain.
3. Busybody.

drei mihr niht kein kawp
1. Literally, "Don't turn my head."
2. Don't confuse me!
3. Don't pester me!

drei zihch
1. Literally, "turn yourself."
2. Keep moving!

drek
1. Feces, manure, excrement, "crap."
2. Inferior merchandise or work.
3. Insincere talk or excessive flattery.

drerd
A contraction of *der erd,* meaning "the earth."

(ihn) drerd main gelt
1. Literally, "My money is in the earth."
2. My money is lost.

(ihn) droisen ihz a glihtsh
Literally, "It's slippery outside."

duchan see *doochn*

dunam see *doonam*

d'var To-ra*
Also *d'var To-raw.*
Also spelled *devar Torah.*
1. Literally, "a word of Torah."
2. A Torah lesson.
3. A study session.

d'vei-koot*
Also *d'vei-koos.*
Also spelled *d'vekut, devekut.*
1. Literally, "attachment, adhesion."
2. Devotion to and communion with God.

dybbuk see *dihbook*
dzhlob see *zhlawb*

E

edel see *eidl*

edelkeit see *eidlkait*

efn
> Also spelled *efen.*
> Open.

ef-nen
> To open.

efshr
> Also *ef-shar,* ef-shawr.*
> Also spelled *efsher.*
> Perhaps, maybe, possibly.

(der) Ei-bihsh-ter
> Also *der Ih-ber-shter.*
> 1. Literally, "the Most High."
> 2. God.

eidelkait see *eidlkait*

eidem see *eidm*

eides zawgn see *eiduhs zawgen*

eidl
> Also spelled *edel, aydel.*
> 1. Courteous, refined, genteel, polite.
> 2. Sometimes used sarcastically, as in *eidl ge-patchket,* meaning "overparticular, perfectionist."

eidl-kait
> Also spelled *eidelkait, edelkeit, aidelkait.*
> Gentility.

eidm
> Also *ei-duhm.*
> Also spelled *eidem, aidem, aydem.*
> Son-in-law.

---

eidm oif kest
Literally, "a son-in-law who boards," referring to one who continues his studies while being supported by his in-laws.

ei-duhs zawgen
Also spelled *eides zawgen, eidus zogen.*
Testify, bear witness.

ei-er kih-chel
Also *ai-er kih-chel.*
Egg biscuit.

ei-ge-ne bloot oon fleish
Also *ai-ge-ne blut oon flaish.*
1. Literally, "one's own blood and flesh."
2. A relative.

Ei-li-ya-hoo Ha-na-vi*
Also *Ei-li-yaw-hu Ha-naw-vi.*
Also spelled *Eliahu Hanavi.*
Elijah the Prophet.

Eil Maw-lei Ra-cha-mihm
Also *El Ma-le Ra-cha-mihm.**
1. Literally, "God abundant in compassion."
2. The memorial prayer recited at funerals, unveilings, and on special occasions in the synagogue.

eilt zich see *ailt zihch*

einbren see *ainbren*

einfahl see *ainfal*

eingemachts see *aingemachts*

eingeshpart see *aingeshpart*

eingetunken see *aingetoonken*

einhore see *ain hawre*

ein klein-ih-keit
Also *ain klain-ih-kait.*
Also spelled *ein kleinikait.*
1. Some trifle!
2. Is that so!
3. Wow!

---

a as in father; aw as in law; ai as in aisle; ei as in neighbor; e as in bet; i as in vaccine; ih as in tin; o as in solar; oi as in void; oo as in food; u as in put; uh as in but; ch as in chutzpa; zh as in Zhivago.

ein oond ein-tsih-ke
1. Literally, "a one and only."
2. A rarity.
3. An only child

ein-red-e-nihsh see *ainredenihsh*

Ein Sof
Also *En Sof.**
1. Literally, "without end."
2. Eternal.
3. A kabbalistic reference to a hidden aspect of God.

eins, tsvei, drai, fir see *ains, tsvai, drai, fir*

ei-ruv
1. The "mixing" (literally) of that which is permitted and that which is prohibited on the Sabbath. By a symbolic action, that which is generally prohibited on the Sabbath becomes permissible.
2. In popular usage, the term refers to an enclosure created around a given area in the public domain in order that individuals may carry on the Sabbath.

ei-ruv tav-shi-lihn
1. Literally, "the merging (mixture) of foods."
2. A religious procedure to enable one to prepare food on a holiday when the Sabbath follows immediately after the holiday.

ei-sek
Also *e-sek.**
1. Business.
2. Occupation.
3. Dabbling.
4. Involvement.

ei-shes cha-yihl
Also *ei-shet cha-yihl.**
Also spelled *eshet chayil.*
1. Literally, "woman of valor" (Proverbs 31:10).
2. The proverbial Jewish woman, respected for her devotion to husband and family.

---

a as in father; aw as in law; ai as in aisle; ei as in neighbor; e as in bet; i as in vaccine; ih as in tin; o as in solar; oi as in void; oo as in food; u as in put; uh as in but; ch as in chutzpa; zh as in Zhivago.

ei-tzuh
> Also *ei-tza.**
> Also spelled *ai-tze.*
> Advice, counsel.

ei-ver
> Also *e-ver.**
> 1. Appendage (part of the body), limb.
> 2. Penis (slang).

eizl
> Also spelled *eizel.*
> 1. Literally, "a goat."
> 2. A fool.

ek velt
> 1. Literally, "the edge of the earth."
> 2. The other side of the world.
> 3. Far away.

El Male Rachamim see *Eil Mawlei Rachamihm*

E-lo-hihm
> Also spelled *Elohim*
> God.

E-lool
> Also spelled *Elul.*
> Sixth month of the Jewish religious calendar, the twelfth and final month of the Civil calendar, corresponding to August-September.

e-mes
> Also *e-met**
> Truth.

(der) e-mes ge-shprawch-en
> 1. Literally, "the truth was spoken."
> 2. The absolute truth.

emet see *emes*

En Sof see *Ein Sof*

e-puhs
> Also spelled *epes, eppes.*
> 1. Something, somewhat.
> 2. An interjection used for emphasis.

---

a as in father; aw as in law; ai as in aisle; ei as in neighbor; e as in bet; i as in vaccine; ih as in tin; o as in solar; oi as in void; oo as in food; u as in put; uh as in but; ch as in chutzpa; zh as in Zhivago.

er
    He, him.

erd
    Earth, ground. See also *drerd,* a combination of *der* (the) and *erd* (earth).

er est vi nuhch a krenk
    Literally, "he eats like one who just recovered from an illness," that is, heartily.

E-retz Yihs-raw-eil
    Also *E-retz Yis-ra-el.**
    The Land of Israel.

e-rev*
    Also *e-ruhv.*
    Evening.

e-rev Sha-bes
    Also *e-rev Sha-baws, e-rev Sha-buhs, erev Sha-bat.**
    Sabbath Eve (Friday at sundown).

e-rev Yom Tov
    The eve of a holiday.

er far-macht niht daws moil
    1. He doesn't close his mouth.
    2. He doesn't stop talking.

es
    1. It.
    2. Eat.

esen see *esn*

es far-drihst mihr
    1. It saddens me.
    2. It disturbs me.

es felt a bihsl fefr
    1. Literally, "Some pepper is missing."
    2. It's not just right.
    3. It's bland.

es felt a bihsl seichel
    1. Literally, "Some brains are lacking."
    2. Reference to a stupid person.

---

a as in father; aw as in law; ai as in aisle; ei as in neighbor; e as in bet; i as in vaccine; ih as in tin; o as in solar; oi as in void; oo as in food; u as in put; uh as in but; ch as in chutzpa; zh as in Zhivago.

es felt a bihsl zaltz
1. Literally, "Some salt is missing."
2. It's not just right.
3. It's bland.

es ge-zoonte heit
Also spelled *es gezunte hait.*
1. Literally, "Eat in a healthy condition."
2. Eat hearty! Enjoy your meal!

eshet chayil see *eishes chayihl*

es-ihg
Also *es-ihk.*
Vinegar.

es-ihg fleish
Also spelled *esig flaish.*
1. Literally, "vinegar meat."
2. A stew with vinegar as one of its ingredients.

es main kihnd
Also spelled *es mein kind.*
Literally, "Eat, my child!"

esn
Also *es-en.*
1. To eat.
2. Food.

esn teg
Also spelled *esen teg.*
Literally, "eating days," referring to *Yeshiva* (seminary) students of Eastern Europe who ate in different homes.

esn vi a chazr
Also spelled *esen vi a chazer.*
To eat like a pig.

esn vi a ferd
To eat like a horse.

esn vi nawch a kihm-piht
1. Literally, "to eat like one who just got over a pregnancy."
2. To eat like a glutton.

---

a as in father; aw as in law; ai as in aisle; ei as in neighbor; e as in bet; i as in vaccine; ih as in tin; o as in solar; oi as in void; oo as in food; u as in put; uh as in but; ch as in chutzpa; zh as in Zhivago.

esn vi nawch a kreink
1. Literally, "to eat like one after an illness."
2. To eat heartily.

es past niht
1. It's not suitable.
2. It's not fitting.

es ret zihch a-zoi
1. Literally, "It speaks that way."
2. It seems that way.
3. So it says (I don't believe it).

es-rihg
Also *es-rog, et-rog.**
Also spelled *esrig*.
A citron, used on the Sukkot holiday.

esrog see *esrihg*

essn see *esn*

etrog see *esrihg*

ez-ras naw-shihm
Also *ez-rat na-shim.**
Women's section in an Orthodox synagogue.

F

fahrdrayen see *fardreien*

(a) fai-er zawl ihm trefn
>Also spelled *a feier zol im trefen.*
>1. Literally, "A fire should happen to him."
>2. Let him disappear!

faifn
>Also spelled *feifen, faifen.*
>To whistle.

faifn oif
>1. Literally, "to whistle on (at) someone."
>2. To show contempt.

faifn oifn yam
>Also spelled *feifen oifen yam.*
>1. Literally, "to whistle on the ocean."
>2. To waste breath, to waste effort.

faifr
>Also spelled *feifer, fifer.*
>One who whistles.

faigel see *feigel*

faigele see *feigele*

faind
>Also spelled *faint, feind.*
>Enemy, foe.

faind hawbn
>Also *faint hawbn.*
>Also spelled *feind hoben.*
>To hate, loathe, abhor.

faind krihgn
>Also spelled *faint krign, feint krigen.*
>To hate, abhor, dislike, detest.

fain-kuchn
>Also spelled *fainkuchen, feinkuchen.*

---

a as in father; aw as in law; ai as in aisle: ei as in neighbor; e as in bet; i as in vaccine; ih as in tin; o as in solar; oi as in void; oo as in food; u as in put; uh as in but; ch as in chutzpa; zh as in Zhivago.

1. Literally, "fine cooking."
2. An omelet.

fain-shmekr
Also spelled *fainshmeker, feinshmeker.*
1. Literally, "fine-sniffing."
2. Elite, uppity.

faint see *faind*

Falashas
Dark-skinned Jews who live in Ethiopia.

fangn uhn
Also spelled *fangen un.*
1. Literally, "to start in."
2. To begin.
3. To create a scene.
Also expressed in reverse: *uhn-fangn.*

fang shoin un
1. Literally, "Begin already!"
2. Stop procrastinating!

fangst shoin uhn?
Are you starting in again? Are you starting trouble again?

fan-taz-yawr
A visionary, a dreamer.

far-ain
Also spelled *farein.*
1. From the German *verein,* "an organization."
2. A social group.
3. A club.

far-baitn di Yoitz-res
Also spelled *farbeiten di Yoitzruhs.*
1. Literally, "to confuse the *Yotzer* prayers" (part of the morning prayer service), that is, to recite them in the wrong order.
2. To mix things up.

far-baitn
Also spelled *farbaiten, farbeiten.*
1. To supplant, replace, exchange.
2. To mix up.

---

a as in father: aw as in law; ai as in aisle; ei as in neighbor; e as in bet: i as in vaccine: ih as in tin: o as in solar: oi as in void; oo as in food; u as in put; uh as in but; ch as in chutzpa: zh as in Zhivago.

far-bihs-en
Also spelled *farbissen.*
Embittered, bitter, caustic, angry.

far-bihs-enr
Also spelled *farbisener.*
1. An embittered person.
2. A mean person.

far-blun-jet
Also spelled *farblonjet.*
1. Lost.
2. Misguided.
3. Bewildered, confused.

far-breing-en
Also *far-braing-ung.*
Also spelled *farbraingen, farbraingung.*
1. To get together, to celebrate
2. A Chasidic cultural and social gathering with
the *rebbe.*

far-brentr
Also spelled *farbrenter.*
1. Literally, "a burnt one."
2. A devotee, disciple, fan.

far-dai-get
1. Worried, anxious.
2. Distressed.
3. Careworn.

far-dart
Dried out, withered.

fardihnen
Also spelled *fardinen.*
1. To earn.
2. To be deserving.

far-dih-nen a mihtz-vuh
Also spelled *fardinen a mitzvah.*
To earn (merit) a good deed.

far-dih-ner
Also spelled *fardinr, fardiner.*
A provider, breadwinner.

---

a as in father; aw as in law; ai as in aisle; ei as in neighbor; e as in bet; i as in vaccine; ih as in tin; o as in
solar; oi as in void; oo as in food; u as in put; uh as in but; ch as in chutzpa; zh as in Zhivago.

fardraien see *fardreien*

far-draws
Also *far-drus.*
Also spelled *fardross.*
1. Distress, annoyance.
2. Chagrin, resentment. Used with *hawbn* (to have): *hawbn fardraws* or *fardrus,* "to be distressed."

far-drei-en
Also *far-drai-en.*
Also spelled *fardrayen, fardrehen.*
1. To turn, twist.
2. To distort, misrepresent.

far-drei-en a kawp
Also spelled *fardrehen a kop.*
1. Literally, "to twist a head."
2. To confuse.

far-drei-e-nihsh
1. A bothersome situation.
2. Confusion created by another person.

far-drei zihch dain ei-ge-ne kawp
1. Literally, "twist your own head."
2. Drive yourself crazy!
3. Don't bother me!

far-drihs
Also *far-dris.*
1. Hurt, irked, peeved, distressed.
2. A sad situation.

far-drihsn
Also *far-dris-en.*
To aggravate, distress, as in *es fardrihst mihr,* "it distresses me."

fardross see *fardraws*

fardrus see *fardraws*

farein see *farain*

far-faln
Also spelled *farfalen.*

---

a as in father; aw as in law; ai as in aisle; ei as in neighbor; e as in bet; i as in vaccine; ih as in tin; o as in solar; oi as in void; oo as in food; u as in put; uh as in but; ch as in chutzpa; zh as in Zhivago.

1. Doomed, lost.
2. Hopeless.

farfel see *farfl*

farfl
Also spelled *farfel.*
1. Broken-up pieces of *matza.*
2. Noodle dough chopped or grated into barley-like pieces.

far-foiln
Also spelled *farfoilen.*
Rotten, decayed, putrid.

far-froi-ren
Frozen.

far-ge-ni-gen
Also *far-ge-nihgn.*
A pleasure, delight.

far-gesn
Also spelled *fargesen.*
Forgotten.

far-gloost
Also *far-glust, far-gluhst.*
1. To desire.
2. To crave.

far-kawchn a ka-she
1. Literally, "to cook up a pot of *kashe* (buckwheat kernels)"
2. To cook up a storm.
3. To make a mess.

far-kert
1. Opposite.
2. Vice versa.
For emphasis *punkt farkert* is used. See *punkt farkert.*

far-kil-en
1. To cool.
2. To catch cold.

far-libt
Also *far-lihbt.*

---

a as in father; aw as in law; ai as in aisle: ei as in neighbor; e as in bet; i as in vaccine; ih as in tin; o as in solar; oi as in void; oo as in food; u as in put; uh as in but; ch as in chutzpa; zh as in Zhivago.

1. To fall in love with someone.
2. To fall in love with a thing.

far-mach daws moil
1. Literally, "shut your mouth."
2. Shut up!

far-machn
Also spelled *farmachen.*
To close, to shut.

far-matrt
Also spelled *farmatert.*
Weary, tired.

far-mihshn
Also spelled *farmishen.*
To mix up, confuse.

far-mihsh niht di Yoitz-res
1. Literally, "Don't mix up the prayers."
2. Don't mix things up.
See also *farbaiten di Yoitzres.*

far-mihsht
Mixed up, confused, befuddled.

far-mut-shet
Fatigued, exhausted, worn out.

far-nemt zihch
Beat it! Go away!

far-patsh-ket
Also spelled *farpotshket.*
1. Messed up.
2. Sloppy.
3. Mixed up.

far-pootzt
Also spelled *farputzt.*
1. Dressed up.
2. Adorned, decorated.

(a) far-shlep-te kreink
Also spelled *(a) farshlepte krenk.*
1. A drawn-out sickness.
2. A chronic condition.

---

far-shmai-et
Busy, active.

far-shmai-e-ter
One who is always on the go.

far-shnawsh-ket
Drunk, tipsy.

far-shtawpt
Also spelled *farshtopt.*
1. Stuffed, cluttered, clogged.
2. Constipated.

far-shtawp-te kawp
1. Literally, "a clogged head."
2. Dumb, stupid.

far-shtei-en
To understand, comprehend.

far-shteist?
Do you understand?

farshtinken see *farshtoonken*

far-shtoonk-en
Also *far-shtin-ken.*
Also spelled *farshtunken.*
Stinking, smelly.

farshtopt see *farshtawpt*

far-shvihtzt
Also spelled *farshvitzt.*
Sweated, sweaty.

far-tihg
Also spelled *fartig.*
1. Ended, completed.
2. It's all over.

far-tih-ge-heit
1. In the end.
2. Eventually.

far-tshad-et
1. Confused.
2. Charmed, taken in.
3. Surprised.

---

a as in father; aw as in law; ai as in aisle; ei as in neighbor; e as in bet; i as in vaccine; ih as in tin; o as in solar; oi as in void; oo as in food; u as in put; uh as in but; ch as in chutzpa; zh as in Zhivago.

far-tutst
 Bewildered, confused.
fartz
 A fart.
fartzen see *fartzn*
fartzn
 Also spelled *fartzen.*
 To fart.
far-zawr-ger
 Also spelled *farzorger.*
 1. Literally, "a provider."
 2. Head of the family.
far-zawrgn
 Also spelled *farzorgen.*
 1. To be concerned.
 2. To be angry.
 3. To be upset.
far-zooch-en
 Also spelled *farzuchen.*
 1. To examine.
 2. To taste.
farzorgen see *farzawrgn*
fawdm
 Also spelled *fawdem.*
 A thread.
fawlg mihch a gang
 1. Literally, "It follows me on a walk."
 2. It's worthless, a waste of time.
 3. Some distance!
 Also expressed as *s'fawlgt* (or *es fawlgt*) *mihch a gang.*
fawlgn
 Also spelled *folgn* and *folgen.*
 1. To follow.
 2. To obey.
fawlks-mensh
 Also spelled *folks-mentsh.*

a as in father; aw as in law; ai as in aisle; ei as in neighbor; e as in bet; i as in vaccine; ih as in tin; o as in solar; oi as in void; oo as in food; u as in put; uh as in but; ch as in chutzpa; zh as in Zhivago.

1. Literally, "a folk-person," a folksy person.
2. An average person.

fawnfn
Also spelled *fawnfen, fonfen.*
1. To speak with a nasal twang.
2. To mumble.
3. Double-talk.

fawnfn oon-ter
Also spelled *fonfen unter.*
To incite, instigate.

fawnfr
Also spelled *fawnfer, fonfer, fuhnfr.*
1. One who speaks with a twang.
2. A mumbler, one who speaks unclearly.

fawr-shpais
Also spelled *forshpeis.*
An appetizer.

fawr-shtel-oong
Also spelled *forstellung.*
A performance, a play.

fawrt ge-zoont-er-heit
Also spelled *fort gezunter hait.*
1. Literally, "travel in good health."
2. Have a good trip!

fawrt vaiter
Also spelled *fort veiter.*
1. Literally, "travel further."
2. Move ahead! Go on!

fawr-vertz see *Forvets*

fawtr
Also spelled *foter.*
Daddy, father.

faygehleh see *feigele*

fe
Also spelled *feh.*
1. An expression of distaste.
2. Phooey!

---

fees-e-lach
>Also *fihs-e-lach*.
>Small feet.

fefr
>Also spelled *feffer*.
>Pepper.

feh see *fe*

(a) feier zol im trefen see *a faier zawl ihm trefn*

feifen see *faifn*

feifer see *faifr*

fei-gel see *feigl*

fei-ge-le
>Also spelled *faygeleh, faigele*.
>1. Literally, "little bird."
>2. A gay, a homosexual (slang).

feigl
>Also spelled *feigel, faigel*.
>A bird.

feilen
>1. To fail.
>2. To be missing.

feilt
>Past tense of *feilen*, as in *es feilt a bihsl zaltz*, "A bit of salt is missing."

fein see *fain*

feind see *faind*

feind hoben see *faind hawbn*

feinkuchen see *fainkoochen*

feinshmeker see *fainshmekr*

feint see *faind*

feint krigen see *faint krihgn*

feln
>Also spelled *felen*.
>1. To be wanting.
>2. Missing.

---

fenstr
>Also spelled *fenster.*
>A window.

ferd
>1. A horse.
>2. A boor.
>3. A fool.

fer-gihn-en
>To begrudge.

fer-machn di moil
>1. Literally, "Close the mouth."
>2. Shut up!

fet
>Fat, greasy.

fetr
>Also spelled *feter.*
>Uncle.

fifer see *faifr*

fih-lan-trup
>A philanthropist.

fihnf
>Also *fih-nef.*
>Five.

(a) fihnfer
>A fiver, a five-dollar bill.

(a) fihn-ste-ren sawf
>1. Literally, "a dark ending."
>2. (May you have) a miserable end (to your life).

(a) fihn-ste-re yawr
>1. Literally, "a dark year."
>2. A miserable year.

fihn-ster-nihsh
>1. Darkness.
>2. A plague, a curse.

fihnstr
>Also spelled *finster.*
>1. Dark.

---

a as in father; aw as in law; ai as in aisle; ei as in neighbor; e as in bet; i as in vaccine; ih as in tin; o as in solar; oi as in void; oo as in food; u as in put; uh as in but; ch as in chutzpa; zh as in Zhivago.

2. Sinister.
3. Bleak.
4. Foreboding.

fihnstr ihn di oi-gen
Also spelled *finster in di oigen.*
1. Literally, "dark in the eyes."
2. Faint, fainting.
3. Hopeless.

fihnstr oond glihtch-ihk
1. Literally, "dark and slippery."
2. Miserable.

fihselach see *feeselach*

flaishig see *fleishihg*

flaishik see *fleishihg*

flankn
Also spelled *flanken.*
1. A cut of meat from the side (flank) of the animal.
2. Short ribs.

fleish-e-dihg
A variant form of *fleishihg.* See *fleishihg.*

fleish-ihg
Also *fleish-ihk.*
Also spelled *flaishig, flaishik, flayshig.*
Meat or meat products as well as utensils that have been used in the preparation or serving of meat products. In contrast to *mihlchihk.* See *mihlchihk.*

fligel
Wing of fowl.

flihgn ihn nuhz
Also spelled *fligen in nuz.*
1. Literally, "flies in one's nose."
2. An uppity person.

floim
A plum.

fluden
Dessert made by alternating layers of thin pancakes *(crepes)* with a filling.

---

a as in father; aw as in law; ai as in aisle; ei as in neighbor; e as in bet; i as in vaccine; ih as in tin; o as in solar; oi as in void; oo as in food; u as in put; uh as in but; ch as in chutzpa; zh as in Zhivago.

foiln zihch
Also spelled *foilen zich.*
To be lazy.

foilr
Also spelled *foiler.*
A lazy person.

folgn see *fawlgn*

folksmentsh see *fawlksmensh*

fonfen see *fawnfn*

fonfer see *fawnfr*

foon
Also spelled *fun.*
From.

foon ai-er moil ihn Gawtz oi-ren
1. Literally, "From your mouth into God's ears."
2. May God hear you!

foon dest-veign
Also spelled *fun destvegen.*
1. Nevertheless, however.
2. Still, yet.

foon va-nen
Also *fun vanen.*
From where?

foos
Also spelled *fus.*
Foot, leg.

forshpeis see *fawrshpais*

forstellung see *fawrshteloong*

fort gezunter hait see *fawrt gezoonterheit*

fort veiter see *fawrt vaiter*

Forverts
A Yiddish newspaper founded in New York City in 1897. Pronounced: *Fawr-vertz.* English: *Forward.*

foter see *fawtr*

fra-ge
Question, query.

---

a as in father; aw as in law; ai as in aisle; ei as in neighbor; e as in bet; i as in vaccine; ih as in tin; o as in solar; oi as in void; oo as in food; u as in put; uh as in but; ch as in chutzpa; zh as in Zhivago.

frai
> Also spelled *frei.*
> 1. Free, no charge.
> 2. Not enslaved.

fraid see *freid*

frailich see *freilihch*

fraind
> Also spelled *freind.*
> Friend.

Frankists
> Followers of the Sabbatean pseudomessiah Joseph
> Frank (1726-1791), who eventually converted to Ca-
> tholicism.

frask
> Also spelled *frosk.*
> A strong slap, usually in the face.

a frask ihn fressr
> Literally, "a smack in the eater (face)."

frau see *froi*

freg
> Ask, inquire

fregn
> Also spelled *fregen.*
> To ask.

frei see *frai*

freid
> Also spelled *fraid.*
> Happiness, delight, joy.

freilach
> 1. Happy, cheerful, merry.
> 2. A Jewish folk dance.

frei-lihch
> Also spelled *frailich.*
> Cheerful, merry.

freind see *fraind*

fremdr
> Also spelled *fremder.*

1. A stranger
2. A foreigner, an alien.

fres
To eat like a glutton. See also *fresn.*

fresn
Also spelled *fresen.*
1. To devour.
2. To gorge oneself.

fresn vi a ferd
1. Literally, "to eat like a horse."
2. To gorge oneself.

fresr
Also spelled *fresser.*
1. A big eater.
2. A glutton.

frihtz
Also spelled *fritz.*
1. A novice.
2. A blockhead.

fri-shtihk
Also spelled *frishtik.*
Breakfast.

froi
Also spelled *frau.*
1. Woman.
2. Wife.

froocht
Also spelled *frucht.*
Fruit.

froom
Also spelled *frum.*
1. Devout, pious.
2. A religious person.

froom-ak
Also spelled *frumak.*
1. A hypocritically pious person
2. A hypocrite.

frosk see *frask*

---

a as in father; aw as in law; ai as in aisle; ei as in neighbor; e as in bet; i as in vaccine; ih as in tin; o as in solar; oi as in void; oo as in food; u as in put; uh as in but; ch as in chutzpa; zh as in Zhivago.

frucht see *froocht*

frum see *froom*

frumak see *froomak*

fuhnfn
> Also spelled *funfen*.
> 1. To speak with a twang.
> 2. To mimic.
> 3. To mock.

fuhnfr see *fawnfr*

fun destvegen see *foon destveign*

funfen see *fuhnfn*

fun vanen see *foon vanen*

fus see *foos*

fussnogge
> A jellied soup, usually garlic-flavored.

G

ga-bai
 Also spelled *gabbai.*
 1. A synagogue trustee or treasurer.
 2. The fiscal head of a Jewish community.
 3. A manager for Chassidic rabbis.
 4. Originally, a dues collector.

Ga-lihtz-i-a-ner
 Also spelled *Glitzianer.*
 A Jew of Galician origin, as opposed to a *Litvak,* a Jew of Lithuanian origin. *Glitz* and *Glihtz* are short forms.

galoot see *gawlus*

galuptze see *holishkes*

galut see *gawluhs*

gam a-tem
 1. Literally, "you too."
 2. The same to you! A response to one who has been wished well.

gam zoo l'to-va*
 Also *gam zu le-to-vaw.*
 1. Literally, "This also is for the best."
 2. An expression addressed to one who has had an unpleasant experience.

ganef
 A distorted form of *ganuhv.* See *ganuhv.*

Gan Ei-den
 Also spelled *Gan Eden.*
 1. Literally, "Garden of Eden."
 2. Heaven, paradise.

(a) gang
 1. Walk, gait.
 2. An errand
 3. A walkway, a path.

---

a as in father; aw as in law; ai as in aisle; ei as in neighbor; e as in bet; i as in vaccine; ih as in tin; o as in solar; oi as in void; oo as in food; u as in put; uh as in but; ch as in chutzpa; zh as in Zhivago.

gantz
> Entire, whole, all, complete.

(a) gantz-e ge-shihch-te
> 1. Literally, "a whole story."
> 2. A long, involved tale.
> 3. The entire matter.

(a) gantz-e mai-se
> Also spelled *gantze meiseh*.
> The entire story.

(a) gantz-e me-gih-luh
> Also spelled *a gantze megilla*.
> 1. Literally, "an entire scroll."
> 2. A whole, long story.

(a) gantz-er knakr
> 1. Literally, "a whole knocker."
> 2. A bigshot.

gantz-er mach-er
> 1. Literally, "a whole maker."
> 2. A bigshot.

gantz gut
> Quite good.

ga-nuhv
> Also *ga-nav,* ga-nawv, ga-nef*.
> Also spelled *gonef, gonif*.
> 1. A thief.
> 2. A swindler.
> 3. A burglar.

ganz
> Goose.

ga-on see *gawon*

gartl
> Also spelled *gartel*.
> A silk waistband or sash worn by *Chasidim*, particularly during prayertime.

gas
> 1. A street.
> 2. A thoroughfare in the Jewish section of an East European town.

---

a as in father; aw as in law; ai as in aisle; ei as in neighbor; e as in bet; i as in vaccine; ih as in tin; o as in solar; oi as in void; oo as in food; u as in put; uh as in but; ch as in chutzpa; zh as in Zhivago.

gat-kes
Also spelled *gotkes, gotkis.*
Underwear.

gawld-e-ne
Also spelled *goldene.*
Golden.

gawld-e-ne cha-se-ne
Also spelled *goldene chasseneh.*
1. Literally, "golden wedding."
2. Fiftieth wedding anniversary.

gawld-e-ne me-di-ne
Also spelled *goldene medina, goldeneh medineh.*
1. Literally, "golden country."
2. The United States.

gawld-e-ne yawr-en
1. Literally, "golden years."
2. Old age.

gaw-luhs
Also ga-lut*, ga-loot, gaw-loos.
Also spelled *galus.*
1. Literally, "expulsion, dispersion."
2. The exile, the Diaspora.

gawl-yas
1. The Philistine giant slain by David (I Samuel 17:48-51).
2. A strong man.

gaw-on
Also *ga-on.**
1. The head of an academy of higher learning in Babylonia in the post-Talmudic period.
2. An exceptionally erudite scholar.
3. A genius.
Geonim is the plural form.

gawrgl
Also spelled *gawrgel, gorgel.*
1. Throat, Adam's apple.
2. The neck of a chicken or other fowl.

---

a as in father; aw as in law; ai as in aisle· ei as in neighbor; e as in bet; i as in vaccine; ih as in tin; o as in solar; oi as in void; oo as in food; u as in put; uh as in but; ch as in chutzpa; zh as in Zhivago.

gawr-nihsht
Also spelled *gornisht.*
Nothing, nil.

gawr-niht
Also spelled *gornit.*
A variant form of *gawrnihsht.*
1. Nothing.
2. Absolutely nothing.

Gawt
Also spelled *Gott.*
God.

Gawt-en-yoo
Also spelled *Gottenyu.*
1. Oh God!
2. Dear God!

Gawt hiht up di na-a-raw-nihm
God watches out for fools.

Gawt ihn hihml
Also spelled *Gott in himmel.*
1. Literally, "God in heaven."
2. My God!

Gawt tsoo dankn
Also spelled *Gott tsu danken.*
Thank God!

Gawt veist
Also spelled *Gott vaist.*
1. Literally, "God knows."
2. God only knows!

Gawt vet shtrawfn
Also spelled *Gott vet shtrofen.*
God will punish!

Gawt zai dank
1. Literally, "God be thanked!"
2. God bless!

Gawt zawl up-hihtn
Also spelled *Gott zol uphiten.*
1. Literally, "God should protect!"

2. May God prevent!
3. God forbid!

gazln
Also *gaz-lawn, gaz-lan.* *
Also spelled *gazlin, gazlen.*
A robber, crook, bandit.

ge-beks
Also *ge-baks.*
1. Something baked.
2. Pastry.

geben see *gebn*

ge-bensht
Blessed.

ge-bentsht miht kind-er
Literally, "blessed with children."

ge-bentsh-ter
A blessed person.

gebn
Also spelled *geben.*
Give.

gebn a klap
1. Literally, "to give a blow."
2. To hit someone or something.

gebn an ain haw-re
Also *gebn an ein haw-ruh.*
1. Literally, "to give an evil eye."
2. To nix someone by superfluous praise.

gebn shoi-ched
To bribe.

gebrattens see *gebrawtens*

ge-brawch-en-er Eing-lihsh
Also spelled *gebrochener English.*
1. Literally, "broken English."
2. English spoken with an accent.

ge-brawks
Also spelled *gebroks.*
A mixture of *matza* or *matza* meal and a liquid.

ge-brawt-ens
Also spelled *gebrottens, gebrattens.*
Roasted meat.

ge-bren-te tzaw-res
Also *ge-bren-te tzaw-ruhs.*
1. Literally, "incinerated troubles."
2. Utter misery.

gebroks see *gebrawks*

gebrottens see *gebrawtens*

ge-chrawp-et
Also spelled *gechropet.*
Snored.

ge-dacht
1. Thought.
2. Contemplated.
3. Imagined.

ge-dank
A thought.

ge-dempt-e fleish
Also *ge-demf-te flaish.*
Also spelled *gedempte flaishe.*
Stewed meat.

ge-denkn
Also spelled *gedenken.*
Remember.

gedihle see *gedule*

gedoold see *geduld*

ge-duld
Also spelled *gedoold.*
1. Patience.
2. Temper.

ge-du-le
Also *ge-dihle.*
Also spelled *geduluh, geduleh.*
1. A great thing.
2. Something to exult about.
3. (Sarcastically) a big deal.

---

ge-feln
Also spelled *gefelen.*
1. To suit, satisfy.
2. To appeal to, please.

ge-felt
Past tense of *gefelen,* as in *es gefelt mihr nit,* "I'm not satisfied."

(es) ge-felt mihr
It satisfies me. It pleases me.

ge-fer-lech
Also *ge-fer-lihch.*
Terrible, dangerous.

ge-fihlte fihsh
Also spelled *gefilte fish, gefulte fish.*
1. Literally, "stuffed fish."
2. A mixture of several varieties of fish chopped together and seasoned. Originally the mixture was stuffed into the head or the skin of the fish.

ge-fihlte helzl
Also spelled *gefilte helzel.*
1. Literally, "stuffed neck."
2. Stuffed derma.

ge-hak-te
1. Chopped.
2. Minced.

ge-hak-te Einglihsh
"Chopped" (broken) English.

ge-hak-te herring
Chopped herring.

ge-hak-te lebr
Also *ge-hak-te leibr.*
Also spelled *gehakter leber.*
Chopped liver.

ge-hak-te tzaw-res
Also *ge-hak-te tzaw-ruhs.*
Also spelled *gehakte tzores.*
1. Literally, "chopped troubles."

2. Terrible troubles.
3. Utter misery.

ge-harg-et zawlst doo ver-en
1. Literally, "You should get killed!"
2. Drop dead!

ge-hargn
Also spelled *gehargen.*
Killed. *Derhargnen* is a variant form.

Ge-he-na
Also *Ge-hih-nom.**
Also spelled *Gehenna.*
1. Literally, "the Valley of Hinnom" (near Jerusalem).
2. Hell, inferno.

Gehihnom see *Gehena*

gei a-rois
Go out! Leave!

gei-en
Also *gein.*
1. Go.
2. Walk.
3. Function.

gei ge-zoont-er-heit
1. Literally, "Go in good health!"
2. Goodbye.

gei ihn drerd
1. Literally, "Go into the earth!"
2. Go to hell!

gein tzoo kihnd
Also spelled *gei-en tzu kind.*
1. Literally,"going to child."
2. Going into labor to give birth.

geit
The present tense of *geien,* as in *es geit mihr goot,* "things are going well."

geit es niht
1. Literally, "It doesn't go."
2. It doesn't work well.

a as in father; aw as in law; ai as in aisle; ei as in neighbor; e as in bet; i as in vaccine; ih as in tin; o as in solar; oi as in void; oo as in food; u as in put; uh as in but; ch as in chutzpa; zh as in Zhivago

ge-klih-be-ne verk
  1. Selected writings.
  2. Anthology.

ge-klihbn
  Also spelled *gekliben.*
  1. Selected, chosen.
  2. Gathered.

gel
  Yellow.

gelaimt see *geleimt*

ge-lasn
  Also spelled *gelassen.*
  1. Tender.
  2. Compassionate.
  Gelashn is a distorted form.

ge-lechtr
  Also spelled *gelechter.*
  Laughter.

ge-leimt
  Also spelled *gelaimt.*
  1. Numb.
  2. Paralyzed.

ge-lihb-te
  Also spelled *gelibte.*
  1. Sweetheart (feminine).
  2. Lover.

gelila see *gliluh*

ge-loint
  1. Worth it.
  2. Appropriate, suitable.

gelt
  Money, funds.

ge-malt
  Circumcised.

gemar tov see *gmar tov*

Gemara see *Gemawruh*

ge-mat-ria see *gihmatriyaw*

Ge-maw-ruh
Also *Ge-ma-ra,* Ge-maw-raw.*
Also spelled *Gemarah.*
1. Literally, "completion."
2. The second part of the Talmud, that which is a commentary on the Mishna, the first part of the Talmud.
3. A designation for the whole of the Talmud.

ge-mihsh
Also spelled *gemish.*
Mixture.

ge-miht-lech
Also spelled *gemitlech.*
1. Cozy.
2. Unhurried.

ge-mi-las che-sed
Also *ge-mi-lat che-sed.**
1. Literally, "an act of kindness."
2. A good deed.
3. Jewish Free Loan society.

gemish see *gemihsh*

gemitlech see *gemihtlech*

ge-mut-shet
1. Suffering.
2. Tortured, tormented.
3. Inconvenienced.

ge-nawsn
Also spelled *genawsen, genossen.*
To sneeze, sneezed.

geneiva see *gneivuh*

geneivas daas see *gneivas daas*

geneivishe shtik see *gneivihshe shtihk*

geniza*
Also *ge-ni-zaw.*
1. Literally, "hidden, stored away."
2. A storage place for sacred books and religious articles.
3. The Cairo Geniza, most famous of such deposito-

---

a as in father; aw as in law; ai as in aisle; ei as in neighbor; e as in bet; i as in vaccine; ih as in tin; o as in solar; oi as in void; oo as in food; u as in put; uh as in but; ch as in chutzpa; zh as in Zhivago.

ries, was located (1896) in the Ben Ezra Synagogue in Fustat (Old Cairo) in Egypt.

genossen see *genawsn*

ge-nug
Enough, sufficient.

ge-nug shoin!
1. Literally, "Enough already!"
2. All right already!

geonim Plural of *gaon.* See *gaon.*

ge-oo-luh
Also *ge-oo-la.**
Also spelled *geula.*
1. Redemption.
2. The arrival of the Messiah.

ger
1. A stranger.
2. A convert to Judaism.

ge-recht
1. Correct, right.
2. Fair, just.

ger tze-dek
1. Literally, "righteous stranger."
2. A sincere proselyte.

ge-rut
Conversion to Judaism.

ge-sel see *gesl*

ge-shat
1. Affected.
2. Damaged.

ge-sheft
Business

Ge-shem
A prayer for rain recited on Shemini Atzeret.

ge-shihch-te
Also spelled *geshichte.*
1. History.

a as in father; aw as in law; ai as in aisle· ei as in neighbor; e as in bet; i as in vaccine; ih as in tin; o as in solar; oi as in void; oo as in food; u as in put; uh as in but; ch as in chutzpa; zh as in Zhivago.

2. A story.
3. A long narrative.
ge-shmak
Delicious, tasty.
ge-shmak-e
A very tasty dish.
geshrai see *geshrei*
ʒe-shrei
Also spelled *geshrai*.
A scream, yell, shout.
ge-shtank
Foul odor, stench.
ge-shtawr-ben
Also spelled *geshtorben*.
Deceased.
ge-shtroft
Cursed, punished.
ge-shvawln
Also spelled *geshvollen*.
1. Swollen, puffed up.
2. Haughty.
ge-shvoondn
Also spelled *geshvunden*.
Fainted.
gesl
Also *gas-el*
A diminutive form of *gas*.
1. A short street.
2. An alley.
gesundheit see *gezunthait*
get
A Jewish religious bill of divorcement.
geula see *geooluh*
gevald
A variant form of *gevalt*. See *gevalt*.
ge-vald-ihg
Terrible, awful. *Gevaldihk* is a variant form.

ge-vald-ihg
> Terrible, awful.
> *Gevaldihk* is a variant form.

gevalt
> A cry of frustration, dismay, horror.
> *Gevald* is a variant form.

gevir see *gvihr*

gezl
> Also spelled *gezel*.
> Thievery, stolen merchandise.

ge-zunt
> Also spelled *gezoont, gesund, gesunt, gezund.*
> 1. Health.
> 2. Healthy.

(a) ge-zunt dirh ihn pu-pihk
> 1. Literally, "Good health to your belly button!"
> 2. Thanks for nothing!

(a) ge-zunte
> 1. A healthy person.
> 2. A strong person.

ge-zunt-er-heit
> Also spelled *gezunterhait.*
> Let it happen (or do it) in good health!

ge-zunt-hait
> Also spelled *gesundhait, gesundheit.*
> 1. Literally, "Good health to you!
> 2. God bless you!
> An expression used when one sneezes, originally to ward off evil spirits.

ge-zunt oif dain kawp
> 1. Literally, "Good health upon your head!"
> 2. More power to you!

ge-zunt vi a ferd
> 1. Healthy as a horse.
> 2. Strong as a horse.

gich see *gihch*

a as in father; aw as in law; ai as in aisle; ei as in neighbor; e as in bet; i as in vaccine; ih as in tin; o as in solar; oi as in void; oo as in food; u as in put; uh as in but; ch as in chutzpa; zh as in Zhivago.

gihb sihch a rihr
1. Literally, "Give yourself a move!"
2. Get a move on you!

gihb zihch a shawkl
Also spelled *gib zich a shokl.*
1. Literally, "Give yourself a shake!"
2. Get a move on you!
3. Hurry up!

gihch
Also spelled *gich.*
Soon, fast, speedy, quick.

gihl-gul
Also spelled *gilgul.*
1. Literally, "rolling, revolving."
2. A human being or animal into whom the soul of a deceased person may enter to atone for past sins.

gih-mat-ri-yaw
Also *gih-mat-ri-ya.* *
Also spelled *gimatriya, gematria.*
From the Greek meaning "measurement."
A form of cryptograph in which a word derives its meaning from the numerical value of its Hebrew letters. Widely employed by devotees of Kabbala.

gihml
Also spelled *gimmel.*
The third letter of the Hebrew alphabet.

gihtz see *gutz*

gilgul see *gihlgul*

gil-gul ne-sha-mot*
Also *gil-gool ne-shaw-mos.*
The reincarnation of souls.

gimatriya see *gihmatriyaw*

gimmel see *gihml*

gi-o-ret*
Also *gi-o-res.*
A female convert to Judaism.

---

a as in father; aw as in law; ai as in aisle; ei as in neighbor; e as in bet; i as in vaccine; ih as in tin; o as in solar; oi as in void; oo as in food; u as in put; uh as in but; ch as in chutzpa; zh as in Zhivago.

gi-tihn
>Also spelled *gittin, gitin.*
>1. The plural of *get.*
>2. A tractate of the Talmud.

glaich
>Also spelled *gleich.*
>1. Equal to.
>2. Like.
>3. Straight.

glaich-tzait-ihk
>Also spelled *gleichtseitik*
>Simultaneously.

glaich-vawrt
>Also spelled *gleichvort.*
>Witticism, wisecrack.

glaich-vertl
>Also spelled *gleichvertel.*
>A *bon mot,* a clever remark.

glat kawshr
>Also *glat ka-sher.*
>Also spelled *glatt kosher.*
>1. Literally, "smooth kosher," referring to an animal that has perfectly smooth lungs, as opposed to one that has lungs containing scar tissue. The latter is unacceptable to very Orthodox Jews.
>2. Used in recent years to indicate the highest degree of *kashrut.* See *kashrut.*

glawz
>Also spelled *gloz.*
>1. Glass.
>2. A drinking glass.

gleich see *glaich*

gleichtseitik see *glaichtzaitihk*

gleichvertel see *glaichvertl*

gleichvort see *glaichvawrt*

glez
>A glass.

---

a as in father; aw as in law; ai as in aisle; ei as in neighbor; e as in bet; i as in vaccine; ih as in tin; o as in solar; oi as in void; oo as in food; u as in put; uh as in but; ch as in chutzpa; zh as in Zhivago.

(a) glez-e-le tei
A small glass of tea.

(a) gle-ze-le var-ems
1. Literally, "a glass of warmth."
2. Tea.

(a) glez tei
A glass of tea.

glihk
Also spelled *glick*.
Good luck, good fortune.

(a) glihk hawt dihr ge-trawf-en
Also spelled *(a) glick hot dir getrofen*.
1. Literally, "a bit of luck met up with you."
2. (Sarcastically) Big deal!

glihtsh-ihk
Also spelled *glitshik*.
Slippery.

Glihtz see *Galihtzianer*

gli-luh
Also *gli-la,** *gli-law*.
Also spelled *geliluh, gelila*.
1. Literally, "rolling up."
2. The final Torah honor, in which the recipient rolls the Torah scroll together, ties it with a special band, and then drapes the Torah mantle over it.

glitshik see *glihtshihk*

Glitzianer see *Galihtzianer*

gloib mihr
Also spelled *gloib mir*.
Believe me.

gloibn
Also spelled *gloiben*.
1. Belief.
2. Conviction.
3. Faith.

gloz see *glawz*

---

a as in father: aw as in law; ai as in aisle; ei as in neighbor; e as in bet; i as in vaccine; ih as in tin: o as in solar; oi as in void; oo as in food; u as in put; uh as in but; ch as in chutzpa: zh as in Zhivago.

glustn
Also spelled *glusten.*
1. To lust.
2. To desire, covet.

gmar tov
Also spelled *gemar tov.*
1. Literally "a happy conclusion."
2. Yom Kippur holiday greeting (at the conclusion of the Days of Awe).

gnawsn
Also spelled *genawsen, gnossen.*
Sneezed.

gnawsn oifn e-mes
1. Literally, "sneezed upon (about) the truth."
2. Agreement or confirmation of a statement made.

gneiva see *gneivuh*

gnei-vas da-as
Also *ge-nei-vat da-at.**
1. Literally, "robbing the mind."
2. Deception.

gnei-vih-she shtihk
Also spelled *geneivishe shtik.*
1. Literally, "thieving ways."
2. Dirty tricks.
3. Crooked activities.

gnei-vuh
Also *gnei-vaw, gnei-va.**
Also spelled *geneivuh.*
Theft, robbery.

gnossen see *gnawsn*

goi
Also spelled *goy.*
1. Literally, "a nation."
2. A non-Jewish person.

goi-ihsh
Also spelled *goyish.*
1. Non-Jewish.
2. Gentile in attitude, appearance, or actions.

---

a as in father; aw as in law; ai as in aisle; ei as in neighbor; e as in bet; i as in vaccine; ih as in tin; o as in solar; oi as in void; oo as in food; u as in put; uh as in but; ch as in chutzpa; zh as in Zhivago.

goi-im
Also spelled *goyim*.
Plural of *goi*. See *goi*.

goi-lem
Also *go-lem.**
1. Automaton.
2. An artificial man of legend created by magical
means in Prague in the sixteenth century.
3. A clumsy person.

goi-seis
Also *go-seis.**
A dying person.

goldene see *gawldene*

golem see *goilem*

Go-mel
A prayer of thanksgiving recited in the synagogue
for having been saved from a precarious situation
or on the safe return from a hazardous trip.

gonif
A distorted form of *ganuhv*. See *ganuhv*.

good Shabbos see *gut Shabes*

(a) gootn tawg
Also spelled *(a) guten tag*.
1. Literally, "a good day."
2. Have a good day!

gorgel see *gargl*

gornisht see *gawrnihsht*

gornit see *gawrniht*

gotkes see *gatkes*

Gott see *Gawt*

Gottenyu see *Gawtenyoo*

goy see *goi*

goyim see *goiim*

goyish see *goiihsh*

gragr
Also spelled *grager, grogger*.

---

a as in father; aw as in law; ai as in aisle; ei as in neighbor; e as in bet; i as in vaccine; ih as in tin; o as in
solar; oi as in void; oo as in food; u as in put; uh as in but; ch as in chutzpa; zh as in Zhivago.

A noisemaker used in the synagogue on the Purim holiday during the reading of the Megilla, to denigrate the name of Haman whenever it is mentioned.

(a) greener see *(a) grihner*

greptz
A belch, burp.

gribenes see *grihbenes*

grieben
A variant form of *grivn*. See *grivn*.

grih-be-nes
Also spelled *gribenes*.
A variant form of *grivn*. See *grivn*.

grihn
Also *grin*.
Green.

(a) grihn-er
Also spelled *(a) greener*.
1. Literally, "a green person."
2. A newly-arrived immigrant.

grihns
Also spelled *grins*.
1. Green vegetables.
2. Green plants.

grihs
Also *grus*.
Also spelled *gris*.
1. Greetings.
2. Regards.

grihzh-ih-dihk-er
Also spelled *grizhidiker*.
1. One who gnaws away.
2. A nag.

grihzhn
Also spelled *grizhen*.
1. To gnaw at, nibble.
2. Grind.
3. Annoy.

grihzhn miht di tsein
Also spelled *grizhen mit di tsain*.
Grind one's teeth.

grins see *grihns*

gris see *grihs*

grivn
Also *grihbn*.
Also spelled *grieven, griven*.
Crisp, fried pieces of poultry fat or skin after rendering.

grizhen see *grihzhn*

grizhidiker see *grihzhihdihker*

gro
Also *groi*.
Gray.

grob see *gruhb*

grobber finger see *gruhber fingr*

grobber yung see *gruhber yoong*

grogger see *gragr*

groi see *gro*

grois
Large, big, great, grand.

(a) grois-e ge-du-le
1. Literally, "great glory."
2. Big deal!

(a) grois-e me-tzi-e
Also spelled *(a) groise metzia*.
1. A great find.
2. A big bargain.

grois-haltr
Also spelled *groishalter*.
1. Literally, "one who holds himself big."
2. Conceited, boastful.

(a) groisr far-dihn-er
Also spelled *groiser fardihner*.
1. Literally, "big wage earner!"
2. (Sarcastically) A great breadwinner.

a as in father: aw as in law; ai as in aisle; ei as in neighbor; e as in bet; i as in vaccine; ih as in tin; o as in solar; oi as in void; oo as in food; u as in put; uh as in but; ch as in chutzpa; zh as in Zhivago.

(a) groisr gawr-nihsht
Also spelled *groiser gornisht.*
A big nothing.

(a) groisr knakr
Also spelled *groiser knaker.*
1. Literally, "big knocker."
2. A big shot.

groisr shihsr
Also spelled *groiser shisser.*
1. Literally, "big shot."
2. A big talker, a braggart.

grois vi a barg
As big as a mountain.

groschen see *gruhshn*

gruhb
Also spelled *grob.*
1. Fat.
2. Uncouth.
3. Rude, coarse.
4. Obscene.

gruh-ber fingr
Also spelled *grobber finger.*
1. Literally, "thick (fat) finger."
2. Thumb.

gruhb-er yoong
Also spelled *grobber yung.*
1. Literally, "an uncouth young man."
2. A boorish, coarse, rude person.

gruhb-yan
A boor. A contraction of *gruhber yoong.*

gruhshn
Also spelled *groschen.*
A small coin having the value of a penny.

grus see *grihs*

(a) grus fun der heim
1. Literally, "a greeting from home."
2. Regards from home.

gut
> 1. Good.
> 2. Well.

gut awvnt
> Also spelled *gut ovent*.
> Popularly expressed as *a gutn awvnt*.
> Good evening!

(a) gut-e nacht
> Good night!

gut far ihm
> 1. Good for him!
> 2. Serves him right!

gut ge-nug
> Good enough!

gut ge-zawgt
> Also spelled *gut gezogt*.
> Well said! Well stated!

gut mawrgen
> Also spelled *gut morgen*.
> Popularly expressed as *a gutn mawrgen*.
> Good morning!

(a) gutn tawg
> Also spelled *a guten tag*.
> Also expressed as *a guter tawg*.
> 1. Literally, "a good day."
> 2. A greeting.

gut Sha-bes
> Also *gut Sha-buhs*.
> Also spelled *good Shabbos*.
> Popularly expressed as *a gutn Shabbes*.
> Literally, "good Sabbath," a greeting equivalent to
> *Shabbat shalom,** used in Israel and elsewhere.

gut vawch
> Also spelled *gut voch*.
> 1. Literally, "good week."
> 2. A Saturday night, end-of-Sabbath greeting.

---

a as in father: aw as in law; ai as in aisle; ei as in neighbor; e as in bet: i as in vaccine: ih as in tin: o as in solar; oi as in void; oo as in food; u as in put; uh as in but; ch as in chutzpa: zh as in Zhivago.

(a) gut yawr
    Also expressed as *a gutn yawr.*
    1. Literally, "a good year."
    2. A New Year (Rosh Hashana) greeting.

gut yon tov
    Popularly expressed as *a gutn yontif (yawntif).*
    1. Literally, "a good holiday."
    2. A holiday greeting.

gutz
    Also *gihtz.*
    1. Good things.
    2. Goodies, sweets.
    3. Good news.

(a) gvihr
    Also spelled *gvier, gevir.*
    A wealthy person.

H

ha-ba-chur ha-cha-tan*
Also *ha-baw-chur ha-chaw-sawn.*
1. Literally, "the young bridegroom."
2. A phrase used to call up a bridegroom to the Torah for an *aliya* on the Sabbath before his wedding.

Habad see *Chabad*

haben see *hawbn*

hach-naw-sas or-chihm
Also *hach-na-sat or-chim.**
1. Literally, "taking in, receiving travelers."
2. Granting hospitality to wayfarers.
3. The hospitality committee set up in Jewish communities to attend to needs of visitors.

hach-sha-ra*
Also *hach-shaw-raw.*
1. Literally, "preparation."
2. Agricultural training of pioneer settlers in preparation for their settlement in Israel.

ha-das
Myrtle, one of the species used with the *lulav* on the Sukkot festival. *Hadasim* is the plural form.

Ha-da-sa*
Also *Ha-da-saw.*
Also spelled *Hadassah.*
1. A myrtle.
2. Jewish women's organization supporting medical services in Israel, founded in the United States by Henrietta Szold on Purim, 1912.
3. Hebrew name of Esther, the heroine of Purim story as recorded in the biblical Scroll of Esther.

ha-da-sihm*
Also spelled *hadasim.*

Plural of *hadas.* Myrtle branches held with the *lulav* on Sukkot.

Hadassah see *Hadasa*

Haf-to-raw
Also *Haf-ta-ra.**
Also spelled *Haftorah, Haftarah.*
1. A selection from the books of the Hebrew Prophets which follows the reading of the Pentateuch in synagogues on the Sabbath and holidays.
2. The prophetic portion read by *Bar Mitzva* boys and *Bat Mitzva* girls.

hag see *chag*

Hagada see *Hagawdaw*

Ha-ga-na*
Also *Ha-gaw-naw.*
1. Literally, "protection."
2. A Jewish self-defense underground in Palestine under the British Mandate which evolved into the army of the State of Israel.

Ha-gaw-daw
Also *Ha-ga-da*.*
Also spelled *Haggada, Haggadah.*
1. Literally, "the telling, narration."
2. The Passover Seder prayerbook, in which the story of the Exodus is told. Used at the family celebrations on the first two nights of Passover.
3. A synonym for *Agada.* See *Agada.*

hag-baw
Also *hag-ba.**
The honor bestowed upon one called to lift up the Torah scroll so it can be bound before restoring it to the Ark.

Haggada see *Hagawdaw*

haham see *chacham*

hailn zihch
Also spelled *hailen zich.*
To hurry.

hailt zihch see *ailt zihch*

haim see *heim*

haimihsh see *heimihsh*

haint
Also spelled *heint.*
Today.

haint ihz Purim
Also spelled *heint iz Purim.*
Literally,. "today is (the holiday of) Purim."

hais see *heis*

haisen see *heisn*

haise vanne see *heise vane*

haisr
Also spelled *haizer.*
Houses. Plural of *hoiz.*

haizer see *haisr*

hakafa see *hakawfe*

ha-kaw-fe
Also *ha-kaw-faw, ha-ka-fa.**
1. Literally, "to encircle."
2. The procession of congregants inside the synagogue on Sukkot, each holding a *lulav,* and on
Simchat Torah, each holding a Torah scroll.

hak-fleish
Also spelled *hakflaish.*
Chopped meat, hash.

hak mesr
Also spelled *hak messer.*
A chopping knife, used with a wooden bowl.

hak mihr niht ihn kawp
Also spelled *hak mir nit in kop.*
1. Literally, "Stop chopping on my head!"
2. Stop annoying me!

hak mihr niht kain tchai-nihk
Also *hak mihr niht kein tchai-nihk.*
1. Literally, "Don't bang me on a kettle!"
2. Don't bother me!

---

hakn
>Also spelled *haken*.
>To chop, hew.

hakn a chai-nihk
>1. Literally, "to chop (bang) on a tea kettle."
>2. To drivel, babble.

hak un pak
>1. Literally, "kit and caboodle."
>2. Everything, the whole lot.

halacha*
>Also *ha-law-chaw*.
>Also spelled *halakhah, halachah*.
>1. Rabbinic law.
>2. Those parts of the Talmud devoted to legal matters as contrasted with *agada* (historical and folkloristic subjects).

ha-la-chot*
>Also *ha-law-chos*.
>Plural form of *halacha*.

haldzvetik see *haltzveitihk*

Ha-leil
>Also spelled *Hallel*.
>1. Literally, "praise."
>2. Psalms of thanksgiving, part of the holiday liturgy.

haleva see *haluhva*

ha-le-vai
>Often pronounced *a-le-vai*.
>Also spelled *halevei*.
>1. Perhaps.
>2. May it only happen!

Halitza see *Chalitzuh*

halke
>Grated potato dumpling.

Hallel see *Haleil*

haltz
>Also spelled *halz*.
>Neck, throat.

---

a as in father; aw as in law; ai as in aisle; ei as in neighbor; e as in bet; i as in vaccine; ih as in tin; o as in solar; oi as in void; oo as in food; u as in put; uh as in but; ch as in chutzpa; zh as in Zhivago.

haltz-vei-tihk
Also spelled *haldzvetik.*
1. Literally, "throat pain."
2. A sore throat.

ha-luh-va
Also spelled *haleva, halva, halvah.*
A confection made with ground sesame seeds.

halutz see *chalootz*

halva see *haluhva*

hal-vaw-yas ha-meis-ihm
Also *hal-va-yat ha-mei-tihm.**
1. Literally, "escorting the dead."
2. A funeral procession, often referred to as a *leva'ye.*

haltz
Also spelled *halz.*
Neck, throat.

hamantash see *hawmentash*

hamantashen
Plural of *hawmentash.* See *hawmentash.*

hametz see *chawmetz*

ha-mon
1. The masses.
2. Common people.

Ha-mo-tzi
1. Literally, "He (God) who brings forth."
2. The blessing recited before eating bread.
3. Grace Before the Meal.

ha-na-a*
Also *ha-nuh-uh, ha-naw-aw.*
1. Pleasure, enjoyment.
2. Fun.

handln
Also spelled *handlen.*
1. To do business, to trade.
2. To bargain.

hanukat habayit see *chanookas habayihs*

hanukia see *chanookiyaw*

Hanukkah see *Chanookuh*

hargn
Murder, kill.

haroset see *charoses*

hartz
Heart.

hartz-en-yoo
Also spelled *hartzenyu.*
Sweetheart, darling.

hartz-ihg
1. Hearty.
2. Sincere.
3. Cordial.

hartz-vei-tihk
Also spelled *hartzvaitik.*
Heartache.

ha-saw-gas ge-vool
Also *ha-sa-gat ge-vul.**
1. Literally, "encroachment upon (a neighbor's) boundary (land)."
2. Unfair competition in business.

ha-Sheim
Also *ha-Shem.**
1. Literally, "the (Divine) Name."
2. God, used as a substitute for Adonai.

hash-ga-cha*
Also *hash-gaw-chaw.*
Religious supervision, particularly in the preparation of food.

Hash-ka-ba*
Memorial prayer recited in Sephardic congregations.

hasid see *chuhsihd*

hasidei Ashkenaz see *chasidei Ashkenaz*

hasidism see *chasihdihzm*

Has-kaw-law
> Also *Has-ka-la.**
> 1. Literally, "enlightenment."
> 2. A movement that flourished from 1750 to 1880 to disseminate European culture among Jews.

Ha-tihk-va*
> Also *Ha-tihk-vaw.*
> Also spelled *Hatikva* and *Hatikvah.*
> 1. Literally, "the hope."
> 2. The anthem of the Zionist movement and State of Israel, with lyrics composed in 1878 by Naphtali Herz Imber and music based on a Moldavian-Rumanian folk song.

Hatzi Kaddish see *Chatzi Kadihsh*

Hava Nagila see *hawvaw nawgilaw*

Hav-duh-luh
> Also *Hav-daw-law, Hav-da-la.**
> Also spelled *Havdalah, Habdalah.*
> 1. Literally, "separation."
> 2. The ceremony that marks the conclusion of the Sabbath.

ha-veil ha-vaw-lihm
> Also *hav-eil ha-va-lihm.**
> 1. Literally, "vanity of vanities."
> 2. The second verse of the Book of Ecclesiastes.

haver see *chawvr*

havera see *chaveira*

havura see *chavoora*

haw-ben far-drus
> Also *haw-ben far-dris.*
> 1. To harbor resentment.
> 2. To be angry.
> 3. To be distressed.

haw-ben tzoo zingn oon tzoo zawgn
> Also spelled *hoben tzu zingen un tzu zogen.*
> 1. Literally, "to have what to sing and what to talk about."
> 2. To have no end of trouble.

---

a as in father; aw as in law; ai as in aisle; ei as in neighbor; e as in bet; i as in vaccine; ih as in tin; o as in solar; oi as in void; oo as in food; u as in put; uh as in but; ch as in chutzpa; zh as in Zhivago.

hawbn
Also *haw-ben.*
Also spelled *hoben, haben.*
To have.

hawbn de-rech e-retz
1. To have good manners.
2. To be respectful.

hawl-ep-tches
Also spelled *holeptzes, holopches.*
Stuffed cabbage.

hawltz
Wood.

haw-men-tash
Also *ha-man-tash.*
Also spelled *homentash, hamantash.*
A triangular pastry filled with poppy seeds, prunes, or cheese and eaten on Purim; named after Haman, the Purim villain. *Hamantashen* is the plural form.

hawn
A rooster.

haw-nihg
Also *haw-nihk.*
Also spelled *honik.*
Honey.

hawst doo bai mihr an av-luh
Also spelled *host du bei mir an avla.*
1. Literally, "So you have a grievance against me!"
2. So I made a mistake, so what!

hawt niht kain dai-ges
Also *hawt niht kein deiges.*
Don't be concerned! Don't worry!

hawt niht kain fa-rihbl oif mihr
Also *hawt niht kein fa-ribl oif mihr.*
Don't be angry with me!

hawt niht kain zawrg
Also *hawt niht kein zawrg.*
Don't worry!

---

a as in father; aw as in law; ai as in aisle; ei as in neighbor; e as in bet; i as in vaccine; ih as in tin; o as in solar; oi as in void; oo as in food; u as in put; uh as in but; ch as in chutzpa; zh as in Zhivago.

hawtz-en-plawtz
Also spelled *hotzenplotz*.
1. A faraway town in Central Europe.
2. Way out in the "sticks."

hawtz mihch oon zatz mihch
You should live and be well!

Haw-vaw Naw-gi-law
Also *Ha-va Na-gi-la.**
1. Literally, "Come, let's be joyous."
2. A popular Hebrew song.

hayim see *chayihm*

Hazarat Hashatz see *Chazawras Hashatz*

Haz-kaw-ras Ne-shaw-mos
Also *Haz-ka-rat Ne-sha-mot.**
1. Literally, "remembrance of souls."
2. The memorial service held on the Day of Atonement and on the final days of Pesach, Shavuot, and Sukkot.
Also called *Yizkor*.

hazzan see *chazn*

he see *hei*

hechshr
Also *hech-sher.**
1. Literally, "certification."
2. Rabbinical approval or validation, especially of *kosher* food.

heder see *cheidr*

hei
Also spelled *he*.
1. The fifth letter of the Hebrew alphabet.
2. A Hebrew letter used as a neck charm because of its association with the name of God.

Hei-chal Shlo-mo
1. Literally, "palace of Solomon."
2. Seat of Israel's Chief Rabbinate in Jerusalem.

heiln zihch
Also spelled *hailen zich*.
To care for oneself, to heal oneself.

---

a as in father; aw as in law; ai as in aisle; ei as in neighbor; e as in bet; i as in vaccine; ih as in tin; o as in solar; oi as in void; oo as in food; u as in put; uh as in but; ch as in chutzpa; zh as in Zhivago.

heim
Also *haim*.
1. Home.
2. Native land, as in *in der alter heim,* "in the old country."

heim-ihsh
Also *haim-ihsh*.
1. Homey, cozy, intimate, snug.
2. Informal.

heim-ihsh paw-nihm
Also *haim-ihsh paw-nihm*.
1. Literally, "a homey face."
2. A familiar face.

heint see *haint*

heis
Also spelled *hais*.
1. Hot, torrid.
2. Fervent, devoted.

hei-se va-ne
Also spelled *haise vanne*.
A hot bath.

heisn
Also spelled *haisęn*.
1. To tell.
2. To order.
3. To direct, command.

heizl
Also spelled *heizel*.
1. Literally, "a small house."
2. House of ill repute.

heizr gei-er
Also spelled *heizer gaier*.
1. Literally, "house-goer."
2. Beggar.

hek-deish
Also *hek-desh*.*
1. A forsaken place or thing.
2. A slum.

---

a as in father; aw as in law; ai as in aisle: ei as in neighbor; e as in bet; i as in vaccine; ih as in tin; o as in solar; oi as in void; oo as in food; u as in put; uh as in but; ch as in chutzpa; zh as in Zhivago.

3. A poorhouse.
4. A mess.

held
1. A hero
2. A protagonist.

helfn
Help.

helfn vi a toitn bank-es
1. Literally, "It will be of as much help as performing cupping (to draw blood) on a corpse."
2. It's of no use.
See also *bankes*.

helzl
Also *held-zel*.
Also spelled *helzel*.
1. Neck.
2. Stuffed neck of a fowl, usually chicken.

hemd
A shirt.

her
1. Hear.
2. Listen.

herem see *cheirem*

hern
Also spelled *heren*.
1. To hear.
2. To listen.
3. To obey.

hern a rei-ach
1. Literally, "to hear an odor."
2. To give off an odor.

herr
German for "sir, mister, gentleman." Used by German-speaking Jews.

hert oif
1. Stop!
2. Cease!
3. Cut it out!

---

a as in father: aw as in law; ai as in aisle; ei as in neighbor: e as in bet: i as in vaccine: ih as in tin: o as in solar: oi as in void; oo as in food; u as in put; uh as in but; ch as in chutzpa: zh as in Zhivago.

hert ois
    Literally, "hear out," hear me out.

hert zihch ain
    1. Listen attentively!
    2. Listen (to me) carefully!

hert zihch tzoo
    Listen carefully.

hesdr
    Also spelled *hesder.*
    Orthodox *yeshiva* students in Israel serving in the
    army and carrying on their studies.

hesed see *chesed*

hes-peid
    Also *he-sped.**
    1. A funeral eulogy.
    2. An obituary.

het see *cheit*

hetzn
    Also *hihtzn.*
    Also spelled *hetzen.*
    Incite.

hetzn oon-ter
    1. Bait, heckle.
    2. To incite.

hetzn zihch
    Also spelled *hetzen zich.*
    1. Bounce.
    2. Shake.
    3. Dance with joy.

he-vel
    1. A breath.
    2. Vanity.
    3. Nonsense.

Hevra Kaddisha see *Chevruh Kadishuh*

(a) hihbsh bisl
    Also spelled *a hibsh bissel.*
    1. A considerable amount.
    2. A large quantity.

---

a as in father; aw as in law; ai as in aisle: ei as in neighbor; e as in bet; i as in vaccine; ih as in tin; o as in
solar; oi as in void; oo as in food; u as in put; uh as in but; ch as in chutzpa; zh as in Zhivago.

hihml
Also spelled *himmel.*
1. Heaven.
2. Sky.

hihnkedihk
One who limps, a lame person.

hihnkn
Also spelled *hinken.*
To limp.

hihntehn see *hinten*

hihntn
Also spelled *hinten.*
1. Buttock, the behind.
2. Below.
3. In back of.

hihpsh
Also spelled *hipsh.*
1. Substantial.
2. Sizeable.
3. Considerable.

hihp-sher bisl
Also spelled *hipsher bisl.*
An extremely large amount.

hihs-la-ha-vus
Also *hit-la-ha-vut.**
1. Enthusiasm, excitement.
2. Fervor.
3. Inspiration.

Hihs-tad-rus
Also *Hihs-tad-rut.**
Also spelled *Histadrut.*
1. Literally, "an association, organization."
2. The Federation of Labor in Israel.

hihtl
Also spelled *hitel.*
A cap, hat.

hiht zihch
Also spelled *hit zich.*

---

1. Watch it! Look out!
2. Be careful!

hihtz-kuhp
Also spelled *hitzkop*.
A hothead, an excitable person.

hihtzn see *hetzn*

hilul ha-Shem see *chilool ha-Sheim*

hi-lu-la*
Also *hi-loo-law*.
1. Rejoicing.
2. A day of singing praises *(Hallel)*.
3. A day commemorating the death of a parent or a famous man (in the Sephardic tradition).

hilul Shabbat see *chilool Shabes*

himmel see *hihml*

hin-dig
Turkey.

hinken see *hihnkn*

hinten see *hihntn*

hipsh see *hihpsh*

hipsher bisel see *hihpshėr bihsl*

Histadrut see *Hihstadrus*

hitel see *hihtl*

hitlahavut see *hihslahavus*

hitn
Also spelled *hitten*.
1. To protect oneself.
2. To guard, watch.

hit zich see *hiht zihch*

hitzkop see *hihtzkuhp*

hoben see *hawbn*

hock-messr
A chopping knife, used with a wooden bowl.

hodesh see *chodesh*

---

hoi-cher drung
Also *hoich-er drong.*
1. Literally, "high pole."
2. A tall person.

hoit
Skin.

hoiz
House.

hokhma see *chawchme*

hold-up-nihk
A Yiddish form of "holdup-man," that is, a robber.

holeptzes see *hawleptches*

Hol Hamoed see *Chol Hamoeid*

holishkes
Chopped meat rolled in cabbage or grape leaves.
Also known as *galuptze* or *prokes.*

Holocaust see *Shoa*

holopches see *hawleptches*

homentash see *hawmentash*

honik see *hawnihg*

hoo-ha
An expression of surprise, astonishment, admiration.

hoon-ger-ihk
Also spelled *hungerik.*
Hungry.

ho-raw
Also *ho-ra.**
An Israeli circle folk-dance of Balkan origin.

Ho-sha-na Ra-ba*
Also *Ho-shaw-naw Ra-baw.*
Also spelled *Hoshana Rabba.*
1. Literally, "Great Hosanna."
2. The seventh day of the Sukkot festival.

Ho-sha-not*
Also *Ho-sha-nos.*

Hymns sung during the *hakafot* on Hoshana Rabba.

Ho-shi-a-na
Hymn sung during the *hakafot* of Simchat Torah.

host du bei mir an avla see *hawst doo bai mihr an avluh*

hotzenplotz
See *hawtzenplawtz.*
1. A faraway town in Central Europe.
2. Way out in the "sticks."

hotz-mach
1. Good-natured.
2. A good-natured peddler in a Yiddish play by Abraham Goldfaden.

huhbn chei-shek tzoo
Also spelled *hoben chaishek tzu.*
Have a desire for.

hul-ya-kes
Also spelled *huliakes.*
Roisterers.

hul-yen
Frolic, revel, carouse.

hul-ye-ven
A form of *hulyen.* See *hulyen.*

Humash see *Chumuhsh*

hun
A hen.

hungerik see *hoongerihk*

huppa see *chupuh*

hurban see *choorbn*

hutzpa see *chootzpuh*

I

iberchazeren see *ihberhazren*

ibersetzen see *ihberzetzn*

Ibershter see *Eibershter*

ich see *ihch*

ihber-chazern
>Also spelled *iberchazeren*.
>1 To repeat.
>2. To review by repetition.

ih-ber-zetzn
>Also spelled *iberzetzen*.
>1. To translate.
>2. To transpose.

ihch
>Also spelled *ich*.
>I, me.

ihch bihn
>Also spelled *ich bin*.
>I am.

ihch bihn dihr niht me-ka-ne
>I don't envy you.

ihch darf es
>Also spelled *ich darf es*.
>I need it.

ihch faif oif dihr
>Also spelled *ich feif oif dir*.
>1. Literally, "I whistle upon you."
>2. I despise you!

ihch fihl zihch uhp-ge-nart
>Also spelled *ich fil zich opgenart*.
>1. Literally, "I feel like I have been made to look like a fool."
>2. I was tricked, deceived.

---

a as in father; aw as in law; ai as in aisle; ei as in neighbor; e as in bet; i as in vaccine; ih as in tin; o as in solar; oi as in void; oo as in food; u as in put; uh as in but; ch as in chutzpa; zh as in Zhivago.

ihch hail zihch niht
Also *ich eil zich nit.*
1 I'm in no hurry.
2. Don't rush me!

ihch heis
Also spelled *ich hais.*
1. Literally, "I am called."
2. My name is.

ihch huhb dihr faint
Also spelled *ich hob dir feint.*
I hate you!

ihch huhb dihr ihn buhd
Also spelled *ich hob dir in bod.*
1. Literally, "I have you in the bath (bathhouse)."
2. I despise you!

ihch huhb dihr ihn drerd
Also spelled *ich huhb dir in drerd.*
1. Literally, "I have you in the ground."
2. Go to hell!

ihch huhb dihr ihn tuh-ches
Also spelled *ich hob dir in toches.*
1. Literally, "I have you in my buttocks."
2. I have no use for you!

ihch huhb zihch ge-mutsh-et
Also spelled *ich hob zich gemutshet.*
1. I tortured (troubled) myself.
2. I agonized, suffered.

ihch veis
Also spelled *ich vais,*
1. I know.
2. I am aware.

ihch veis niht
Also spelled *ich vais nit.*
I don't know.

ihch vel dihr gebn ka-daw-ches
Also spelled *ich vell dir geben kadoches.*
1. Literally, "I'll give you a fever, the chills."
2. I'll give you nothing.

---

a as in father; aw as in law; ai as in aisle; ei as in neighbor; e as in bet; i as in vaccine; ih as in tin; o as in solar; oi as in void; oo as in food; u as in put; uh as in but; ch as in chutzpa; zh as in Zhivago.

ihch yawg zihch
Also spelled *ich yog zich.*
1. Literally, "I'm chasing myself."
2. I'm rushing.

ihch yawg zihch niht
Also spelled *ich yog zich nit.*
1. Literally, "I'm not chasing myself."
2. I'm not rushing.
3. I'm in no hurry.

ihch zawl a-zoi vihsn foon tsaw-res
Also spelled *ich zol azoi vissen fun tsores.*
1. Literally, "I should know as little about trouble (as I know about what you are asking me)."
2. I'm totally ignorant of the matter.

ihm-be-shri-en
Also *oom-be-shri-en.*
1. Literally, "unbewitched."
2. God forbid!
3. It shouldn't happen!
Sometimes said when praising a child, to ward off evil.

ihm yihr-tse ha-Shem*
Also spelled *im yirtse ha-Shem.*
1. Literally, "If the (Divine) Name wills it!"
2. God willing!
Contracted to *mirtzishem* and *mihrtzeshem.*

ihn a nuh-ve-ne
Also *ihn a naw-vih-ne.*
Also spelled *in a noveneh.*
1. Literally, "in time for something new."
2. For a change.
3. Once in a blue moon.

ihn buhd
Also spelled *in bod.*
1. In the bath.
2. In the bathhouse.

ihn der erd
Also *ihn drerd.*

---

a as in father; aw as in law; ai as in aisle; ei as in neighbor; e as in bet; i as in vaccine; ih as in tin; o as in solar; oi as in void; oo as in food; u as in put; uh as in but; ch as in chutzpa; zh as in Zhivago.

1. Literally, "in the earth."
2. Of no value.

ihn di al-te gut-e tzaitn
Also spelled *in di alte gute tzeiten.*
In the good old days.

ihn di al-te yawr-en
Also spelled *in di alte yoren.*
1. Literally, "in the elderly years."
2. In (one's) old age.

ihndihg
Also *hihndihk.*
A turkey.

ihn drerd see *ihn der erd*

ihn drerd a-rain
1. Literally, "into the earth with you."
2. Go to hell!

ihn drerd main gelt
Also *drerd mein gelt.*
1. Literally, "My money is in the earth (in hell)."
2. My money went down the drain.

ihn droisn ihz a glihtsh
Also spelled *in droisen iz a glitsh.*
It's slippery outside.

ihn es-ihg oon ihn haw-nihg
Also *ihn es-ihk oon ihn haw-nihk.*
1. Literally, "in vinegar and in honey."
2. Dressed in finery.

ihn ka-as oif
To be angry with.

ihn mihtn der-ihn-en
Also spelled *in mitten derinin.*
1. In the midst of.
2. Suddenly.

ihn miht-she der-ihn-en
A variant form of *ihn mihtn derihnen.* See above.

ihn-yen
Also *ihn-yan.**

---

a as in father; aw as in law; ai as in aisle; ei as in neighbor; e as in bet; i as in vaccine; ih as in tin; o as in solar; oi as in void; oo as in food; u as in put; uh as in but; ch as in chutzpa; zh as in Zhivago.

1. A subject.
2. A concern.
3. A theme (in Talmudic study).

ihp-uhsh
Also *ihp-esh.*
Also spelled *ipush.*
1. Stench.
2. Mold.

ihr ge-felt mihr
Also spelled *ir gefelt mir.*
You please me.

ihr ge-felt mihr zeir
Also spelled *ir gefelt mir zaier.*
You please me greatly.

Ihr-gun*
Short for *Ihr-gun Tsva-i Le-oo-mi.**
Also spelled *Irgun Z'vai Leumi, Irgun.*
"National Military Organization." The name of the underground Jewish military group in Palestine, founded in 1931. From 1937 to 1948 it engaged in attacks against Arabs and British mandatory officials.

ihtst
Also *yetzt.*
Also spelled *itzt.*
Now, presently.

Ihv-ri
Also spelled *Ivri.*
1. Literally, "one from across (the Euphrates River)."
2. A member of a Semitic people that traces its origins to the patriarchs Abraham, Isaac, and Jacob.
3. A Hebrew.

Ihv-rihs
Also *Ihv-riht,** *Iv-rit.*
Hebrew, the Hebrew language.

ihz nihsht ge-fer-lach
Also spelled *iz nisht geferlach.*
It's not so terrible!

i-kuhr
Also spelled *i-kar.* *
1. Essence
2. Principle.
3. Fundamental tenet.

i-looy
Also spelled *ilui.*
1. A genius.
2. A Talmudic prodigy.

im yirtse ha-Shem see *ihm yihrtze ha-Sheim*

in a noveneh see *ihn a nuhvene*

in bod see *ihn buhd*

in di alte gute tzeiten see *ihn di alte gute tzaitn*

in di alte yoren see *ihn di alte yawren*

in esik un in honik see *ihn esihk oon ihn hawnihk*

ing-ber
Ginger.

ing-ber lei-kach
Also *ing-ber le-kach.*
Gingerbread.

ing-ber vasr
Ginger water, ginger ale.

in mitten derinin see *ihn mihtn derihnen*

ipush see *ihpuhsh*

ir gefelt mir see *ihr gefelt mihr*

Irgun Z'vai Leumi see *Ihrgun*

Israel
English for *Yihsraweil.* See *Yihsraweil.*
1. Literally, "contender with God."
2. The Holy Land.
3. The Jewish people.
4. The name assigned to Jacob after he contended
   with a divine emissary (Genesis 32:39).

itzt see *ihtst*
Ivri see *Ihvri*
Ivrit see *Ihvrihs*
I-yar*
    Also *I-yawr.*
    Also spelled *Iyyar.*
    The second month of the Jewish religious calendar, eighth of the Civil calendar, corresponding to April-May.
I-ze-vel
    Also spelled *Jezebel.*
    1. Wife of King Ahab of Israel (I Kings 16:31).
    2. A shameless, wicked woman.
iz nisht geferlach see *ihz nihsht gerferlach*

a as in father; aw as in law; ai as in aisle; ei as in neighbor; e as in bet; i as in vaccine; ih as in tin; o as in solar; oi as in void; oo as in food; u as in put; uh as in but; ch as in chutzpa; zh as in Zhivago.

J

jahrzeit see *yartzait*

Jehovah
1. God.
2. The English form of YHVH.

Jezebel see *Izevel*

Judenrat
German for the "Jewish Council" ordered by Nazis to carry out their orders.

Judeo-German
Yiddish

Judeo-Spanish
Ladino.

Judezmo
Also spelled *Judesmo*.
The Ladino word for Judeo-Spanish.

K

kaas see *kas*

Ka-ba-la*

Also *Ka-baw-law.*

Also spelled *Kabbalah, Cabala, Cabbala.*

1. Literally, "receipt, receiving."
2. Jewish mysticism.
3. A document certifying a *shochet* to slaughter animals.

ka-ba-lat mihtz-vot*

Also *ka-baw-las mihtz-vos.*

Acceptance of the commandments, a necessary prelude to conversion to Judaism.

Ka-baw-las Sha-buhs

Also *Ka-ba-lat Sha-bat,* *Ka-baw-las Sha-bes.*

The Friday evening prayer service ushering in the Sabbath.

kab-tzaw-nihm

Plural of *kabtzn.* See below.

kabtzn

Also *kab-tzan.**

Also spelled *kabtzen, kabtzin, kobtzen, koptzen, koptzin.*

1. A pauper.
2. A mendicant, a beggar.

ka-daw-ches see *kaduhches*

Ka-dihsh

Also spelled *kaddish.*

1. Literally, "sanctification."
2. Doxology.
3. Mourner's Prayer.
4. An orphan, often referred to as a *kadihshl.*
5. A person hired to say the Mourner's Prayer.

---

a as in father; aw as in law; ai as in aisle; ei as in neighbor; e as in bet; i as in vaccine; ih as in tin; o as in solar; oi as in void; oo as in food; u as in put; uh as in but; ch as in chutzpa; zh as in Zhivago.

ka-dihshl
A young orphan. See also *Kadihsh.*

Ka-dihsh Tihs-ka-beil
Also *Ka-dihsh Tiht-ka-bel**
The full Kaddish, which includes the petition beginning with *Tihtkabel:* "May the prayers of the House of Israel be accepted."

kadosh see *kawdosh*

ka-duh-ches
Also *ka-da-chat.**
Also spelled *kadoches, kadawches.*
1. Fever, ague, malaria.
2. A bad situation.

ka-duh-ches miht kuh-sher-e fuh-dem
1. Literally, "a fever with *kosher* thread."
2. Absolutely nothing.
3. Of no value.

kaf*
Also *kawf.*
1. A spoon, a ladle.
2. The eleventh letter of the Hebrew alphabet.

kaf-tan*
Also *kaf-tuhn.*
The long, black overgarment worn by observant Jewish men in Eastern Europe. Also called *kapawtuh.*

kahal see *kawhawl*

kailihke see *kalihke*

kain see *kein*

kainainhore see *kein ayihn huruh*

kain ayin hore see *kein ayihn huhruh*

kain mal see *kein muhl*

kai oon shpai
Literally, "chew and spit."

kairuh see *ke'ara*

ka-la see *kale*

kalb fleish
>Veal meat.

ka-le
>Also *ka-la,* ka-law.*
>Also spelled *kalle.*
>Bride.

ka-lih-ke
>Also *kai-lih-ke, kal-yih-ke.*
>A handicapped person.

kam see *kum*

kam-puht
>Also *kam-pot, kam-put.*
>Also spelled *kampote, campote.*
>Stewed fruit.

kamtzn
>Also *kam-tzawn, kam-tzan.**
>1. A skinflint.
>2. A miser.

ka-nuh
>Also spelled *kaneh.*
>An enema.

kapara see *kapawruh.*

ka-pa-rot*
>Also *ka-paw-res.*
>1. Literally, "atonements."
>2. Hens and roosters used as symbols of atonement before Yom Kippur.
>*Kapara* is the singular form.

ka-paw-ruh
>Also *ka-pa-ra,* ka-paw-raw.*
>Also spelled *kapora, kapore.*
>1. Literally, "atonement."
>2. A fowl used for atonement.
>3. A scapegoat.

ka-paw-tuh
>Also spelled *caputa, kapote.*
>1. A robe.
>2. A long, black overgarment.

---

a as in father; aw as in law; ai as in aisle; ei as in neighbor; e as in bet; i as in vaccine; ih as in tin; o as in solar; oi as in void; oo as in food; u as in put; uh as in but; ch as in chutzpa; zh as in Zhivago.

ka-pe-le
A small skullcap. See also *kapl.*

kapl
Also spelled *kappel, koppel.*
A skullcap.

ka-poi-e
Also *ka-poir.*
1. Reverse.
2. Inside out.
3. Backwards.
4. One who is contrary.

kapora see *kapawruh*

kapote see *kapawtuh*

kappel see *kapl*

Karaim see *Karaite*

Karaite
A member of a Jewish settlement founded in the eighth century. These Jews, known as *Karaim* in Hebrew, rejected the Oral Law (Talmud) and followed the Written Law (Bible) literally.

kargr
Also spelled *karger.*
1. A miser.
2. Cheapskate, tightwad.

kar-kuh
Also *kar-ka.**
Earth, ground, soil, land.

karnatzlach
Hamburgers in the shape of frankfurters.

karov see *kawrov*

kar-pas
A green vegetable eaten at the Passover *Seder.*

kar-tawfl
Also spelled *kartofel, kartoffel.*
Potato.

kas
Also *ka-as.**

---

a as in father; aw as in law; ai as in aisle: ei as in neighbor; e as in bet; i as in vaccine; ih as in tin; o as in solar; oi as in void; oo as in food; u as in put; uh as in but; ch as in chutzpa; zh as in Zhivago.

1. Anger, wrath, ire.
2. Sorrow, vexation.

kasha see *kashuh*

kashe varnihshkaz see *kashuh varnihshkez*

kasher see *kosher*

kashering see *koshering*

kash-rus
Also *kash-rut.**
Also spelled *kashruth.*
The state or condition of being kosher, in accordance with Jewish dietary laws as specified in Leviticus 11 and elaborated upon in the Talmud and later codes.

kashrut see *kashrus*

ka-shuh
Also spelled *kasha, kashe.*
1. Buckwheat kernels, cereal, porridge.
2. A mess, a mix-up.

ka-shuh var-nihsh-kez
Also *ka-she var-nihsh-kaz.*
Buckwheat groats with pasta.

ka-suh-ke
Also spelled *kasoke.*
Cross-eyed.

katch-ke
Duck.

katz-ih-sher kawp
Also spelled *katzisher kop.*
1. Literally, "cat-head."
2. Forgetful.
3. Lame-brain.

kaufen see *koifn*

kavana see *kavuhne*

ka-ve
Coffee.

kavod see *kuhved*

---

a as in father; aw as in law; ai as in aisle; ei as in neighbor; e as in bet; i as in vaccine; ih as in tin; o as in solar; oi as in void; oo as in food; u as in put; uh as in but; ch as in chutzpa; zh as in Zhivago.

ka-vuh-ne
> Also *ka-va-na,** *ka-vaw-naw.*
> Also spelled *kavanah.*
> 1. Intention.
> 2. Concentration.
> 3. In Jewish mysticism, "to turn oneself" toward God in prayer.

kawch-a-lein
> Also spelled *kochalain, kochalayn.*
> 1. Literally, "to cook alone."
> 2. A boarding house with cooking privileges.

kawch-lefl
> Also spelled *kochleffel.*
> 1. Literally, "cooking ladle."
> 2. Busybody, meddler.

kawchn
> Also spelled *kawchen, kochen.*
> 1. Cook, boil, seethe.
> 2. Cooked food.

kaw-dosh
> Also *ka-dosh.**
> Holy, sacred. See also *kodesh.*

kawf see *kaf*

kaw-hawl
> Also *ka-hal.**
> Congregation.

kawl-boi-nihk
> Also *kolbonik.*
> 1. A religious leader who can perform many religious functions.
> 2. A know-it-all.
> 3. A jack-of-all-trades.

(ihm) kawl ha-ne-aw-rihm
> Also *(ihm) kal ha-n'a-rihm.**
> 1. Literally, "with all the lads."
> 2. A collective *aliya* on Simchat Torah for boys under age thirteen.

kawp see *kuhp*

k'awraw see *ke'ara*

kaw-rov
Also *ka-rov.**
1. Near, nearby.
2. A relative.

kawrt
1. A card.
2. A playing card.
Kawrtn is the plural form.

kawvod see *kuhved*

kayn see *kein*

k'dei-shuh
Also spelled *kedeisha,** *kedeishaw.*
1. A prostitute
2. A priestess.

K'doo-shas Ha-yom
Also *Ke-doo-shat Ha-yom.**
1. Literally, "the holiness of the day."
2. A blessing recited during the *Amida* on Sabbaths and holidays.

K'du-shuh
Also *Ke-du-shaw, Ke-du-sha.**
1. Holiness.
2. A portion of the liturgy consisting of verses praising God.

ke-a-ra*
Also *kai-ruh, k'aw-raw.*
A special plate used for the Passover *Seder.*

kefar see *k'far*

ke-hi-luh
Also *ke-hi-la,** *ke-hi-law.*
Also spelled *kehilla.**
1. A Jewish congregation.
2. An organized Jewish community.

kei-lihtsh
Also spelled *keylitch.*
A large *chalah* used on special occasions.

---

a as in father: aw as in law: ai as in aisle: ei as in neighbor: e as in bet: i as in vaccine: ih as in tin: o as in solar: oi as in void: oo as in food: u as in put: uh as in but: ch as in chutzpa: zh as in Zhivago.

kein
Also *kain, kayn.*
1. No, none.
2. Nobody.

kein a-yihn huh-ruh
Also spelled *kainainhore, kine-ahora, kain ayin hore. Kaineinhora* and *kenahora* are contracted forms.
1. Literally, "no evil eye."
2. May no evil befall you!

kein muhl
Also *kain mal.*
At no time, never.

keivr
Also *ke-ver.**
A grave.

kelipa see *klipaw*

kelipot see *klipot*

kelnr
Also spelled *kelner.*
A waiter.

kempfr
Also spelled *kempfer.*
1. A fighter.
2. One who battles for a cause.

ken*
Also *kein.*
1. Yes.
2. Correct.

kenahora see *kein ayihn huhruh*

kenen see *kenuhn*

ken ge-moolt zain
It's imaginable. It's conceivable.

ken-uhn
Also *ken-en.*
1. To know how.
2. To recognize.
3. To be able.

ken zain
Could be, maybe.

ke-puh-le
A small head. A diminutive form of *kuhp*.

ker-en ih-ber di velt
1. Literally, "to turn the world upside down."
2. To perform the impossible.
3. To carry on joyfully.

Ke-ren Ka-ye-met L'Yis-ra-el*
Also *Ke-ren Ka-ye-mes L'Yis-raw-eil.*
Jewish National Fund, the tree planting and afforestation agency for Israel.

keria see *kriuh*

kerias haTorah see *k'rias haToraw*

kerias Shema see *k'rias Shema*

ke-ro-va*
Also *ke-ro-vaw.*
Also spelled *kerovah.*
1. Literally, "nearness (to God)."
2. A prayer-poem.

kerovim see *kroivihm*

kerovot*
The plural of *kerovah.*

kertl
Also spelled *kertel.*
A playing card.

kesubah see *k'subuh*

ke-too-vihm*
Also *ke-su-vim.*
Also spelled *ketubim.*
1. Literally, "writings."
2. The third part of the Hebrew Bible, called "Sacred Writings."

ketuba see *k'subuh*

ketuva see *k'subuh*

ketuvim see *ketoovihm*

---

a as in father; aw as in law; ai as in aisle; ei as in neighbor; e as in bet; i as in vaccine; ih as in tin; o as in solar; oi as in void; oo as in food; u as in put; uh as in but; ch as in chutzpa; zh as in Zhivago.

kever see *keivr*

ke-vod ha-be-ri-yot
Respect for human beings.

ke-vod ha-meis
Also *ke-vod ha-met.**
Respect for the dead.

ke-voo-ra*
Also spelled *k'vura.*
1. Burial.
2. Grave.

ke-voo-tza*
Also spelled *kevutza, kvutza.*
A cooperative farming settlement in Israel.

keylitch see *keilihtsh*

kezayit see *k'zayiht*

k'far
Also spelled *kefar.*
A village, especially in Israel.

Khazars
A Tatar people who allegedly converted to Judaism in the ninth century.

kibbetz see *kihbetz*

kibbutz see *kibutz*

ki-bood*
Also *ki-bud.*
1. Honor, respect.
2. A ritual honor, such as being called to Torah in synagogue.

ki-bood awv
Also spelled *kibud av.**
Honoring one's father.

ki-bood eim
Also spelled *kibud aym.*
Honoring one's mother.

ki-butz
Also spelled *kibbutz.*

---

a as in father; aw as in law; ai as in aisle; ei as in neighbor; e as in bet; i as in vaccine; ih as in tin; o as in solar; oi as in void; oo as in food; u as in put; uh as in but; ch as in chutzpa; zh as in Zhivago.

A commune in Israel.
Kibbutzihm is the plural form.

ki-butz ga-loo-yot*
Also *ki-bootz gaw-loo-yos.*
Also spelled *kibbutz galuyot.*
1. Literally, "ingathering of the exiles."
2. Return of Jews from the Diaspora to Israel.

kibutznik
A member of a *kibutz.*

kichl see *kihchl*

kichlach see *kihchlach*

kiddush see *kihdoosh*

kiddushin see *kihdooshihn*

kih-betz
Also spelled *kibbetz, kibutz.*
1. To joke, kid around.
2. Tease.
3. To offer unsolicited advice as a spectator.

kih-betzr
Also spelled *kibbetzer, kibbitzer.*
1. One who offers unsolicited advice.
2. A meddlesome spectator.
3. One who teases.
4. A buttinsky.
5. One who annoys others.

kihchl
Also spelled *kichl.*
A cookie, wafer.

kihch-lach
Also spelled *kichlach.*
Light, airy cookies.

Kih-doosh*
Also *Ki-doosh.*
Also spelled *Kiddush.*
1. Literally, "sanctification."
2. The blessing recited over wine on the Sabbath and holidays.

a as in father; aw as in law; ai as in aisle; ei as in neighbor; e as in bet; i as in vaccine; ih as in tin; o as in solar; oi as in void; oo as in food; u as in put; uh as in but; ch as in chutzpa; zh as in Zhivago.

kih-doosh ha-Shem*
Also *ki-doosh ha-Shem.*
Also spelled *kiddush haShem, kiddush haShaym.*
1. Literally, "sanctification of the Name (of God)."
2. An act of Jewish martyrdom.

Kih-doo-shihn*
Also *Ki-doo-shihn.*
Also spelled *Kiddushin.*
1. Marriage.
2. A tractate of the Talmud dealing with matrimony.

kih-doosh Le-vuh-nuh
Also *ki-doosh Levawnaw, ki-doosh Le-va-na.**
Also spelled *kiddush Levana.*
Blessing of the New Moon, said between the third and sixteenth days of the Jewish month.

kihm miht tzuris
Also *kum mit tzores.*
1. Literally, "barely with trouble."
2. Barely made it.

kihm-puht
Also *kim-pet.*
1. A woman in labor.
2. Childbirth.
3. Confinement.

kihm-puht tzetl
Also spelled *kimpet tzetel.*
Childbirth amulet or charm containing Psalm 121 and names of angels and patriarchs.

kih-nas chi-nawm
Also *kihn-at chi-nam.**
Also spelled *kinas chinawm.*
Unwarranted jealousy.

kihnd
Also spelled *kind.*
A child, youngster.

kihn-der-lach
Also spelled *kinderlach.*
Little children.

kihnd-oon-keit
Also spelled *kind-un-keit*.
Kith and kin; kit and caboodle.

kihndr
Also spelled *kinder*.
Children.

kih-ne
Also *ki-naw, ki-na*.*
1. Jealousy, envy.
2. A lamentation.

kihn-yan*
Also *kihn-yuhn*.
Also spelled *kinyan*.
1. A purchase.
2. The finalizing of an agreement whereby both parties grasp a garment at the same time.
3. Consideration, as in a contract.

kih-shef
Also *ki-shoof*.*
Also spelled *kishuf*.
Magic.

kih-shef ma-cher-ihn
1. A witch.
2. Title of a play by Abraham Goldfaden (1840-1908), the father of Yiddish theater.

kih-shef machr
Also spelled *kishef macher*.
1. Literally, "magic maker."
2. A male magician.

kihsh-kih
Also spelled *kishka, kishke*.
1. Intestines, guts.
2. Stuffed derma.

Kihs-lev
Also *Kihs-leiv*.
Also spelled *Kislev, Kislayv*.
Ninth month of the Jewish religious calendar, third of the Civil calendar, corresponding to No-

---

a as in father; aw as in law; ai as in aisle; ei as in neighbor; e as in bet; i as in vaccine; ih as in tin; o as in solar; oi as in void; oo as in food; u as in put; uh as in but; ch as in chutzpa; zh as in Zhivago.

vember-December, the month in which Chanukah falls.

kihtl
Also spelled *kittel.*
The white linen robe worn by Jewish men at High Holiday services and often also by the leader at the Passover *Seder.*

kiht-ni-ot*
Also *kiht-ni-os.*
Also spelled *kitniot, kitnios.*
The lesser grains—such as rice, beans, and maize—forbidden to Ashkenazim on Passover but permitted to most Sephardim.

kihtzl
Also spelled *kitzel.*
To tickle.

kike
An epithet for "Jew," much like the usage of "wop" or "dago" for Italians and "spik" for Spaniards. The origin is unknown but may be related to the Yiddish word *kaikel (kikel),* meaning "a circle." Not willing to sign their names with a cross (or an "X," which is similar to a cross), some Jews used a circle (a *kaikel*) instead.

kimpet see *kihmpuht*

kina see *kihne*

kind see *kihnd*

kinder see *kihndr*

kindunkeit see *kihndoonkeit*

kine-ahora see *kein ayihn huruh*

ki-not*
Also *ki-nos.*
Also spelled *kinoth, kinnot.*
1. Lamentations.
2. The biblical book Lamentations, recited on Tisha b'Av.

ki-nui
1. Appellation.

2. The name by which a Jew is known in non-Jewish life, not his "Jewish" name.

kinyan see *kihnyan*

kipa*
Also *ki-paw.*
A skullcap.

ki-sei shel Ei-li-yaw-hoo ha-naw-vi
Also *ki-se shel E-li-a-hoo ha-na-vi.**
Also spelled *kise shel Eliyahu hanavi.*
Literally, "the chair of the Prophet Elijah," on which a baby boy is placed before his circumcision.

kishef macher see *kihshef machr*

kishke see *kihshkuh*

Kislev see *Kihslev*

kitniot see *kihtniot*

kittel see *kihtl*

kitzel see *kihtzl*

klai zemer see *klei zemr*

klaid see *kleid*

klain see *klein*

(a) klainer gornisht see *(a) kleiner gawrnihsht*

klainikeit see *kleinihkait*

klal Yihs-raw-ayl
Also *klal Yis-ra-el.**
1. Literally, "the totality of the Jewish people."
2. The Jewish community.

klap
Also spelled *klop.*
Slap, hit, rap.

klap zihch kawp ihn vant
1. Literally, "Bang your head against the wall!"
2. Don't bother me!

klas
1. Class, classroom.
2. Grade in school.

klaus see *kloiz*

---

a as in father: aw as in law: ai as in aisle; ei as in neighbor; e as in bet; i as in vaccine: ih as in tin: o as in solar; oi as in void; oo as in food; u as in put; uh as in but; ch as in chutzpa; zh as in Zhivago.

klawg
>Also *kluhg, klug.*
>Also spelled *klog.*
>1. A curse.
>2. A lament.

(a) klawg ihz mihr
>Also *a klug iz mir.*
>1. Literally, "A curse is (on) me!"
>2. Woe is me!

klawgn
>Also spelled *klogen.*
>Complain, wail, lament.

(a) klawg tzoo Columbus
>Also spelled *a klog tzu Columbus.*
>1. Literally, "A curse on Columbus!"
>2. Damn Columbus! Spoken by Jewish immigrants
>from Eastern Europe around the turn of the
>twentieth century when they found that the
>streets of the New World were not "paved with
>gold."

(a) klawg tzoo main-e saw-nihm
>Also spelled *(a) klog tzu meine sonim.*
>A curse on my enemies!

klawtz
>Also spelled *kluhtz, klotz.*
>1. Foolish.
>2. Clumsy, awkward.
>3. A bungler.

klawtz ka-she
>Also spelled *klotz kashe.*
>1. A foolish question.
>2. A question intended to annoy someone.

kleid
>Also spelled *klaid.*
>Dress, apparel, clothing.

klein
>Also *klain.*
>Small, short.

---

a as in father; aw as in law; ai as in aisle; ei as in neighbor; e as in bet; i as in vaccine; ih as in tin; o as in
solar; oi as in void; oo as in food; u as in put; uh as in but; ch as in chutzpa; zh as in Zhivago.

(a) klein-er gawr-nihsht
Also spelled *(a) klainer gornisht.*
1. Literally, "a little nothing."
2. A nobody, a nonentity.

klein-ih-kait
Also spelled *klainikeit.*
Trifle.

kleis
A *matza*-meal dumpling. Synonymous with *kneidl (knaidel).*

klei zemr
Also spelled *klai zemer.*
1. Literally, "musical instruments."
2. Musicians.
3. A band, combo.

klekn
Also spelled *kleken.*
To suffice.

klepn tzoo
To adhere, to stick to.

(es) klept zihch vi arbes ihn vant
1. Literally, "It sticks (applies) like peas to a wall."
2. Irrelevant.
3. Incoherent.

klez-muhr
Also *klez-mihr, klez-mer.*
1. Derived from *klei zemr,* "musical instruments."
2. Musicians.
3. Itinerant musicians in Europe.

kli-paw
Also *kli-pa,* klih-puh.*
Also spelled *kelipa.*
1. Literally, "husk"
2. Used in Jewish mysticism to denote the forces of evil.
3. A shrew.
4. A gabby woman.
5. A female demon.
Klipot and *kelipot* are plural forms.

kli-pot*
> Also *ke-li-pot.*
> Plural of *klipaw.*

klogen see *klawgn*

kloi-mersht
> 1. Ostensibly.
> 2. As it were.

kloiz
> Also *klowz, klaus.*
> 1. A club, group.
> 2. A meeting place.
> 3. A small synagogue.

kloog
> Also *kluhg, klug.*
> Smart, clever.

klop see *klap*

klotz see *klawtz*

klowz see *kloiz*

klug see *klawg*

klupr
> Also spelled *klupper.*
> 1. A slow worker.
> 2. A slow thinker.

klutz see *klawtz*

knaidel see *kneidl*

knakr
> Also spelled *knaker, knocker.*
> 1. Literally, "one who snaps (his fingers, the whip)."
> 2. Big shot, showoff, big wheel.

kneidl
> Also spelled *knaydl, knaidel, knaidle, knaidl, kneidl.*
> A dumpling, usually made with *matza* meal, eggs, water, and chicken fat. Served in chicken soup, most often on Passover.
> Kneidlach and *knaidlach* are plural forms.

---

a as in father; aw as in law; ai as in aisle; ei as in neighbor; e as in bet; i as in vaccine; ih as in tin; o as in solar; oi as in void; oo as in food; u as in put; uh as in but; ch as in chutzpa; zh as in Zhivago.

kneppel see *knihpl*

Kne-set*
Also *Knes-es.*
Also spelled *Knesset.*
1. Literally, "an assembly."
2. Unicameral parliament of the State of Israel.

knihp
Also spelled *knip.*
To nip, pinch.

knihpl
Also spelled *knipl, knippel, kneppel.*
1. Button.
2. Knot.
3. Savings, a nest egg, because women often placed money in a handkerchief and tied it into a knot.

knihsh
Also spelled *knish.*
Crisp dough filled with potatoes, meat, or buckwheat, served hot.

knihsh-es
Also spelled *knishes.*
Plural of *knihsh.*

knip see *knihp*

knoble
Garlic.

knocker see *knakr*

kobtzen see *kabtzn*

kochalain see *kawchalein*

kochedik see *kuhchedihk*

kochen see *kawchn*

kochleffel see *kawchlefl*

ko-desh*
Also *koi-desh.*
1. Literally, "holy."
2. Holy objects.

kodoches see *kaduhches*

Ko-hein*
Also *ko-han, Ko-hen.*
Also spelled *Kohayn.*
1. A priest.
2. A descendant of a priestly family.

koifn
Also spelled *koifen, kaufen.*
To buy, purchase.

koileil see *koleil*

koim see *kum*

kolbonik see *kawlboinihk*

ko-leil
Also *koi-leil.*
Also spelled *kolel.*
1. An assembly, a gathering.
2. An institution for or group engaged in advanced
Torah study.

Kol Nihd-rei
Also spelled *Kol Nidre.*
1. Literally, "all vows."
2. The opening prayer of the Yom Kippur Eve service, which ushers in the Day of Atonement.

koo
Also *ki.*
A cow.

koof
The nineteenth letter of the Hebrew alphabet,
sounded "k."

koogel see *kugl*

kook ihm uhn see *kuk ihm awn*

koomt a-her
Also spelled *kumt aher.*
Come here.

koomt a-rain
Also spelled *kumt arein.*
Come in.

a as in father; aw as in law; ai as in aisle; ei as in neighbor; e as in bet; i as in vaccine; ih as in tin; o as in solar; oi as in void; oo as in food; u as in put; uh as in but; ch as in chutzpa; zh as in Zhivago.

koomt tzoo-rihk
 Also spelled *kumt tzurik.*
 Come back.

koo-ni leml
 Also spelled *kuni lemel.* Probably related to the
 German *lummel,* meaning "bumpkin."
 1. A naive person.
 2. A nincompoop.
 3. A simpleton in a satiric comedy (1880) by Abraham Goldfaden.

koontz
 Also spelled *kuntz.*
 1. Trick.
 2. Trickery.

koontzn
 Also spelled *koontzen, kuntzen.*
 Plural of *koontz.* See above.

koontzn machr
 1. Magician.
 2. Trickster.

kop see *kuhp*

kopdraienish see *kuhpdreienihsh*

koppel see *kapl*

koptzen see *kabtzn*

kopvaitik see *kuhpveitig*

ko-sel
 Also *ko-tel.**
 A wall.

Kosel Maarawvi see *Kotel Maaravi*

kosher
 Also *ka-sher,* kuhshr, ka-sheir.*
 1. Literally, "fit, proper."
 2. Descriptive of a ritual article or food item that is
 fit for use in accordance with Jewish law.
 3. To make an article kosher. See *koshering.*
 4. (Vernacular) good, all right.

---

a as in father; aw as in law; ai as in aisle; ei as in neighbor; e as in bet; i as in vaccine; ih as in tin; o as in
solar; oi as in void; oo as in food; u as in put; uh as in but; ch as in chutzpa; zh as in Zhivago.

koshering
Also *ka-sher-ing.*
1. An Anglicized form for the process of making kosher meats permissible for cooking by first soaking and salting in accordance with the laws of *kashrus.* See *kashrus.*
2. The process whereby certain utensils used during the year for cooking and eating are rendered permissible for use on Passover. This process involves glowing or soaking. Non-kosher utensils are also rendered kosher by this process.

ko-sher l'Pe-sach
Also *ka-sher l'Pe-sach.**
Kosher for Passover use.

kotel see *kosel*

Ko-tel Ma-a-ra-vi*
Also *Ko-sel Ma-a-raw-vi.*
1. Literally, "Western Wall" of the Temple destroyed in 70 C.E.
2. The Wailing Wall.

koved see *kuhved*

kovid see *kuhved*

kraftihg see *kreftihg*

krank
To be sick, ill.

krank-hait
Also spelled *krankeit, cronkite.*
Sickness, illness.

kra-sa-vih-tze
Also spelled *krasavitse.*
Beautiful woman.

kratz
To scratch.

krechtz
To groan, moan.

kref-tihg
Also *kraf-tihg, kref-tihk.*

1. Robust, sturdy, strong, husky.
2. Full-bodied.
3. Valid.

(a) kreink
Also spelled *krenk.*
A sickness, illness, disease.

kreml
A store, a shop.

krenk see *(a) kreink*

krenkn
Also spelled *krenken.*
1. To be sick (for a time).
2. To suffer.

kre-pi-ren
To die.

krepl
Also spelled *krepel*
A dumpling, filled with meat or cheese, then boiled or fried.

krep-lach
Also *krep-lech.*
Plural of *krepl.* See *krepl.*

kriah see *kriuh*

k'ri-as ha-To-raw
Also *k'ri-at ha-To-ra.**
Also spelled *kerias haTorah.*
Literally, "the reading of the Torah," performed publicly on Monday, Thursday, Saturday, and on all holiday mornings.

k'ri-as She-ma
Also *k'ri-at She-ma.**
Also spelled *kerias Sh'ma.*
1. Literally, "the reading of the Shema."
2. A prayer from the Bible (Deuteronomy 6:4-9) recited at most prayer services and at bedtime.

k'rias She-ma al ha-mi-taw
Also *k'ri-at She-ma al ha-mi-ta.**
Literally, "the recital of the *Shema* at bedtime."

---

a as in father; **aw** as in law; **ai** as in aisle; **ei** as in neighbor; **e** as in bet; **i** as in vaccine; **ih** as in tin; **o** as in solar; **oi** as in void; **oo** as in food; **u** as in put; **uh** as in but; **ch** as in chutzpa; **zh** as in Zhivago.

krihchn
 Also spelled *krichen.*
 Crawl, creep.

krihchn a-rein ihn di bein-er
 1. Literally, "to creep into the bones."
 2. To annoy, to irritate.

krihchn ihn di hoi-che fen-ster
 1. Literally, "crawl into high windows."
 2. Aspire to high position and status.
 3. A social climber.

krihchn oif di glai-che vent
 1. Literally, "climb up straight walls."
 2. A trouble-maker
 3. One who mixes in unduly.

krihch vi a vantz
 1. Literally, "creep like a bedbug."
 2. Slow-moving.

Kristallnacht
 German for "night of broken glass," so named
 because of what happened in Germany on Novem-
 ber 9-10, 1938 when Nazis broke windows of synagogues and Jewish shops.

k'ri-uh
 Also *kri-a,* kri-aw.*
 Also spelled *keria.*
 1. Literally, "tearing."
 2. Tearing of one's garment at the graveside or in
    the chapel as an act of mourning.

kroi-vihm
 Also *kro-vihm.**
 Also spelled *krovim, kerovim.*
 Plural of *kawrov.* See *kawrov.*

kruhm
 Also spelled *krom.*
 Store, shop.

krup-nihk
 Also spelled *krupnick.*
 Barley soup.

---

a as in father; aw as in law; ai as in aisle: ei as in neighbor; e as in bet; i as in vaccine: ih as in tin; o as in
solar; oi as in void; oo as in food; u as in put; uh as in but; ch as in chutzpa; zh as in Zhivago.

k'su-buh
>Also *k'tu-va,* k'su-ba, k'su-baw.*
>Also spelled *ketuba, ketubah, ketuva, ketuvah.*
>A Jewish marriage contract, written in Aramaic
>and read at the wedding ceremony.

k'tuva see *ksubuh*

kugl
>Also spelled *kugel, koo-gel.*
>A pudding, sweet or savory, usually made with
>noodles or potatoes.

kuh-che-dihk
>Also spelled *kochedik.*
>1. Boiling, seething.
>2. Excitable.

kuhm
>Barely.

kuhm der-lebt
>Also *kum der-leibt.*
>Literally, "barely alive to see (or enjoy) it."

kuhm vaws er krihcht
>Also *kum vos er kricht.*
>1. Barely able to creep.
>2. A slowpoke.

kuhm vaws er leibt
>Also *kum vaws er lebt.*
>He's barely alive.

kuhp
>Also spelled *kawp, kop, kopf.*
>1. Head.
>2. Brains, intelligence.

kuhp-drei-en-ihsh
>Also spelled *kawpdreienihsh, kopdrayenish,
>kopdraienish.*
>1. Literally, "head-turning."
>2. A troublesome matter.
>3. Bother, worry.

kuhp ihn drerd
>Literally, "head in the earth." Usually used as a

a as in father; aw as in law; ai as in aisle; ei as in neighbor; e as in bet; i as in vaccine; ih as in tin; o as in solar; oi as in void; oo as in food; u as in put; uh as in but; ch as in chutzpa; zh as in Zhivago.

curse, as in *zawl er vaksn vi a tzihbele mitn kawp in drerd,* "May he grow like an onion, with his head in the ground!"

(a) kuhp oif di plei-tzes
Also spelled *(a) kop oif di plaitzes.*
1. Literally, "a head on the shoulders."
2. Level-headed.
3. Good sense, common sense.

kuhp-vei-tig
Also *kuhp-vei-tik.*
Also spelled *kopvaitik.*
Headache.

kuhpveitik see *kuhpveitig*

kuhshr v'yuhshr
1. Literally, "kosher and straight."
2. Fair and square.
3. Legitimate.

kuhved
Also *ka-vod,* kaw-vod.*
Also spelled *koved, kovid.*
1. Honor.
2. Respect.
3. Glory.
4. Dignity.

kuk ihm awn
Also spelled *kook ihm uhn.*
Look at him!

kukn
Also spelled *kuken.*
To look, view.

kum
Also *kam, koim.*
Hardly, barely.

kum derleibt see *kuhm derlebt*

kumen
Come, arrive.

kum ihch niht haint, kim ihch mawr-gen
Also spelled *kum ich nit heint, kum ich morgen.*

---

a as in father; aw as in law; ai as in aisle· ei as in neighbor; e as in bet; i as in vaccine; ih as in tin; o as in solar; oi as in void; oo as in food; u as in put; uh as in but; ch as in chutzpa; zh as in Zhivago.

1. Literally, "If I don't come today, I'll come tomorrow."
2. A procrastinator.

kum mit tzores see *kihm miht tzuris*

kum vos er kricht see *kuhm vaws er krihcht*

kumn tzoo gast
  Also spelled *kumen tzu gast.*
  1. Literally, "come to be a guest."
  2. Come to visit.

kumn tzu Gawt bawr-ves
  Also spelled *kumen tsu Gawt bawrves.*
  1. Literally, "come before God barefoot."
  2. Be humble.

kumsitz see *kumzihtz*

kumt aher see *koomt aher*

kumt arein see *koomt arain*

kumt tzurik see *koomt tzoorihk*

kum-zihtz
  Also spelled *kumsitz.*
  1. Literally, "come sit."
  2. An informal get-together.
  3. A social hour.

kuni lemel see *kooni leml*

kuntz see *koontz*

kuntzen see *koontzn*

kur-vuh
  Also spelled *kurve, kurveh.*
  A prostitute.

kvat-er
  Also spelled *kvatter.*
  The man who brings the child to the *sondek* at the time of circumcision.

kvat-er-ihn
  Also spelled *kvatterin.*
  Feminine of *kvater.* See above.

kvel
> 1. To derive pleasure.
> 2. To swell with pride.

kvetsh
> 1. To complain, whine.
> 2. One who complains a great deal, also called *a kvetsher.*

kvetsh-er-ke
> Feminine of *kvetsh.*

kvitl
> Also spelled *kvitel, kvitle.*
> 1. A slip.
> 2. A ticket.
> 3. A receipt.
> 4. A prescription.
> 5. A note slipped into the cracks of the Western Wall on which a petition or prayer has been inscribed.

kvitsh
> To scream, shriek, screech.

kvura see *kevoorah*

k'za-yiht*
> Also *ke-za-yihs.*
> Also spelled *kezayit.*
> 1. Literally, "like an olive."
> 2. A piece (usually of food) the size of an olive, the minimum required for certain blessings.

---

a as in father; aw as in law; ai as in aisle ei as in neighbor; e as in bet; i as in vaccine; ih as in tin; o as in solar; oi as in void; oo as in food; u as in put; uh as in but; ch as in chutzpa; zh as in Zhivago.

L

lachn
Also spelled *lachen.*
To laugh.

Ladino
A mixture of Spanish and Hebrew, written in Hebrew characters and spoken by Sephardic Jews of Turkey, Iberia, and the Middle East.

Lag Ba-o-mer*
Also *Lag Boi-mer, Lag Baw-o-mer.*
Also spelled *Lag B'Omer.*
Literally, "the thirty-third day of the *Omer*," a semi-holiday between Passover and Shavuot, occuring on the thirty-third day after the second day of Passover.

laid
Also spelled *leid.*
Pain, anguish.

laidik see *leidihg*

laidik geher see *leidihk geier*

laidn
Also spelled *leiden.*
1. To suffer.
2. To endure.

laigen zich shlofen see *leign zihch shlawfn*

laing see *lang*

lamdn
Also *lam-dan.**
1. A Talmudic scholar.
2. One who is erudite.

la-muhd
Also *la-med.**

---

a as in father; aw as in law; ai as in aisle; ei as in neighbor; e as in bet; i as in vaccine; ih as in tin; o as in solar; oi as in void; oo as in food; u as in put; uh as in but; ch as in chutzpa; zh as in Zhivago.

The twelfth letter of the Hebrew alphabet, corresponding to "l."

la-muhd vawv-nihk
Also spelled *lamed vawvnihk, lamed vovnick.*
See *lamuhd vawv tzadikim.*

la-muhd vawv tza-di-kim
Also *la-med vav tza-di-kihm.**
Literally, "thirty-six saintly people."
According to a tradition, the world continues to exist because of the merit of thirty-six righteous persons whose identity is not known. Each such individual is referred to as a *lamed vovnick.* (The numerical value of the Hebrew letters *lamed* and *vawv* is thirty-six.)

lands-leit
Plural of *landsman.* See *landsman.*

lang
Also *laing.*
Long, referring to time and distance.

lang leibn zawlt ihr
Also spelled *lang leben zolt ir.*
Long may you live!

lashon see *luhshn*

lashon hakodesh see *l'shon hakodesh*

lashon hara see *luhshn hawruh*

lashon kodesh see *luhshn koidesh*

latke see *latkuh*

lat-kes
Pancakes. Plural of *latkuh.*

lat-kuh
Also *lat-ke, lat-ka.*
Potato pancakes, traditionally associated with Chanukah. *Latkes* is the plural form.

lawch see *luhch*

lawshon see *luhshn*

lawshon hawraw see *luhshn hawruh*

lawz mihr tzoo roo
Also spelled *loz mir tzu ru.*
1. Literally, "Let me be in peace."
2. Leave me alone! Let me be!

laytz see *letz*

l'cha-yihm
Also spelled *l'chaim, l'chayim, lechayim.*
1. Literally, "to life."
2. A toast offered before drinking liquor or wine.

(a) le-be-dih-ke velt
A lively world, a spirited world.

lebedik see *leibedihk*

leber
Liver.

lebn
Also spelled *leben.*
1. Living.
2. To live.

lebn a cha-zihr-she tawg
Also spelled *leben a chazershen tog.*
1. Literally, "living a pig's day."
2. Living high off the hog.
3. Uninhibited pleasure.

lebn a-zoi vi Gawt ihn Aw-des
Also spelled *leben azi vi Gott in Odess.*
1. Literally, "living like God in Odessa."
2. Living like a king.

(a) lebn oif dain kawp
Also spelled a *leben oif dein kop.*
1. Literally, "a life upon your head."
2. Live and be well!
3. Well said!
4. Well done!

le-chat-chi-law
Also *l'chat-chi-la.**
1. From the outset.
2. A priori.
See also *bihd'eved.*

---

a as in father: **aw** as in law; **ai** as in aisle; **ei** as in neighbor; **e** as in bet: **i** as in vaccine: **ih** as in tin: **o** as in solar: **oi** as in void; **oo** as in food; **u** as in put; **uh** as in but; **ch** as in chutzpa: **zh** as in Zhivago.

Le-chi
Also spelled *LeHi*.
An acronym for Lochamei Cherut Yisrael ("Figh-ters for the Freedom of Israel"), the anti-British underground in pre-Israel Palestine, formerly part of the Irgun.

lef-e-le
A small spoon.

lefl
Also spelled *lefel*.
A teaspoon.

le-hach-ihs
Also spelled *l'hachis*.
To annoy, anger, irritate, provoke.

lehavdil see *l'havdihl*

LeHi see *Lechi*

lehveiyeh see *levaya*

lei-be-dihk
Also spelled *lebedik*.
1. Lively, alive.
2. Sprightly.

leid see *laid*

leiden see *laidn*

lei-dihg
Also *lei-dihk*.
Also spelled *laidik*.
1. Empty.
2. Vacant.

lei-dihk gei-er
Also spelled *laidik geher*.
1. Literally, "idle goer."
2. Idler.
3. Vagabond.

leign t'fihlihn
Also spelled *legen tefilin*.
To don phylacteries.

leign zihch shlawfn
Also spelled *laigen zich shlofen.*
1. Literally, "to lay oneself (down) to sleep."
2. To go to bed.

lei-kuhch
Also *lei-kech, lei-kach.*
Also spelled *lekach, lekech.*
A sweet cake, usually honey cake.

lei-kuhch-el
A cookie. A diminutive form of *leikuhch.*

lei-men-er goi-lem
1. Literally, "clumsy robot."
2. A clumsy person.

lekach see *leikuhch*

lekn
Also spelled *leken.*
To lick.

(a) lek oon a shmek
1. A lick and a sniff.
2. A little bit.

lekr
Also spelled *leker.*
Literally, "one who licks."

lemech
Plural of *leml.*

le-mihsh-ke
Also spelled *lemishke.*
1. Literally, "porridge."
2. A naive, wishy-washy person.

leml
Also spelled *lemel.*
1. Literally, "a lamb."
2. Meek, mild.
3. A nincompoop.

leshon hakodesh see *l'shon hakodesh*

le-shon tar-gum*
Also *law-shon tar-goom.*

---

a as in father; aw as in law; ai as in aisle; ei as in neighbor; e as in bet; i as in vaccine; ih as in tin; o as in solar; oi as in void; oo as in food; u as in put; uh as in but; ch as in chutzpa; zh as in Zhivago.

1. Aramaic language.
2. Aramaic translation.

letz*

Also *laytz.*
1. A prankster, jester, wag, buffoon, clown.
2. A mocker, scorner, scoffer.

le-va-yuh

Also *le-va-ya**
Also spelled *levaiye, levahyah, leveiyeh.*
1. Literally, "accompaniment."
2. A funeral procession, cortege.

le-va-yat ha-met*

Also *le-vaw-yas ha-meis.*
Literally, "accompanying the deceased" (in the funeral cortege).

Le-vi*

Also *Lei-vi.*
1. A descendant of the tribe of Levi, who were assistants to the priests in Temple times.
2. A Torah honor bestowed upon the non-priestly members of the tribe of Levi.

Levirate marriage

A biblical law requiring the brother of a childless widow either to marry her or to submit to the ritual *chalitza.* See *chalitza.*

Levite

A descendant of the tribe of Levi, including both priests and Levites. See *Levi.*

l'hachis see *lehachihs*

l'hav-dihl*

Also spelled *lehavdil.*
1. To differentiate, distinguish.
2. To establish a distinction between the sacred and profane, between the Sabbath and weekdays, between the living and the dead.
See also *havdala.*

li-al-ke

Doll.

lib hawben see *lihb huhbn*

libe see *lihbe*

libn
>Also spelled *liben.*
>To love.

licht see *lihcht*

liebe see *lihbe*

lieb hoben see *lihb huhbn*

ligen see *lihgn*

ligner see *lihgner*

lihb huhbn
>Also spelled *lieb hoben, lib hawben.*
>1. To love.
>2. To be fond of.
>3. To care for.

lih-be
>Also spelled *libe, liebe.*
>1. Love.
>2. Beloved.
>3. A romance, a love affair.

lihcht
>Also spelled *licht.*
>Candle, light.

lihcht benshen
>Also spelled *licht bentshen.*
>1. Candle blessing.
>2. Candlelighting ceremony conducted to usher in Sabbaths and holidays.

lihcht-ihg
>Also spelled *lichtig.*
>Bright, lighted.

lihgn
>Also spelled *ligen.*
>1. Lay down.
>2. Be situated.

lihgnen
>To lie, to prevaricate.

---

a as in father; aw as in law; ai as in aisle; ei as in neighbor; e as in bet; i as in vaccine; ih as in tin; o as in solar; oi as in void; oo as in food; u as in put; uh as in but; ch as in chutzpa; zh as in Zhivago.

lihg-ner
> Also spelled *ligner.*
> Liar, prevaricator.

lihgn ihn zih-nen
> 1. Literally, "to lay on one's mind."
> 2. To be concerned with, to think of.

lih-liht
> Also *li-liht.*
> Also spelled *Lilith.*
> 1. Literally, "of the night."
> 2. In Semitic folklore, a female demon.
> 3. A magazine published by and for Jewish women *(Lilith).*

Liht-vak
> Also spelled *Litvak.*
> 1. A Jewish native of Lithuania.
> 2. A descendant of Lithuanian Jews.

Lilith see *lihliht*

Litvak see *Lihtvak*

lo a-lei-chem
> 1. Literally, "not upon you."
> 2. May it not happen to you!

loch see *luhch*

loch in kop see *lawch ihn kawp*

loifn
> To run.

loksh see *luhksh*

lokshn see *luhkshen*

loo-ach
> Also spelled *luach* and *luah.*
> 1. Calendar.
> 2. Tablet.
> 3. Timetable.

loo-chos
> Also *loo-chot,** *lu-chot.*
> Plural of *looach.* See *looach.*

---

a as in father; aw as in law; ai as in aisle; ei as in neighbor; e as in bet; i as in vaccine; ih as in tin; o as in solar; oi as in void; oo as in food; u as in put; uh as in but; ch as in chutzpa; zh as in Zhivago.

loo-luhv
Also *loo-lav.**
Also spelled *lulav.*
1. A palm branch.
2. One of the four species of plants used in the ritual of the Sukkot festival.

loong
Also spelled *lung.*
Lung.

(a) loong oon le-ber oif der nawz
Also spelled *(a) lung un leber oif der noz.*
1. Literally, "a lung and a liver on your nose."
2. Stop being a hypochondriac!
3. Stop imagining things!

lox
Pronounced *laks.*
Smoked salmon, usually eaten on a bagel with cream cheese. From the German *Lachs,* "salmon."

loz mir tzu ru see *lawz mihr tzoo roo*

l'shaw-naw to-vaw
Also *l'sha-na to-va.**
Literally, "a good year." An abbreviated form of the salutation *l'shana tova tikateivu.*

l'shaw-naw to-vaw ti-chaw-sei-moo
Also *l'sha-na to-va ti-cha-tei-mu.**
1. Literally, "May you be sealed in the Book of Life!"
2. A Yom Kippur greeting.

l'shaw-naw to-vaw ti-kaw-sei-voo
Also *l'sha-na to-va ti-ka-tei-vu.**
1. Literally, "May you be inscribed for a good year!"
2. A Jewish New Year greeting, often abbreviated to *l'shuhnuh toivuh* or *l'shana tova.**

l'shon ha-ko-desh
Also *la-shon ha-ko-desh.**
Also spelled *leshon hakodesh.*
1. Literally, "holy tongue."
2. Hebrew language.

---

a as in father; aw as in law; ai as in aisle; ei as in neighbor; e as in bet; i as in vaccine; ih as in tin; o as in solar; oi as in void; oo as in food; u as in put; uh as in but; ch as in chutzpa; zh as in Zhivago.

l'shon hawraw see *luhshuhn hawruh*
luach see *looach*
luchot see *loochos*
luft
>Air, atmosphere.
luft-mensh
>1. Literally, "air man."
>2. A person without an occupation or income, improvising for a livelihood.
>3. A dreamer.
luhch
>Also *lawch.*
>Also spelled *loch.*
>1. Hole, aperture.
>2. Cavity.
luhch ihn kawp
>Also spelled *loch in kop.*
>1. Literally, "a hole in the head."
>2. A person whose mental faculties are not in tact.
>3. Something unwanted.
luhksh
>Also spelled *loksh.*
>1. Noodle.
>2. (Slang) a tall, thin person.
luhk-shen
>Also spelled *lokshn, lokshen, luhkshn.*
>Noodles. Plural of *luhksh.*
luhkshn kugl
>Also spelled *lukshen kugel.*
>Noodle pudding.
luhshn
>Also *law-shon, la-shon.**
>Also spelled *luhshen.*
>1. Language.
>2. Tongue.
>3. Speech.
luhshn haw-ruh
>Also *lawshn haw-ruh, l'shon haw-raw,*

and *la-shon ha-ra.**
1. Literally, "evil tongue."
2. Gossip, slander.
3. Bad-mouthing.

luhshn koi-desh
Also *law-shon ko-desh, la-shon ko-desh.**
1. Literally, "holy language."
2. Hebrew.

lukshen kugel see *luhkshn kugl*

lulav see *looluhv*

lump
A scoundrel.

lung see *loong*

(a) lung un leber oif der noz see *(a) loong oon leber oif der nawz*

M

maachal see *maichl*

maala see *mailuh*

maalos
Also *ma-a-lot.**
Steps.

Maariv see *Marihv*

maase see *maisuh*

maaser see *maisr*

ma-ba-ra*
Also *ma-baw-raw.*
A transit camp for immigrants to Israel, following statehood in 1948.

ma-ba-rot*
Also *ma-baw-ros.*
Plural of *mabara*. See above.

ma-cha-shei-fuh
Also *ma-cha-shei-fa.**
1. A witch.
2. A sorceress.
Mechasheif is the masculine form.

machateinihste see *mechuteneste*

machen see *machn*

macher see *machr*

mach-er-ai-ke
Also spelled *machereike.*
A gimmick, contraption.

mach es kail-ech-dihk oon shpihtz-ihk
Also spelled *mach es keilechdik un shpitzik.*
1. Literally, "Make it round and pointed."
2. Come to the point! Stop beating around the bush!

mach es shnel
Make it quick! Hurry up!

---

a as in father; aw as in law; ai as in aisle; ei as in neighbor; e as in bet; i as in vaccine; ih as in tin; o as in solar; oi as in void; oo as in food; u as in put; uh as in but; ch as in chutzpa; zh as in Zhivago.

machn
Also spelled *machen*.
1. To make.
2. To do.
3. To feel.

machn a ge-vald
Also spelled *machen a gevald*.
1. To shout, make an outcry.
2. To call for help.

machn a lebn
Also spelled *machen a leben*.
To make a living.

machn a tsih-mes
Also spelled *ma-chen a tzimmes*.
1. Literally, "to make a stew".
2. To make a fuss.
See also *tzihmes*.

machn bluh-te foon
Also spelled *machen blote fun*.
1. To make a mess of.
2. To take someone apart.
3. To vilify.
4. To reprimand.

mach niht kein tsih-mes fun dem
Also spelled *mach nit kain tzimmes fun dem*.
1. Literally, "Don't get into a stew over this."
2. Don't make a big fuss over this!

machn ois
Also spelled *ma-chen ois*.
Literally, "to make out," used in the negative sense:
es macht mihr niht ois, "It doesn't matter to me."

machn Shabuhs far zihch
1. Literally, "to make (prepare) Sabbath for one-self."
2. To do something one's own way.

machn zihch ba-kvem
Also spelled *machen zich bakvem*.
To make oneself comfortable.

machn zihch niht vihs-en-dihk
Also spelled *machen zich nit visendik.*
To pretend not to know (about a matter).

machr
Also spelled *macher.*
1. Literally, "a maker," one who makes things happen.
2. A wheeler-dealer.

machzor see *machzuhr*

Mach-zuhr
Also *Mach-zor.**
Also spelled *Mahzor.*
1. Literally, "cycle."
2. The Jewish prayerbook containing the holiday and festival liturgies, as contrasted with the *Siddur,* which contains the daily and Sabbath prayers.

maf-tir
Also spelled *maphtir.*
1. Literally, "conclusion."
2. The concluding portion of the Torah reading on Sabbaths and holidays.
3. The person who receives the final Torah reading honor *(aliya)* on Sabbaths and holidays.

(a) ma-gei-fuh zawl dihch trefn
Also spelled *a magaife zol dich trefen.*
1. Literally, "A pestilence should befall you!"
2. May you enjoy bad luck!

Magen David see *Muhgn Duhvihd*

ma-gihd
Also spelled *magid, maggid.*
1. An itinerant preacher.
2. An orator.

mahyofisnik see *mayawfihsnihk*

Mahzor see *Machzuhr*

maichl
Also *ma-a-chal.**
Also spelled *meichel.*

---

a as in father; aw as in law; ai as in aisle; ei as in neighbor; e as in bet; i as in vaccine; ih as in tin; o as in solar; oi as in void; oo as in food; u as in put; uh as in but; ch as in chutzpa; zh as in Zhivago.

1. Food, delicacy.
2. A gourmet delight.

maidel see *meidl*

mai-luh
Also *ma-a-law, ma-a-la.**
Also spelled *meileh.*
1. Virtue, good quality.
2. Merit.
3. An asset.

Mai-mu-na
A feast held by Moroccan Jews celebrating the end of Passover

main baw-buhz tam
Also spelled *mein bobe's tam.*
1. Literally, "my grandma's taste."
2. Bad taste, tacky.

mainen see *meinen*

mai-ne suh-nihm zawl-en a-zoi lebn
Also *meine sonim zolen azoi leben.*
1. Literally, "My enemies should live so."
2. It will never happen!

mainung see *meinung*

Mairihv see *Marihv*

mais see *meis*

maise see *maisuh*

maisr
Also *ma-a-ser.**
Also spelled *maiser.*
The taking of a tithe or a tenth of the farmer's first fruits (of the field and livestock) for the upkeep of the Temple and for the support of the Levites.

mai-suh
Also *mai-se, ma-a-se*.*
Also spelled *meiseh.*
1. A story.
2. An episode.

---

mai-suh she-haw-yaw
An old story.

mait mitzvah see *meis mihtsvuh*

maivin see *meivihn*

ma-kes
Plural of *makuh.*

ma-kuh
Also *ma-ka.**
1. A pestilence.
2. A plague.
3. A scourge.
4. A wound.

(a) ma-kuh un-ter yen-emz uhr-em ihz niht shver tzoo trawgn
1. Literally, "an abscess under another's arm is not hard to bear."
2. Someone else's afflication is easy to endure.

malach see *maluhch*

Malach Hamavet see *Maluhch Hamawves*

Mal-choo-yos
Also *Mal-choo-yot.**
Also spelled *Malchuyos, Malkhuyot, Malchuyot.*
1. Literally, "Sovereignty."
2. Part of the *Musaf* prayer of the Rosh Hashana service.

mal-shi-noos
Also *mal-shi-nes, mal-shi-nut.**
1. Slander.
2. Calumny.
3. Libel.

mal-uhch
Also *mal-awch, mal-ach**
Angel.

Mal-uhch Ha-maw-ves
Also *Mal-ach ha-Ma-vet.**
Angel of Death.

mamalige see *mamelihge*

---

mama loshen see *mame lawshn*

mamash see *mamuhsh*

ma-maw-shus
Also *ma-ma-shut.**
1. Literally "substance."
2. Reality, concreteness.

ma-me lawshn
Also spelled *mama loshen, mameh loshen.*
1. Literally, "mother tongue" (of East European Jews and their descendants).
2. Yiddish.

ma-me-lih-ge
Also spelled *mamalige, mamelige.*
Cornmeal pudding, of Rumanian origin.

ma-men-yoo
Also spelled *mamenyu.*
A pet form of *mamuh.* See below.

ma-muh
Also *ma-me.*
Mother, mama, mom.

ma-muhsh
Also *ma-mash.**
1. Actually.
2. The way it happened.
3. Truly.
4. Absolutely.

mam-zei-rus
Also *mam-zei-rut**
Also spelled *mamzerus.*
Bastardy, the state of being a *mamzr.*

mamzr
Also *mam-zer.**
Bastard.

man
1. Man.
2. Husband.

mandel see *mandl*

---

man-del-brot
Sweet, almond-flavored pastry, baked in long strips, cut into thin slices, then usually toasted in the oven.

mandl
Also spelled *mandel.*
Almond.

mand-len
Also *mand-lin, mandln.*
Plural of *mandl.* See above.

ma nihsh-ta-naw
Also *ma nihsh-ta-na.**
1. Literally, "What is the difference?"
2. The opening words of the "Four Questions" in the Haggada, asked by the youngest child at the Passover *Seder.*

mantl
Also spelled *mantel.*
1. Covering (garment).
2. Cloak.
3. Torah covering.

maot chitihm see *mawos chitihm*

ma-paw
Also *ma-pa.**
Also spelled *mapah, mappah.*
1. Literally, "a tablecloth."
2. The name of a commentary on the *Shulchan Aruch.*

(a) ma-paw-luh
Also *a ma-paw-law, a ma-puh-le.*
1. A downfall.
2. A catastrophe.
3. A miscarriage.

mappah see *mapaw*

mapuhle see *mapawluh*

Mar Chesh-van*
Also *Mar Chesh-von.*
Also spelled *Mar Heshvan.*

---

a as in father; aw as in law; ai as in aisle· ei as in neighbor; e as in bet; i as in vaccine; ih as in tin; o as in solar; oi as in void; oo as in food; u as in put; uh as in but; ch as in chutzpa; zh as in Zhivago.

1. Literally, "bitter (sad) Cheshvan," a month in which there are no Jewish holidays.
2. A synonym for the Hebrew month Cheshvan, which follows Tishri, a month filled with holidays.

Ma-rihv
Also *Ma-a-rihv,* Mai-rihv.*
Also spelled *Maariv.*
1. The daily evening prayer service.
2. An Israeli afternoon newspaper.

maror see *mawror*

Marrano
1. From the Spanish meaning "pig."
2. In fifteenth-century Spain and Portugal, a contemptuous designation for Jewish converts to Christianity who clandestinely practised Judaism.
3. A secret Jew.

masechta see *mesihchtuh*

ma-ser*
Also spelled *masser.*
1. Literally, "to hand over."
2. To betray.
3. To denounce to the authorities.
4. To tattle.

mash-gi-ach
1. Watchman, observer.
2. *Kashrut* inspector, an overseer who attests to the kosher status of the food that is prepared and served.

mashiach see *meshiach*

mash-ke
1. Any alcoholic liquor.
2. In modern Hebrew, any beverage.

mas-kihl
Also spelled *maskil.*
1. A serious student.
2. An enlightened person.

mas-ki-lihm
Also spelled *maskilim*.
Plural of *maskil*.

mas-mihd
Also *mat-mihd*.*
Also spelled *masmid, matmid*.
1. Diligent, zealous.
2. An industrious student.

ma-so-ruh
Also *ma-so-raw, me-so-ra, ma-so-ra,** me-so-ruh*.
1. Tradition.
2. The accumulation of tradition concerning the correct Hebrew text of the Bible.

massekhet
A variant form of *mesihchtuh*. See *mesihchtuh*.

masser see *maser*

matmid see *masmihd*

mat-ri-ach
1. To burden.
2. To impose upon.
3. To trouble.

mat-ri-ach zain
Also spelled *matriach zein*.
1. To trouble oneself, burden oneself.
2. To take pains.
3. To be so good as to.
4. To take the trouble to.

matseivah see *matzeivuh*

matza see *matzuh*

ma-tza she-mu-ra*
Also *ma-tzuh shmoo-ruh*.
Literally, "guarded *matza*," made under specially rigorous supervision in which moisture is kept off the grain from the time of reaping until the time of baking. See also *matzuh (matza)*.

ma-tzei-vuh
Also *ma-tzei-va,** ma-tzei-vaw*.
Also spelled *matseiva*.

---

a as in father; aw as in law; ai as in aisle: ei as in neighbor; e as in bet; i as in vaccine; ih as in tin; o as in solar; oi as in void; oo as in food; u as in put; uh as in but; ch as in chutzpa; zh as in Zhivago.

1. Pillar.
2. Tombstone.

ma-tzot*
Also *ma-tzuhs, ma-tzos.*
Also spelled *matzas.*
Plural of *matzuh.* See *matzuh.*

ma-tzot shel mihtz-va*
Also *ma-tzos shel mihtz-vaw.*
Three symbolic *matzot* used at the *Seder.*

ma-tzuh
Also *ma-tzaw, ma-tza**
Also spelled *matzo, matsa, matzah.*
Unleavened bread eaten particularly during Passover.

ma-tzuh balls
Dumplings made with *matza* meal.

maven see *meivihn*

mawd-ne
Also spelled *modne.*
Odd, strange.

mawd-ne draw-chihm
Odd ways, peculiar habits.

Mawgein Dawvihd see *Muhgn Duhvihd*

mawgn kugl
Also spelled *mogen kugel.*
1. Literally, "stuffed pudding."
2. Another term for stuffed derma, also referred to as *kishke.*

mawl-en ge-mawl-ene mel
1. Literally, "to grind ground flour."
2. To repeat, rehash things.

maw-os chi-tihm
Also *ma-ot chi-tihm.**
Also spelled *maos chitim.*
Literally, "wheat money," collected before Passover and distributed to the poor so that they can buy *matza* and other articles for the holiday.

mawrgn
Also spelled *mawrgen, morgen.*
1. Morning.
2. Tomorrow.

maw-ror
Also *ma-ror.**
Also spelled *moror.*
Bitter herbs, primarily horseradish, eaten at the
Passover *Seder.*

mawshiach see *meshiach*

ma yaw-fihs-nihk
Also spelled *mah yofisnik.*
1. Literally, "a how-beautiful, how-lovely one."
2. A cringing, servile Jew who plays up to non-
Jews by telling them how wonderful they are.
3. A pollyana.

ma-yihm
Also spelled *mayim.*
Water.

ma-yihm ach-ro-nihm
Also spelled *mayim acharonim.*
1. Literally, "final water."
2. Water used at the end of a meal to rinse the
fingers before reciting Grace After Meals.

mazal see *mazl*

mazal tov see *mazl tuhv*

ma-zihk
Also spelled *mazik.*
One who is destructive mischievous, especially a
child.

mazl
Also *ma-zawl, ma-zal.**
Also spelled *mazel.*
1. Literally, "a star, planet."
2. Luck.
3. Destiny.

mazl tuhv
Also *ma-zawl tov, ma-zal tov.**

---

a as in father; aw as in law; al as in aisle ei as in neighbor; e as in bet; i as in vaccine; ih as in tin; o as in
solar; oi as in void; oo as in food; u as in put; uh as in but; ch as in chutzpa; zh as in Zhivago.

Also spelled *mazel tov, mazzeltov.*
1. A good star.
2. Good fortune.
3. Good luck!
4. Congratulations!

m'cha-leil Sha-buhs
Also *me-cha-leil Sha-baws, me-cha-lel Sha-bat.**
1. One who desecrates the Sabbath.
2. A violator of Sabbath law.

m'cha-ye
Also spelled *mechaye* and *mechaieh.*
1. Literally, "to revive, to bring back to life."
2. A pleasure, delight.

m'cha-ye ha-mei-sihm
Also *m'cha-ye ha-me-tihm.**
Literally, "He (God) revives the dead."

m'darf hawb-en mazl
Also spelled *men darf hoben mazel.*
One has to have luck.

m'darf niht zain shein; m'darf hoben chein
Also spelled *men darf nit zein shain; men darf hoben chain.*
One doesn't have to be pretty; one needs (only) to have charm.

mead see *med*

Mea Shearim
1. Literally, "One Hundred Measures," commonly translated "One Hundred Gates." Based on the verse, "And Isaac sowed the land and it yielded him in that same year a hundredfold *(mea shearim),* for the Lord blessed him" (Genesis 26:12).
2. The ultra-Orthodox quarter of Jerusalem.

mechalel Shabat see *m'chaleil Shabuhs*

me-cha-sheif
1. A sorcerer.
2. A wizard.

a as in father; aw as in law; ai as in aisle; ei as in neighbor; e as in bet; i as in vaccine; ih as in tin; o as in solar; oi as in void; oo as in food; u as in put; uh as in but; ch as in chutzpa; zh as in Zhivago.

3. A magician.
Machasheifa is the feminine form.

mechaye see *m'chaye*

me-chih-tzuh
Also *me-chi-tza,* * *me-chi-tzaw.*
A panel or curtain separating men from women,
particularly in the synagogue.

me-chi-luh
Also *me-chi-law, me-chi-la.* *
Forgiveness, pardon.

me-choo-ta-nihm
Also spelled *mechutanim.*
Plural of *me-chu-tuhn.*

me-chu-luh
Also spelled *mechule.*
1. Sick.
2. Spoiled.
3. Crazy.
4. Wild.
5. Bankrupt.

m-chu-tan-ihm
Also spelled *mechutanim.*
Plural of *mechutan.*

me-chu-ten-es-te
Also *ma-cha-tei-nihs-te.*
1. A female relative.
2. A relative through marriage (mother of a son-in-law or daughter-in-law).

me-chu-tuhn
Also *me-chu-tan,* * *me-chu-tawn.*
1. Related.
2. A relative through marriage (the father of a son-in-law or daughter-in-law).

med
A fermented beverage made of honey, water, and hops.

me-dih-ne
Also *me-di-naw, me-di-na.* *

Also spelled *medine*.
1. Land.
2. Country.

medruhsh see *mihdruhsh*

me-gih-luh
Also *me-gih-le, me-gi-law, me-gi-la.**
Also spelled *megilla*.
1. Literally, "scroll."
2. A generic name of five biblical books: Esther, Ecclesiastes, Song of Songs, Ruth, and Lamentations.
3. "The *Megilla*" is the Book of Esther, read on Purim.
3. Any long, involved, or boring narrative.

Megillat Ester see *M'gilas Ester*

mehren see *merihn*

meichel see *maichl*

meidl
Also spelled *maidel*.
1. A girl.
2. A young, unmarried woman.

meileh see *mailuh*

mein bobe's tam see *main bawbuhz tam*

mein cha-yes geit ois
Also spelled *mein chaies gait ois*.
1. Literally, "My life is ebbing."
2. I'm dying (for it).
3. A yearning.

mei-nen
Also spelled *mainen*.
1. To mean, intend.
2. To believe.
3. To indicate.

meine sonim zolen azoi leben see *maine suhnihm zawlen azoi lebn*

mein-ung
Also spelled *mainung*.

---

a as in father; aw as in law; ai as in aisle; ei as in neighbor; e as in bet; i as in vaccine; ih as in tin; o as in solar; oi as in void; oo as in food; u as in put; uh as in but; ch as in chutzpa; zh as in Zhivago.

1. Meaning.
2. Idea.
3. View, opinion.

meir see *mer*

meirihn see *merihn*

meis
    Also *met,* mes.*
    Also spelled *mais.*
    1. A deceased person.
    2. A corpse.

meiseh see *maisuh*

meis mihtz-vuh
    Also *met mihtz-va.**
    Also spelled *mais mitzvah.*
    1. A good deed honoring the dead.
    2. An "abandoned" corpse. When no one else is available to care for the deceased, the obligation falls upon the first Jew who finds it to arrange for the burial.

mei-vihn
    Also spelled *maven, maivin.*
    1. Expert.
    2. Authority.
    3. Connoisseur.

me-ka-ne*
    Also *me-ka-nei.*
    Jealous, envious.

mek-ler-ke
    The feminine form of *meklr.*

meklr
    Also spelled *mekler.*
    1. A broker.
    2. A go-between.

me-la-muhd
    Also *me-la-med.**
    1. A teacher.
    2. A teacher in a *cheder.* See *cheder.*

---

me-la-ve mal-kuh
Also *me-la-ve mal-ka,** *me-la-ve mal-kaw.*
Also spelled *melaveh malkah.*
1 Literally, "to accompany the queen."
2. To usher out the Sabbath Queen.
3. A repast get-together at the end of the Sabbath.

mel-da-do
A Ladino word describing a get-together of Sephardic Jews at which there are readings from religious literature.

melech* see *meluhch*

Me-lech Mal-chei Ha-me-law-chihm
Literally, "the King of Kings (God)," a phrase used often in the liturgy.

me-lech Sobieski's yawr-en
Also spelled *melech Sobieski's yoren.*
1. Literally, "King (John) Sobieski's years." Sobieski was a seventeenth-century Polish monarch.
2. The good old days.

me-li-tza*
Also *me-li-tzaw.*
Also spelled *melitsa, melizah.*
1. A parable.
2. An elegant, florid style in Hebrew prose writing.

mellah
1. A ghetto.
2. The Jewish quarter in North African cities.

mel-uhch
Also *me-lach, me-lech.**
King, sovereign.

mem
The thirteenth letter of the Hebrew alphabet, corresponding in sound to "m."

men
One (person). Often used as a prefix in the form *m'*——— or *me*———.

---

a as in father: aw as in law; ai as in aisle; ei as in neighbor; e as in bet; i as in vaccine; ih as in tin; o as in solar; oi as in void; oo as in food; u as in put; uh as in but; ch as in chutzpa; zh as in Zhivago.

me-na-cheim aw-vel zain
Also spelled *menachem avel zein.*
1. Literally, "to comfort the mourner."
2. Paying a condolence call.

mench see *mentsh*

men darf hoben mazel see *m'darf hawben mazl*

men darf nit zein shain; men darf hoben chain
see *m'darf niht zain shein; m'darf hoben chein*

men hawt a-lein uhn-ge-kawcht
Also spelled *men hot alain ungekocht*
1. Literally, "you cooked it yourself."
2. You did it yourself!
3. Don't blame anyone but yourself!

men ken brech-en
1. Literally, "One can vomit (from it)."
2. It's disgusting!

men ken d'harg-et ver-en
1. Literally, "One can get killed" (sarcasm).
2. It's dangerous!

men ken es ihn moil niht ne-men
1. Literally, "One can't take it in his/her mouth."
2. It's unpalatable!

men ken leck-en di fing-ers
1. Literally, "One can lick his/her fingers."
2. It's delicious!

men ken me-shu-ge ver-en
1. Literally, "One can go crazy (over it)."
2. It's terrific!

men ken niht puh-ter ver-en
1. Literally, "One can't get rid of it (him/her)."
2. It's an insoluble problem.

men ken niht tansn oif tzvei cha-se-nez miht ein mawl
1. Literally, "One can't dance at two weddings at the same time"
2. We can do only one thing at a time.

men ken tse-zetst ve-ren
Literally, "One can burst."

men ken zihch ba-lekn di fing-ers
Also spelled *men ken baleken di fingers.*
1. Literally, "One can lick the fingers."
2. It's delicious!

men lawzt niht leibn
1. Literally, "They (people) don't let one live."
2. People don't stop pestering one.

me-noo-vuhl
Also *me-nu-vawl, me-nu-val.**
Ugly, corrupt, contemptible person.

menorah see *menoruh*

me-no-ruh
Also *me-no-raw, me-no-ra.**
1. A candelabrum with two or more branches used on the Sabbath and holidays in the home and the synagogue.
2. An eight-branched candelabrum used on Chanuka.

men ret oon ret
They keep on talking and talking (and say nothing).

men ret zihch ois daws hartz
One talks his/her heart out.

men shush-kiht zihch
Also spelled *men shushkit zich.*
They whisper to each other.

mentsh
Also spelled *mench, mensh.*
1. A man.
2. A real person of worth and dignity.

(a) mentsh awn glihk ihz a toi-ter mentsh
A person without luck is a dead person.

menuval see *menoovuhl*

men zugt see *m'zuhgt*

mer
Also *meir.*
Carrot.

mer-ihn
Also *mei-rihn, me-ren.*
Also spelled *meiren, merin, mehren.*
Plural of *mer.* See *mer.*

me-rihn tzih-muhs
Also spelled *mehren tzimmes.*
A sweet dish made with carrots and occasionally
with a combination of other ingredients: sweet potatoes, prunes, meat, etc.

mer-ka-va*
Also *mer-kaw-vaw.*
Also spelled *merkavah.*
Literally, "chariot." Associated in Jewish mysti-
cism with the prophet Ezekiel's vision of the Divine
throne-chariot.

merkavah see *merkava*

mes see *meis*

mesader gitin see *m'sadeir gitihn*

mesader kiddushin see *m'sadeir kidooshihn*

me-shi-ach
Also *maw-shi-ach, ma-shi-ach.***
1. The anointed one.
2. The Messiah.

meshigaas see *meshugaas*

meshigene see *meshugenuh*

me-shih-gas-ihm
Also spelled *mishigasim.*
1. Crazy actions.
2. Foolish deeds.

me-shu-ga-as
Also *me-shu-ga-at.***
Also spelled *mishegaas, meshigaas, m'shugaas.*
Craziness, madness.

me-shu-ga-ner
A variant form of *meshugenuh.*

me-shu-ge
Also *me-shu-guh, me-shu-ga.***

---

a as in father; aw as in law; ai as in aisle; ei as in neighbor; e as in bet; i as in vaccine; ih as in tin; o as in
solar; oi as in void; oo as in food; u as in put; uh as in but; ch as in chutzpa; zh as in Zhivago.

1. Insane.
2. Mad.
3. Crazy.

me-shu-ge bihst du?
Are you crazy?

me-shu-ge bihst du, tzoo chaw-seir dei-uh?
Also spelled *meshuga bistu tzu chasser daie?*
Are you crazy or just of diminished mental capacity?

me-shu-ge-ne genz, me-shu-ge-ne grih-be-nes
Also spelled *meshugane genz, meshugane gribenes.*
1. Literally, "crazy geese, crazy pieces of rendered fat."
2. Like parents, like children.

me-shu-ge-ner
Also spelled *meshuganer.*
Crazy person (masculine).

me-shu-ge-ner mam-zer
Crazy bastard.

(a) me-shu-ge-ne velt
Also spelled *(a) meshugane velt.*
1. A crazy world.
2. A mad world.

me-shu-ge-nuh
Also spelled *meshugane, meshigine, meshigina.*
1. A crazy person.
2. A madman.

me-shu-ge oif toit
Also *me-shu-ge tzum toit.*
Also spelled *meshuga oif toit.*
1. Literally, "dead crazy."
2. Really crazy.

meshuge tzum toit see *meshuge oif toit*

meshuguh see *meshuge*

me-shu-luhch
Also *me-shu-lach.**

---

a as in father; aw as in law; ai as in aisle; ei as in neighbor; e as in bet; i as in vaccine; ih as in tin; o as in solar; oi as in void; oo as in food; u as in put; uh as in but; ch as in chutzpa; zh as in Zhivago.

1. Literally, "one who has been sent forth."
2. A courier, messenger, envoy.
3. A fund-raising emissary for charitable or academic institutions.

me-shu-muhd
Also *me-shu-med, me-shu-mad.**
An apostate, a Jew who converted to another religion.

me-shu-nuh
Also *me-shu-ne, me-shu-na**.
1. Different.
2. Changed.
3. Strange, queer.
4. Curious, eccentric.

me-sihch-tuh
Also *me-sihch-ta*, ma-sech-ta, ma-sech-tuh.*
Also spelled *messekhet.*
A tractate (book) of the Talmud.

mesihvtuh
Also *me-tihv-ta,* me-sihv-taw.*
Also spelled *metivta, mesifta.*
An academy of Jewish learning for advanced Talmudic studies.

me-soo-she-lach
1. The Hebrew name of Methuselah, the biblical character said to have lived 969 years, (Genesis 5:27).
2. An old man.

mesora see *masoruh*

mesr
Also spelled *meser.*
A knife.

met see *meis*

metihvta see *mesihvtuh*

metivta see *mesihvtuh*

met mihtzva see *meis mihtzvuh*

metsia see *metziuh*

---

a as in father; aw as in law; ai as in aisle; ei as in neighbor; e as in bet; i as in vaccine; ih as in tin; o as in solar; oi as in void; oo as in food; u as in put; uh as in but; ch as in chutzpa; zh as in Zhivago.

me-tur-ge-man
Literally, "translator (of the Bible)."

metzitzuh see *m'tzitza*

me-tzi-uh
Also *me-tzi-a,** *me-tzi-aw, m'tzi-uh.*
Also spelled *metziye, metsieh, metsia.*
1. Literally, "a find."
2. A bargain.
3. A discovery.
4. A windfall.

(a) me-tzi-uh foon a ga-nef
Also spelled *(a) metzia fun a ganav.*
1. Literally, "a find from a thief."
2. An extraordinary bargain.

me-ya-eish
Also *me-ya-esh.**
To be sorry.

me-ya-eish zain
Also spelled *meyaesh zein.*
1. To be disappointed.
2. To give up hope.

me-zo-not*
Also *me-zo-nos.*
1. Provisions.
2. Bread and breadlike products over which the *Hamotzi* prayer must be recited.

me-zumn
Also *me-zu-muhn, me-zu-man.**
Also spelled *m'zumen.*
1. Literally, "ready, prepared."
2. Ready cash, money.
3. A quorum of three or more for joining in the *Grace After Meals* prayers.

mezuza see *mezuzuh*

me-zu-zuh
Also *me-zu-ze, me-zu-za,** *mezuzaw.*
Also spelled *mezzuza, m'zooza, mezuzah.*
1. Doorpost.

---

a as in father: aw as in law; ai as in aisle; ei as in neighbor; e as in bet; i as in vaccine; ih as in tin; o as in solar; oi as in void; oo as in food; u as in put; uh as in but; ch as in chutzpa; zh as in Zhivago.

2. A small parchment upon which passages from the Bible are handwritten and placed in a container which is affixed to the right doorpost (as one enters) of a Jewish home and also of each room used for living purposes.
3. A wooden or metal container which holds the parchment upon which are written words (the *Shema*) from Deuteronomy 6:9 and following.

mezzuza see *mezuzuh*

M'gi-las Es-ter
Also *M'gi-lat Es-ter.**
Also spelled *Megillat Esther.*
Literally, "the Scroll of Esther," the biblical Book of Esther.

mich shrekt men nit see *mihch shrekt men niht*

mi-das haw-ra-cha-mihm
Also *mi-dat ha-ra-cha-mim.**
1. Literally, "the quality, measure of mercy."
2. Divine justice tempered with mercy.
3. Compassion.

mi-dat ha-din*
Also *mi-das ha-dihn.*
Also spelled *middat hadin.*
The attribute of Divine justice.

mi-es
Also *mi-uhs, mi-oos.**
Also spelled *mius.*
1. Ugly.
2. Disgusting, revolting.

mi-es-kait
Also spelled *mieskeit.*
1. Ugliness.
2. An ugly thing.
3. An ugly person.

mi-esr ne-fesh
Also spelled *mieser nefesh.*
1. An ugly person.
2. A cheap person.

mihch shrekt men niht
Also spelled *mich shrekt men nit*.
Me, no one scares!

mihd-ruhsh
Also *med-ruhsh, mihd-rash,* mihd-rawsh*.
Also spelled *midrash*.
1. Literally, "investigation" or "interpretation."
2. Commentary on and interpretation of the Bible.
3. A category of books in which various books of
the Bible are interpreted and explained.

Mih-hag Se-far-ad
The Spanish (Sephardic) ritual of Jews of Iberian
and Middle Eastern descent.

mihk-raw
Also *mihk-ra.**
Also spelled *mikra*.
1. Literally, "reading."
2 The written Torah.

mihk-vuh
Also *mihk-vaw, mihk-va.**
Also spelled *mikva, mikvah, mikve, mikveh*.
1. Reservoir, body of water.
2. A pool of water, derived from natural springs, for
use in Jewish ritual purification.

mihl-chihk
Also *mihl-che-dihg, mihl-che-dihk*.
Also spelled *milchik*.
Dairy foods and utensils used specifically in the
preparation and serving of such foods, in contra-
distinction to *fleishihg*.

mihltz
Also spelled *miltz*.
Spleen, milt.

mihncha see *mihnchuh*

Mihn-chuh
Also *Mihn-cha,* Mihn-chaw*.
Also spelled *Mincha, Minha*.
1. Literally, "a gift."
2. The name of the daily afternoon prayer service.

---

a as in father: aw as in law; ai as in aisle; ei as in neighbor; e as in bet; i as in vaccine; ih as in tin; o as in
solar; oi as in void; oo as in food; u as in put; uh as in but; ch as in chutzpa: zh as in Zhivago.

mihn-hawg
>Also *mihn-hag.**
>Also spelled *minhag.*
>1. Custom.
>2. Ritual practice.

mihn-hawg-ihm
>Also *mihn-ha-gihm.**
>Also spelled *minhagim.*
>Customs, practices. Plural of *minhawg.*

mihn-yuhn
>Also *mihn-yan,** *mihn-yawn.*
>Also spelled *minyan, minyon.*
>1. Literally, "count."
>2. A quorum of ten (traditionally male) Jews, over
>the age of thirteen, required for communal wor-
>ship.

mihp-nei dar-kei sha-lom*
>Also spelled *mipne darkay shawlom.*
>1. Literally, "because of the ways of peace."
>2. In order to establish a climate of peace, for the
>sake of peace.

mihr
>Also spelled *mir.*
>We.

mihr-tse-shem
>Also *mihr-tsih-shem.*
>Also spelled *mirtzishem.*
>God willing! A contraction of the Hebrew words
>*ihm yihr-tse ha-Shem.*

mihr veln benshn
>Also spelled *mir velen bentshen.*
>1. Literally, "We will bless."
>2. The invitation to all present to say the *Grace
>After Meals.*

mihr veln ihm ba-graw-ben
>Also spelled *mir velen im bagroben.*
>We will bury him.

a as in father; aw as in law; ai as in aisle; ei as in neighbor; e as in bet; i as in vaccine; ih as in tin; o as in solar; oi as in void; oo as in food; u as in put; uh as in but; ch as in chutzpa; zh as in Zhivago.

mihr zawln der-lebn
> Also spelled *mir zolen derleben.*
> We should only live (to see it)!

mihr zawln zihch ba-geig-nen oif sihm-ches
> May we meet on happy occasions!

mihsh
> Also spelled *mish.*
> Mix.

mihsh-mash
> Also spelled *mish-mash, mish-mosh.*
> 1. A mix-up.
> 2. Mixture.
> 3. Mess, hodge podge.

mihsh-lo-ach maw-nos
> Also *mihsh-lo-ach ma-not.**
> Also spelled *mishloach manot.*
> 1. Literally, "to send portions."
> 2. Gift-giving, usually goodies, on the Purim holiday.

mihshn a-rain
> Also spelled *mishen arein.*
> 1. To mix in (to another's affairs).
> 2. To butt in.

mihshn di Yoitz-res
> 1. Literally, "to mix up the *Yotzer* prayers" of the morning service by reciting them out of order.
> 2. To mix things up.

Mihsh-nuh
> Also *Mihsh-ne, Mihsh-na.**
> Also spelled *Mishna, Mishnah.*
> 1. Literally, "repetitive study."
> 2. The first part of the Talmud, which contains rabbinic oral interpretations of Scriptural ordinances.

mihsh-puh-che
> Also *mihsh-paw-chaw, mihsh-paw-che, mihsh-pa-cha.**
> Also spelled *mishpoche.*

---

a as in father: aw as in law; ai as in aisle; ei as in neighbor; e as in bet; i as in vaccine; ih as in tin: o as in solar; oi as in void; oo as in food; u as in put; uh as in but; ch as in chutzpa: zh as in Zhivago.

1. Family, relatives.
2. Clan.

mihshugaas see *meshugaas*

mihs-nag-dihm
Also *miht-nag-dihm.**
Also spelled *mitnagdim.*
Plural of *mihsnageid.* See below.

mihs-na-geid
Also *miht-na-ged.**
Also spelled *misnaged, mitnaged.*
1. Literally, "opponent."
2. An opponent of the Chassidic movement.

miht a-le mai-les
Also spelled *mit alle meiles.*
1. Literally, "with all good qualities."
2. A talented person.
3. One who is perfection.

miht ein klap
Also spelled *mit ain klap.*
With one stroke, with one blow.

mih-tel-muh-sih-kait
Also spelled *mittelmošikeit.*
Mediocrity.

mih-tel-muh-sih-ker
Also spelled *mittelmosiker.*
Mediocre person.

mihtn
Also spelled *mitten.*
The middle, center.

mihtnagdihm see *mihsnagdihm*

mihtnageid see *mihsnageid*

mihtsva see *mihtsvuh*

mihtsvos see *mihtsvuhs*

mihtsvot see *mihtsvuhs*

mihts-vuh
Also *mihts-ve, mihts-va.**
Also spelled *mitzva, mitzvah, mitsva, mitsvah.*

---

a as in father; aw as in law; ai as in aisle: ei as in neighbor; e as in bet; i as in vaccine; ih as in tin; o as in
solar; oi as in void; oo as in food; u as in put; uh as in but; ch as in chutzpa; zh as in Zhivago.

1. A commandment.
2. A religious obligation.
3. A good deed, considerate act.

mihts-vuhs
Also *mihts-vos, mihts-vot.**
Also spelled *mitzvot, mitsvot.*
Plural of *mihts-vuh.*

mihzrach see *mihzruhch*

mihz-ra-chihm
Also spelled *mizrachim.*
Plural of *mizrach.* See *mizrach.*

Mihz-raw-chi
Also *Mihz-ra-chi.**
Also spelled *Mizrachi.*
1. Literally, "one who comes from the East."
2. A religious Zionist organization.
3. A person who belongs to the Mizrachi Zionist organization.

mihz-ruhch
Also *mihz-rech, mihz-rach.**
Also spelled *mizrach.*
1. East, eastern.
2. The direction of Jerusalem, toward which Jews in the West pray.
3. A decorative object depicting Jerusalem scenes, placed on the eastern wall of a home to indicate the direction of the holy city.

mihz-ruhch bihld
Also spelled *mizrach bild.*
A calligraphic picture hung on the eastern wall of a house.

mihz-ruhch vant
Also spelled *mizrach vant.*
The eastern wall of the synagogue, where the privileged members are usually seated. See *mizrach.*

mikva see *mihkvuh*

mila see *miluh*

milchedik see *mihlchihk*

---

a as in father; aw as in law; ai as in aisle; ei as in neighbor; e as in bet; i as in vaccine; ih as in tin; o as in solar; oi as in void; oo as in food; u as in put; uh as in but; ch as in chutzpa; zh as in Zhivago.

milchik see *mihlchihk*

miltz see *mihltz*

mi-luh
>Also *mi-la,** *mi-law.*
>1. Circumcision.
>2. The rite of circumcision.

mi-mihsh-pa-chat*
>Also *mi-mihsh-pa-chas.*
>Literally, "from the family of."

mimona see *Noche de Mimona*

Mincha see *Mihnchuh*

minhag see *mihnhawg*

minyan see *mihnyuhn*

mioos see *mies*

mipne darkay shawlom see *mihpnei darkei shalom*

mirtzishem see *mihrtseshem*

mir velen bentshen see *mihr veln benshn*

mir velen im bagroben see *mihr veln ihm bagrawben*

mir zolen derleben see *mihr zawln derlebn*

misaw see *misuh*

mise meshunuh see *misuh meshunuh*

mish see *mihsh*

mi she-bei-rach
>Also spelled *mi sheberach.*
>1. Literally, "May He who blessed."
>2. The opening words and name of a prayer offered in the synagogue for the well-being of an individual.

mishegaas see *meshugaas*

mishen see *mishn*

mishigasim see *meshihgasihm*

mishloach manot see *mihshloach mawnos*

mish-mash see *mihsh mash*

mishn
    Also spelled *mishen*.
    To mix.
Mishna see *Mihshnuh*
mishpoche see *mihshpuhche*
mi-suh
    Also *mi-saw* and *mi-ta*.*
    Death, dying.
mi-suh m'shoo-nuh
    Also *mi-saw m'shoo-naw*, *mi-ta m'shoo-na*.*
    Also spelled *misa m'shoone*, *misa meshunuh*.
    1. Literally, "strange death."
    2. Untimely death.
    3. Unnatural death.
    4. A tragic end.

mita see *misuh*
mit ain klap see *miht ein klap*
mit alle meiles see *miht ale mailes*
mitnaged see *mihsnageid*
mitsvot see *mihtsvuhs*
mittelmosikeit see *mihtelmuhsihkait*
mitten see *mihtn*
mitzva see *mihtzvuh*
mitzvoth see *mihtsvuhs*
miuhs see *mies*
mizrach see *mihzruhch*
mizrach bild see *mihzruhch bihld*
Mizrachi see *Mihzrawchi*
mizrachim see *mihzrachihm*
mizrach vant see *mihzruhch vant*
m'ken see *men* and *men ken*
mode ani see *moide ani*
modeh ani see *moide ani*
modne see *mawdne*

---

mogen see *muhgn*

Mogen David see *Muhgn Duhvihd*

mogen kugel see *mawgn kugl*

mohayl see *moil*

mohel see *moil*

moichl
>Also *mo-cheil.*
>Also spelled *moichel.*
>Thanks, but no thanks! Forget it!

moichl zain
>Also spelled *moichel zein.*
>To excuse, forgive, pardon, condone

moid
>Girl. A distorted form of *meidl.*

moi-de a-ni
>Also *mo-de a-ni.*
>Also spelled *modeh ani.*
>1. Literally, "I render thanks."
>2. The first words of prayer uttered by a traditional Jew upon arising in the morning.

moil
>Also *mo-hel,* *mo-heil, mo-hayl.*
>Also spelled *moel.*
>1. Mouth.
>2. A person trained to perform circumcisions according to Jewish law.

moi-she ka-poi-er
>1. Literally, "Moses topsy-turvy."
>2. One who does things wrong or in reverse order.

mooktze see *muktzuh*

moo-sar*
>Also *mu-sar, mu-suhr.*
>1. Literally, "moralization, reproaching."
>2. A nineteenth-century ethical movement among Lithuanian Jews.

moo-suhf
>Also *Mu-saf,* *Mu-sawf.*

Also spelled *Musaph.*
1. Literally, "additional, added."
2. An additional service on Sabbath and festivals.

moo-tihk
Also spelled *mutik.*
Bold, courageous, daring, brave.

mordeven zich see *muhrdeven zihch*

Mo-re Ne-vu-chim
Guide for the Perplexed, a book written in 1190 by
Moses ben Maimon (Maimonides), the RaMBaM.

morgen see *mawrgn*

moror see *mawror*

mo-seir
Also *mo-ser.**
Also spelled *mosser.*
A stool pigeon, betrayer, informer.

mo-shav*
The earliest type of settlement in modern Israel, in
which the individual leases the land, and the farming, equipment, and sale of produce are conducted
collectively.

mo-shav ov-dim*
A workers' *moshav.*

mo-shav shi-tu-fi*
A collective in Israel.

mosser see *moseir*

mo-tsaw-ei Sha-bes
Also *Mo-tsaw-ei Sha-buhs, Mo-tsa-ei Sha-bat.**
Also spelled *Motza'ai Shabbat, Motzei Shabbat.*
1. Literally, "Sabbath's exit."
2. Saturday night.

Motzei Shabbat see *Mo-tsaw-ei Sha-bes*

motzi see *Hamotzi*

m'sadeir gi-tihn
Also spelled *mesader gitin.*
A rabbi who specializes in issuing divorces.

---

a as in father; aw as in law; ai as in aisle; ei as in neighbor; e as in bet; i as in vaccine; ih as in tin; o as in solar; oi as in void; oo as in food; u as in put; uh as in but; ch as in chutzpa; zh as in Zhivago.

m'sa-deir ki-doo-shihn*
Also spelled *mesader kiddushin.*
A rabbi or any Jew qualified to perform marriages.

m'shugaat see *meshugaas*

m'shumad
An apostate from Judaism.

m'tzi-tza*
Also *me-tzi-tzuh, me-tzi-tzaw.*
The drawing of blood from the wound left by circumcision.

m'tziuh see *metziuh*

muhgn
Also spelled *muhgen, mogen.*
Stomach.

Muhgn Duh-vihd
Also *Maw-gein Daw-vihd, Ma-gen Da-vihd.**
Also spelled *Magen David, Mogen David.*
1. Literally, "Shield of David."
2. Six-pointed Star of David.
3. Jewish star.

muhr-de-ven zihch
Also spelled *mordeven zich.*
1. To overwork.
2. To overexert oneself.

muk-tzuh
Also *muk-tze.*
Also spelled *mooktsa, mooktze.*
1. An article that may not be touched on the Sabbath because it was not intended for Sabbath use.
2. An article set aside, not to be used presently.

mum-che
An expert, a specialist.

mu-me
Also *mi-me.*
Aunt.

musaf see *moosuhf*

musar see *moosar*

mutche see *mutshe*

mutik see *mootihk*

mutr
Also *moo-tar.**
1. Permitted, permissible.
2. Mother.

mut-she
Also spelled *mutche.*
1. To nag, pester.
2. To annoy.
3. To torment.

mutshn zihch
Also spelled *mutshen zich.*
1. To overwork.
2. To slave away.
3. To suffer (at a job).

m'zooza see *mezuzuh*

m'zuhgt
Also spelled *men zugt.*
1. They say.
2. People say.
3. It is said.

m'zumen see *mezumn*

---

a as in father; aw as in law; ai as in aisle; ei as in neighbor; e as in bet; i as in vaccine; ih as in tin; o as in
solar; oi as in void; oo as in food; u as in put; uh as in but; ch as in chutzpa; zh as in Zhivago.

N

na
>1. Here (when handing something)!
>2. Take it!

naar see *nar*

NaCH
>An acronym from the initials of the Hebrew words *Nevi'im* (Prophets) and *Ketuvim* (Writings), the second and third parts of the Hebrew Bible.

na-cha-la*
>Death anniversary among Sephardic Jews.

nachas see *nachuhs*

nachat see *nachuhs*

nacht
>Night.

nacht falt tzu
>1. Literally, "Night is falling."
>2. Twilight.

na-chuhs
>Also *nach-es, nach-as, nach-at.**
>1. Ease.
>2. Rest.
>3. Pride.
>4. Satisfaction from another's achievement.

na-chuhs roo-ach
>Also *na-chat ru-ach,** *na-ches roo-ach.*
>1. Literally, "ease of spirit."
>2. Pleasure, satisfaction.

nadn
>Also *na-dan.**
>Dowry.

nad-van*
>Also *nad-vawn.*

---

1. A philanthropist.
2. A donor, benefactor.

naf-ke
Also *naf-ka.**
A prostitute.

nagihd see *nawgihd*

naies see *nais*

naigel vasser see *neigl vaser*

nain see *nein*

nais
Also *nai-es.*
Also spelled *neies.*
News.

nar
Also *na-ar.**
1. A boy (Hebrew).
2. A fool (Yiddish).

na-raw-nihm
Also spelled *naronim.*
Fools, stupid people. Plural of *nar.*

(a) nar fihlt niht
A fool feels nothing.

na-rihsh
Also spelled *narish.*
Foolish, stupid.

na-rihsh-kait
Also spelled *narishkeit.*
Nonsense.

naronim see *narawnihm*

(a) nar vaist men (or **tsaigt men**) **kain nihsht hal-be ar-biht**
1. Literally, "One doesn't show a fool half a task."
2. Don't reveal something half-finished to a fool.

nash
Also spelled *nosh.*
1. A snack.

---

a as in father; aw as in law; ai as in aisle; ei as in neighbor; e as in bet; i as in vaccine; ih as in tin; o as in solar; oi as in void; oo as in food; u as in put; uh as in but; ch as in chutzpa; zh as in Zhivago.

2. A sweet.
3. An in-between-meals treat.

nashen see *nashn*

nasher see nashr

nash-er-ai
Also spelled *nasherei*.
1. Sweets, junk food.
2. A place that serves goodies.

nash-ing
Indulging in a *nash*. See *nash. nashn*
Also spelled *nashen*.
To nibble, especially on sweets.

nashr
Also spelled *nasher, nosher*.
1. A nibbler.
2. A person with a sweet-tooth.

na-si*
Also *naw-si*.
1. Leader, head.
2. Head of an academy of Jewish learning in ancient times.
3. President of the Sanhedrin in ancient times.
4. President of the State of Israel.

navi see *nawvi*

nawch
Also spelled *noch*.
1. Yet.
2. After.
3. Following.
4. Next.

nawch nihsht
Also spelled *noch nisht*.
Not yet.

nawch shlepr
Also spelled *nochshlepper*.
1. An unwanted follower.
2. A hanger-on.

---

a as in father; ew as in law; ai as in aisle: ei as in neighbor; e as in bet; i as in vaccine; ih as in tin; o as in solar; oi as in void; oo as in food; u as in put; uh as in but; ch as in chutzpa; zh as in Zhivago.

naw-gihd
Also *na-gihd*.
Also spelled *nogid*.
1. A prince.
2. A person of high estate.

nawmn
Also spelled *nawmen, nomen*.
Name.

nawr
Merely, only, just.

nawr Gawt veist
Also spelled *nor Gott vaist*.
Only God knows.

naw-vi
Also *na-vi*.*
Prophet.

naw-zihr
Also *na-zihr*.*
Also spelled *nazir*.
1. Nazarite.
2. In the Bible, a person who leads an ascetic life, abstaining from wine and cutting of his hair.

Nazirite
A person following the discipline of a *nawzihr*. See *nawzihr*.

nebech see *nebuhch*

ne-bihsh
Also spelled *nebish*.
1. Ineffective, shy, dull.
2. An inept person.
A variant form of *nebuhch*.

ne-buhch
Also spelled *nebech*.
1. A pity, a pitiful situation.
2. A pitiful individual, a person to be pitied.

ne-buhchl
Also spelled *nebechl*.
A variant form of *nebuhch*. See above.

---

ne-chaw-meh
> Also *ne-cha-ma.**
> 1. Literally, "comfort."
> 2. A feminine personal name.

(a) nech-tihger tawg
> Also spelled *(a) nechtiger tog.*
> 1. Literally, "a yesterday's day."
> 2. Nothing of the kind! Forget it! Nonsense! It never happened!

nedr see *neidr*

ne-duh-ve
> Also *ne-daw-vuh, ne-du-ve, ne-da-va.**
> 1. Literally, "an offering."
> 2. A donation.
> 3. Charity.
> 4. Almsgiving.

ne-fuhsh
> Also *ne-fesh,** *nei-fihsh.*
> Also spelled *nafish, nayfish, nefish.*
> 1. Spirit.
> 2. Soul.
> 3. Breath.

Ne-gev
> The southern region of the State of Israel.

neidr
> Also *nedr.**
> 1. A pledge, vow, promise.
> 2. Charity pledged on the Sabbath or a holiday by someone honored with an *aliya.* See *aliya.*

neies see *nais*

neifish see *nefuhsh*

neigl va-ser
> Also spelled *naigel vasser.*
> Literally, "finger water," used by Orthodox Jews upon rising in the morning.

Ne-i-luh
> Also *Ne-i-law, Ne-i-la.**
> Also spelled *Neilah.*

---

a as in father; aw as in law; ai as in aisle: ei as in neighbor; e as in bet; i as in vaccine; ih as in tin; o as in solar; oi as in void; oo as in food; u as in put; uh as in but; ch as in chutzpa; zh as in Zhivago.

1. Literally, "closing (of the gates of the Temple and forgiveness)."
2. Concluding service of Yom Kippur (Day of Atonement).

nein
Also *nain*.
No, not.

neis see *nes*

neisuhch see *nesech*

nekama see *n'kuhme*

nekeva see *n'keivuh*

nem
Take! .

nemn
Also spelled *nemen*.
To take.

nemn shoi-ched
Also spelled *nemen shoichuhd*.
To take a bribe.

nem zihch a va-ne
Also spelled *nem zich a vanne*.
1. Literally, "take a bath."
2. Don't bother me!

Ner Ta-mid*
Also *Ner Taw-mihd*.
Literally, "perpetual light" or "eternal light," a designation derived from Leviticus 24:2 for the light suspended above the Holy Ark.

nes*
Also *neis*.
Miracle.

ne-sech*
Also *nei-suhch*.
1. Literally, "pouring."
2. Refers to wine poured on the altar in pagan worship.
3. Wine not usable by Jews.

neshama see *neshuhmuh*

ne-shuh-me-le
1. Literally, "little soul."
2. Darling, sweetheart.

ne-shuh-muh
Also *ne-shaw-maw, ne-sha-ma.**
Also spelled *ne-shuh-me*.
1. Soul.
2. Spirit.

ne-shuh-muh y'sei-ruh
Also *ne-shaw-maw ye-sei-raw, ne-sha-ma ye-tei-ra.**
Literally, "an extra soul," which in Jewish tradition is awarded Jews on the Sabbath.

ne-si-at ka-pa-yihm*
Also *ne-si-as ka-pa-yihm*.
1. Literally, "the raising of hands."
2. The Priestly Blessing.

Ne-tu-rei Kar-ta
1. Literally, "Guardians of the City."
2. A group of anti-Zionist, extreme Orthodox Jews living in Jerusalem.

ne-vi-ihm
Also spelled *n'viim, neviim*.
1. Prophets (plural of *navi*).
2. The prophets of the Bible.
3. The name of the second division of the Bible.

ni-chum a-vei-lihm
Also spelled *nichum avelim*.
Literally, "comforting of mourners."

nidda see *niduh*

nider see *nihdr*

nidertrechtik see *nihdertrechtihk*

ni-duh
Also *ni-daw, ni-da.**
Also spelled *nidda*.
A menstruating woman.

---

a as in father; aw as in law; ai as in aisle; ei as in neighbor; e as in bet; i as in vaccine; ih as in tin; o as in solar; oi as in void; oo as in food; u as in put; uh as in but; ch as in chutzpa; zh as in Zhivago.

niftar see *nihftr*

ni-gun*
  Also *nihgn.*
  A wordless Chassidic melody.

(a) nihd-er-ih-ker kerl
  An inferior, a good-for-nothing.

nih-der-trech-tihk
  Also spelled *nidertrechtik.*
  Outrageous, vile.

nihdr
  Also spelled *nider.*
  Down.

nihftr
  Also *nihf-tar.**
  Also spelled *niftar.*
  1. Literally, "one who has departed."
  2. A deceased person.

nihftr-shmihftr, a lebn macht er?
  Also spelled *niftar-schmifter, a leben macht er?*
  Dead or not—what's the difference, so long as he
  makes a living. (A play on the words *niftar,* "deceased," and *leben,* "living.")

nihs
  Also spelled *nis.*
  Nuts.

nihsht duh ge-dacht
  1. May it not happen here!
  2. May it not happen to us!

nihsht ge-fer-lach see *nit geferlich*

nihsht gut
  Not good! It's not good!

nihsht haint, nihsht mawrgn
  Also spelled *nisht heint, nisht morgen.*
  1. Literally, "neither today nor tomorrow."
  2. It will never happen.

nihsht kaw-she
  Also spelled *nishkoshe, nihsht kusher, nish
  kusher.*

a as in father; aw as in law; ai as in aisle; ei as in neighbor; e as in bet; i as in vaccine; ih as in tin: o as in solar; oi as in void; oo as in food; u as in put; uh as in but; ch as in chutzpa; zh as in Zhivago.

1. Combination of the Yiddish *nihsht* ("not") and the Hebrew *kawshe* ("difficult, hard").
2. Not bad.
3. Bearable.

Erroneously associated with *nihsht kuhsher,* meaning "not kosher."

nihsht kuh-sher
Also spelled *nish kushr.*
Not kosher. See also *nihsht kawshe.*

nihsht neitihg see *nit neitihk*

Nihsn
Also *Ni-san.**
The first month of the Jewish religious calendar, seventh of the Civil calendar, corresponding to March-April; the month in which Passover is celebrated.

niht
Also *nihsht.*
Also spelled *nit.*
1. Not.
2. Nothing.

niht a-hihn, niht a-her
Also spelled *nit ahin, nit aher.*
1. Literally, "neither here nor there."
2. Irrelevant.

niht a-zoi gihch
Also spelled *nit azoi gich.*
1. Not so fast!
2. Take it easy!

niht-duh
A contraction of *niht* ("not") and *duh* ("here").
1. Literally, "(there is) nothing here."
2. No one's here.
3. Nothing to it!

niht duh far aich
Also spelled *nit do far eich.*
May this never happen here to you!

niht duh far vaws
Also *nit do far vos.*

---

a as in father; aw as in law; ai as in aisle; ei as in neighbor; e as in bet; i as in vaccine; ih as in tin; o as in solar; oi as in void; oo as in food; u as in put; uh as in but; ch as in chutzpa; zh as in Zhivago.

1. Literally, "not here for what."
2. There's no reason at all (to do something or to be thankful).

niht far kein Yidn ge-dacht
Also spelled *nit far kain yidden gedocht.*
1. It should not befall Jews.
2. Jews don't deserve it.

niht ge-dai-giht
Also spelled *nit gedeiget.*
Not to worry! Don't worry!

niht ge-fer-lich
Also *nihsht ge-fer-lach.*
Also spelled *nit geferlech, niht geferlach.*
Not so terrible!

niht ge-fuhnf-et
Also spelled *nit gefonfet.*
1. Literally, "Don't mumble."
2. Don't use double-talk!
3. Don't hedge!

niht ge-shtoign oon niht ge-floign
Also spelled *nit geshtoigen un nit gefloigen.*
1. Literally, "doesn't stand and doesn't fly."
2. Not true whatsoever, completely false.
3. It never happened!

niht ge-trawfn
Also spelled *nit getrofen.*
1. Literally, "did not meet."
2. Did not guess right.

(a) niht gut-nihk
Also spelled *a nit gutnik.*
A no-account person.

niht-ih-kait
Also spelled *nitikeit.*
1. Nothingness.
2. Worthlessness.
3. Triviality.

niht kein var-shlawf-en-er
Also spelled *nit kain farshloffener.*
1. Not a sleepyhead.
2. A lively person.

niht nei-tihk
Also *nihst nei-tihg.*
Also spelled *nit naitik.*
Unnecessary.

niht oif dihr ge-dacht
We don't wish it on you!

niht oif unz ge-dacht
We don't wish it on ourselves!

niht shat-uhn tsoom shih-duch
Also spelled *nit shatten tsum shidduch.*
1. Literally, "It won't damage the matrimonial arrangement.".
2. It won't interfere with what is underway.

niht vihs-en-dihk
Also spelled *nit vissendik.*
Unknowing.

niht vihsn miht vaws est men daws
Also spelled *nit vissen mit vos est men dos.*
1. Literally, "not know with what one eats it."
2. Not know how to go about doing things.

nis see *nihs*

Nisan see *Nihsn*

nisht see *nihsht*

nisht heint, nisht morgen see *nihsht haint, nihsht mawrgn*

nisht kosher see *nihsht kuhsher*

ni-sihm*
Also spelled *nissim.*
Miracles. Plural of *nes.*

ni-sihm v'nihf-law-os
Also *ni-sihm v'nihf-la-ot.**

---

a as in father; aw as in law; ai as in aisle; ei as in neighbor; e as in bet; i as in vaccine; ih as in tin; o as in solar; oi as in void; oo as in food; u as in put; uh as in but; ch as in chutzpa; zh as in Zhivago.

1. Literally, "miracles and wonders."
2. Something unbelievable.

ni-soo-ihn
Also spelled *nissuin.*
The Jewish marriage ceremony, also called *kidushin.*

nissim see *nisihm*

nissuin see *nisooihn*

nit see *niht*

n'kei-vuh
Also *n'kei-va.**
Also spelled *nekeva.*
1. Female.
2. Feminine.

n'kuh-me
Also *n'kuh-muh, ne-ka-ma.**
Revenge.

noch see *nawch*

Noche de Mimona
Moroccan Jewish feast of sweet foods, held on the last night of Passover.

nochshlepper see *nawch shlepr*

nogid see *nawgihd*

nomen see *nawmn*

noo see *nu*

nor Gott vaist see *nawr Gawt veist*

no-sei ha-mi-taw
Also *no-sei ha-mi-ta.**
Literally, "bearers of the bier," pallbearers.

nosh see *nash*

no-ta-ri-kon
Also *not-ri-kon.*
Method of abbreviating Hebrew words or phrases by writing single letters.

nu
Also *noo*.
1. Well? So? So what? What about it?
2. Let's go! Hurry up!
3. Haven't you finished?

nud-nihk
Also spelled *nudnik*.
1. A pest.
2. A bore.

nudzh
Also *nudj*.
1. A pest.
2. A bore.
3. To pester, be tedious.

nuhch Ne-i-luh
Also spelled *nach Neila*.
1. Literally, "after *Neila*."
2. Too late.

nuhch-shlepr
Also spelled *nuchshlepper*.
1. One who follows or hangs on to someone else.
2. A fawner.

nun
The fourteenth letter of the Hebrew alphabet, corresponding to the "n" sound in English.

nusach see *nusuhch*

Nu-sach Ashkenaz
The liturgy according to the Ashkenazic tradition.
See *Ashkenaz*.

Nu-sach Se-pha-rad
The liturgy according to the Sephardic tradition.
See *Sephardic*.

nu-suhch
Also *nu-sawch, nu-sach,* nu-sech*.
The order and style of the liturgy according to different traditions: *Nusach Ashkenaz, Nusach Sepharad*, etc.

---

a as in father; aw as in law; ai as in aisle: ei as in neighbor; e as in bet; i as in vaccine; ih as in tin; o as in solar; oi as in void; oo as in food; u as in put; uh as in but; ch as in chutzpa; zh as in Zhivago.

nu-zhe
    To pester.

n'viim see *neviihm*

O

ober see *uhber*

och!
> Oh! Ah! or any exclamation of surprise, admiration, dismay, regret, disapproval, anxiety.

och oon vai see *awch un vei*

odem naket see *awdem naket*

oder see *uhder*

o-heiv Yihs-raw-eil
> Also *o-hev Yihs-ra-el.**
> Also spelled *ohev Yisrael.*
> 1. Literally, "lover of Israel."
> 2. Friend of the Jewish people.

oho see *uhhuh*

oi
> Also spelled *oy.*
> 1. Oh!
> 2. Ouch!
> 3. Wow!

oich
> 1. Also.
> 2. Furthermore.
> 3. Too.

oich a ba-shef-e-nihsh
> 1. Literally, "also a creature" (sarcasm).
> 2. An unimportant person.

oich mihr a lebn
> Also spelled *oich mir a leben.*
> 1. Literally, "also a living" (sarcasm).
> 2. You call this making a living?

oier see *oir*

oifen himmel a yarid see *oifn himl a yarihd*

---

a as in father; aw as in law; ai as in aisle; ei as in neighbor; e as in bet; i as in vaccine; ih as in tin; o as in solar; oi as in void; oo as in food; u as in put; uh as in but; ch as in chutzpa; zh as in Zhivago.

oif-ge-ku-men-er
1. An upstart, Johnny-come-lately.
2. A parvenu.

oif-ge-ku-men-er ge-vir a parvenu
A nouveau riche.

oif ka-paw-res
Also spelled *oif kapores.*
1. Literally, "for an atonement sacrifice."
2. Of no value.

oif mai-ne suh-nihm ge-zawgt
Also spelled *oif meine sonim gezogt.*
1. Literally, "(such a fate) should be said about my enemies."
2. May my enemies have my fate!

oif mihr ge-zawgt ge-vawr-en
Also spelled *oif mir gezogt gevoren.*
1. Literally, "May it be said about me!"
2. It should only happen to me!

oif'n ga-nef brent daws hihtl
Also spelled *oif'n ganef brent dos hitel.*
1. Literally, "Upon the thief burns his hat."
2. The wrongdoer has the guilty conscience.

oif'n himl a ya-rihd
Also spelled *oifen himmel a yarid.*
1. Literally, "a fair in the sky."
2. Much ado about nothing.

oifrifung
Also *oif-ruf.*
Literally, "a calling up," with special reference to a bridegroom called to the Torah on the Sabbath before his wedding.

oif tsaw-res
Also spelled *oif tzores.*
1. In trouble.
2. In a bad way.

oif tsuh-luh-chihs
Also spelled *oif tsulochis.*

---

a as in father: **aw** as in law; **ai** as in aisle; **ei** as in neighbor; **e** as in bet; **i** as in vaccine; **ih** as in tin; **o** as in solar; **oi** as in void; **oo** as in food; **u** as in put; **uh** as in but; **ch** as in chutzpa; **zh** as in Zhivago.

1. In order to anger.
2. Despite.

oig

An eye.

oi-lem

Also *oi-luhm, o-lam.**

1. The world.
2. The masses.
3. Crowd, congregation, public, audience.

oiluhm ha-baw

Also *o-lawm ha-baw, o-lam ha-ba.**

1. Literally, "the world to come."
2. The future.

oi-luhm haw-e-mes

Also *oi-lehm haw-e-mes, o-lam ha-e-met.**

1. Literally, "the true world" or "the world of truth."
2. The world (realm) of the dead.
3. A cemetery.

oi-luhm ha-ze

Also *o-lawm ha-ze, o-lam ha-ze.**

1. Literally, "this world."
2. The here and now.

oimer see *omer*

Oineg Shabes see *Oneg Shabat*

oir

Also spelled *oier*.
Ear.

oi-rei-ach

Also *o-rei-ach.**
Also spelled *oreach*.
Visitor, guest.

oi-ren

Also spelled *oieren*.
Ears. Plural of *oir*.

ois

1. Finished, ended.

---

2. No more.
3. All out.

ois-ge-blawz-en
1. To blow out.
2. To end up with nothing, to fizzle out, as in *oisgeblawzene eir,* "a blown-out egg."

ois-ge-dart
Skinny, thin, emaciated.

ois-ge-huhr-e-vet
Also spelled *oisgehorevet.*
Exhausted.

ois-ge-ma-tert
Weary, tired, exhausted.

ois-ge-mutsh-et
1. Exhausted.
2. Tired.

ois-ge-putzt
1. Dressed up.
2. Overdressed.
3. Overadorned, overdecorated.

ois-ge-tsats-ket
Also spelled *oisgetzatzket.*
1. Overdressed.
2. Overadorned.
3. Ostentatious.
4. Ornate.

ois-ge-tsert
Also spelled *oisgetzert.*
Emaciated.

ois-ge-zei-chent
1. Excellent.
2. Outstanding.

ois-heil-en
Also spelled *oishailen.*
To heal, be cured.

ois-hei-len far dem cha-se-ne
1. Literally, "It (the problem) will be cured before the wedding."

a as in father: aw as in law; ai as in aisle; ei as in neighbor: e as in bet: i as in vaccine: ih as in tin: o as in solar; oi as in void; oo as in food; u as in put; uh as in but; ch as in chutzpa; zh as in Zhivago.

2. Things will work out in time.

oi-sher
Also *o-sher.**
Wealth, riches.

ois-kratzn
Also spelled *ois kratzen.*
1. Literally, "to scratch out."
2. To eke out (a living).
3. To move slowly.

ois-presn
Also spelled *ois-pressen.*
1. Literally, "to press out," a term borrowed from the needle trades and garment industry.
2. To work itself out.
3. The problem will be solved.

ois-redn di hartz
1. Literally, "to talk out the heart."
2. To get things off one's chest.

ois-shih-duhch
Also spelled *ois shidduch.*
The marriage is off.

ois-shte-ler
One who flaunts, a showoff, braggart.

ois-vawrf
Also spelled *ois-vorf.*
1. A reject.
2. A scoundrel.
3. An outcast.

ois-vawrfn
Also spelled *ois-vorfen.*
To reproach, rebuke.

oitsr
Also *o-tsar,** *o-tsawr.*
1. A treasure.
2. Treasury.
3. Treasure-trove, abundance.

---

a as in father; aw as in law; ai as in aisle; ei as in neighbor; e as in bet; i as in vaccine; ih as in tin; o as in solar; oi as in void; oo as in food; u as in put; uh as in but; ch as in chutzpa; zh as in Zhivago.

oi vei
　Also spelled *oi vai.*
　Oh my! An expression of sorrow, defeat.

oi vei ihz mihr
　Also spelled *oi vais mir.*
　Oh! Woe is me!

oi-ver-buhtl
　Also spelled *oiverbotel.*
　1. Senile.
　2. Disoriented.
　3. Absent-minded.

olam see *oilem*

olav hasholem see *awluhv hashawluhm*

olawm habaw see *oiluhm habaw*

olawm haze see *oiluhm haze*

omed see *uhmed*

o-mer*
　Also *oi-mer.*
　1. A dry measure mentioned in the Bible.
　2. First sheaf of barley harvest brought to the Temple in Bible days.
　3. The period of forty-nine days from the second day of Passover until Shavuot.

on see *uhn*

O-neg Sha-bat*
　Also *O-neg Sha-buhs, Oi-neg Sha-bes.*
　Also spelled *Oneg Shabbat.*
　1. Literally, "delight of the Sabbath." Based on Isaiah 58:13.
　2. A celebration held on Friday night or Saturday afternoon to honor the Sabbath. Introduced in the 1920s by the Hebrew poet Chayyim Nachman Bialik.

o-nein
　Also *o-nen.**
　1. Bereaved.
　2. A mourner from the time of death until the funeral.

---

a as in father; aw as in law; ai as in aisle; ei as in neighbor; e as in bet; i as in vaccine; ih as in tin; o as in solar; oi as in void; oo as in food; u as in put; uh as in but; ch as in chutzpa; zh as in Zhivago.

ongeblozen see *awngeblawzen*
ongepatshket see *awngepatshket*
ongeshtopt see *awngeshtawpt*
ongevorfen see *awngevawrfn*
on lange hakdomes see *uhn lange hakdawmes*
onshikenish see *awnshihkenihsh*
onzaltzen see *awnzaltzn*
ooduhm hurishoin see *adam harishon*
ooduhr see *Adar*
opgeflikt see *awpgeflihkt*
opgehit see *awpgehiht*
opgekrochen see *awpgekrawchen*
opgelozen see *awpgelawzn*
opgenart see *awpgenart*
ophiten see *awphihtn*
opnaren zich see *awpnaren zihch*
opnarer see *awpnarer*
optshepen see *awptshepn*
oreach see *oireiach*
orem see *awrem*
oremeleit see *awremelait*
oremkeit see *awremkait*
or-la*
> Also *awr-la, awr-law.*
> 1. Literally, "uncircumcised."
> 2. Fruit produced by trees during their first three years of life. According to biblical law such fruit cannot be eaten.

osher see *oisher*
oto ha-ihsh*
> Also *o-so haw-ihsh.*
> Literally, "that man (Jesus)."

otsar see *oitsr*
ovel see *uhvl*

ovent see *awvent*

oy see *oi*

oz-nei Ha-man*
>Also *awz-nei Haw-mawn.*
>1. Literally, "Haman's ears."
>2. The Hebrew name for *hamantashen.*

P

pai see *pei*

paigaren see *peigeren*

paik-ler
>Also spelled *peikler*.
>A drummer.

pai-tan*
>Also *pai-tawn*.
>Composer of a *piyut* (a poem or hymn of a religious nature). *Paitanihm** is the plural form.

Pal-mach
>An acronym for *Pelugot Machatz,** "shock companies," the commando forces of the Hagana in pre-state Israel.

pa-me-lach
>Also *pa-me-lech*.
>1. Slowly.
>2. By degrees.
>3. Little by little.

panim see *pawnihm*

pa-pih-ruhs
>Also spelled *papiros*.
>Cigarette.

parasha see *parshuh*

parch
>1. A scab.
>2. A nasty person.

parech see *parihch*

Pardesi
>Certain light-skinned Jews of Cochin, India.

pa-rev
>Also *pa-re-ve*.

---

1. Neutral.
2. Food products that are neither *milchik* (dairy) nor *flaishik* (meat), including fruit, vegetables, fish, and all meatless and synthetic products.

pa-rihch
Also spelled *parech, paruhch.*
A wig.

par-naws
Also *par-nas.**
Also spelled *parnass.*
1. A supporter.
2. The chief synagogue administrative officer in previous generations.
3. A community representative.

par-naw-saw
Also *par-na-sa.**
Also spelled *parnuse, parnuhse.*
1. Livelihood.
2. Income.

parshe see *parshuh*

par-shih-ve
Also spelled *parshive.*
1. Nasty, ugly.
2. Cheap, vile, mean.

par-shoin
1. Person, personage.
2. Beauty.

par-shuh
Also *paw-raw-shaw, pa-ra-sha.**
Also spelled *parshe.*
1. Section, division, part.
2. One of the sections of the Pentateuch.
3. Among Sephardim, the name by which the Torah reading of a particular week is called.
4. A deviation from the norm.
5. A scandal (modern Israeli usage.)

par-tatsh
A botcher, one who fouls up.

par-tatsh-ihsh
Sloppy, inferior, bungled (merchandise or workmanship).

paruhch see *parihch*

pas-kud-nak
Also *pas-kud-nihk, paskudnyak.*
A nasty person.

pas-kud-ne
Also spelled *paskudnye.*
Vile, nasty, dirty, filthy (referring to a person).

pas-kust-vuh
Also spelled *paskustve.*
Feminine form of *paskudne.* See above.

pasn
Also spelled *pasen, passen.*
1. To suit someone.
2. Appropriate, proper, fitting.

Passover see *Peisuhch*

past niht
Unbecoming. Also used in the form of *s'past niht,* a short form of *es past niht.*

past zihch
Also spelled *past zich.*
Suitable.

past zihch vi a patsh tzoo a goot Sha-bes
1. Literally, "as appropriate as a slap in response to a 'Good Sabbath' greeting."
2. An illogical and unbefitting reaction.

pa-sul*
Also *paw-sul.*
1. Disqualified.
2. Ritually unusable, in reference to things other than food.

patch see *patsh*

pa-ter-en
Also spelled *patern.*
1. To waste, ruin, spoil.
2. To get rid of.

---

a as in father; aw as in law; ai as in aisle; ei as in neighbor; e as in bet; i as in vaccine; ih as in tin; o as in solar; oi as in void; oo as in food; u as in put; uh as in but; ch as in chutzpa; zh as in Zhivago.

pa-ter-en tsait
>Also spelled *pateren zeit.*
>To waste time.

patsh
>Also spelled *patch, potsh.*
>Slap, smack.

patsh-ke
>Also *patsh-ki.*
>Also spelled *potchki.*
>A variant form of *patshkn.* See below.

patshkn
>Also spelled *patshken.*
>1. Literally, "to smear, daub."
>2. To fuss, to play around.
>3. To be slipshod, messy.

pa-vuhl-ye
>Also spelled *pavolye.*
>1. Slowly.
>2. To move with care.

paw-nihm
>Also *pa-nihm.**
>Also spelled *panim.*
>1. A face.
>2. Appearance.

pawrawshaw see *parshuh*

paw-ro-ches
>Also *pa-ro-chet.**
>Also spelled *parokhet.*
>1. Literally, "curtain."
>2. The curtain that hangs in front of the Holy Ark
>   *(Aron Hakodesh).*

pawsul see *pasul*

pay see *pei*

paya see *peia*

payess see *peies*

pei*
>Also spelled *pe, pay, pai.*

The seventeenth letter of the Hebrew alphabet, sounded like "p."

pei-a*
>Also *pei-aw.*
>Also spelled *peah, paya.*
>1. Literally, "corner."
>2. In the Bible, "corners of a field," the produce of which had to be left for the poor.

pei-es
>Also *pei-uhs, pei-os, pei-ot.**
>Also spelled *peiess, payes, payess, peot.*
>Earlocks, sideburns, worn particularly by Chasidim.

pei-ger-en
>Also spelled *paigaren.*
>To die (said of an animal).

pei-ger-en zawl er
>Also spelled *paigaren zol er.*
>1. Literally, "He should only die."
>2. He should drop dead unceremoniously.

peikler see *paikler*

pei nun
>Two Hebrew letters that appear on tombstones as an abbreviation for the Hebrew words *po nihkbar,* "here lies buried," or *po noach,* "here rests."

peiot see *peies*

pei-sach-dihg
>Also *pei-sach-dihk.*
>Also spelled *pesachdik, pesadik.*
>Food and utensils that are maintained in compliance with the laws of Passover.

Pei-suhch
>Also *Pe-sach.**
>Also spelled *Pesah.*
>1. Literally, "to pass over."
>2. Passover, the Festival of Freedom that is observed for seven days in Israel and for eight days by most Jews of the Diaspora.

---

a as in father; aw as in law; ai as in aisle; ei as in neighbor; e as in bet; i as in vaccine; ih as in tin; o as in solar; oi as in void; oo as in food; u as in put; uh as in but; ch as in chutzpa; zh as in Zhivago.

3. The Paschal Lamb, eaten on Passover in ancient times.

pe-ke-she
>A festive robe worn by Chasidim.

pekl
>Also spelled *pekel.*
>Bundle, parcel, package.

peot see *peies*

pe-rek*
>Also *per-uhk.*
>1. Chapter, section.
>2. Abbreviated reference to *Pirkei Avot* (Ethics of the Fathers), a tractate of the Talmud.

periah see *pria*

peruhk see *perek*

Pesach
>Also spelled *Pesah.* See *Peisuhch.*

pesachdik see *peisachdihg*

peshat see *p'shat*

pesichaw see *p'sichuh*

pesil t'cheiles see *p'tihl t'cheilet*

Pesukei D'zihmruh see *P'sukei D'zihmruh*

peticha see *p'sichuh*

pe-ti-ruh
>Also *pe-ti-ra.**
>1. Literally, "freed of, rid of."
>2. Death, demise.

petshai see *p'tsha*

Pharisee
>A member of the association of scholars and laity in the first century B.C.E. and the first century C.E. that observed the Written Law, interpreted Scriptures liberally, and adhered to the Oral Law.

pihd-yon ha-ben
>Also spelled *pidyon haben.*
>Literally, "redemption of the son," a biblical cere-

---

mony of redemption of the mother's firstborn son
so he will not be required to devote his life to Temple
service.

pihd-yon she-vu-yihm
Also spelled *pidyon shevuyim.*
The ransom of captives, hostages.

pihl-puhl
Also spelled *pilpul.*
1. Casuistry, dialectics.
2. A method of Talmudic debate.

pihpihk see *pupihk*

pihr-o-gen
Also *pihr-uh-gen.*
Also spelled *pirogen.*
Turnovers with meat or dairy fillings.

pihr-uhsh-ki
Also spelled *piroshki.*
Turnovers filled with meat, cheese, mashed po-
tatoes, etc.

pih-she pei-she
Also spelled *pisha payshe.*
A card game.

pihshkeh see *pushke*

pihshn
Also spelled *pish-en.*
To urinate.

pihshr
Also spelled *pisher.*
1. A person who urinates.
2. A nobody.
3. A little squirt.

pihsk
Also spelled *pisk.*
1. Mouth.
2. Snout.
3. A big mouth.

pihsk me-luh-che
Also spelled *pisk maloche.*

a as in father; aw as in law; ai as in aisle: ei as in neighbor; e as in bet; i as in vaccine; ih as in tin; o as in solar; oi as in void; oo as in food; u as in put; uh as in but; ch as in chutzpa; zh as in Zhivago.

1. Literally, "mouth worker."
2. A big talker who achieves little.

pihtom see *pihtuhm*

pihts-e-le
Also spelled *pitseιe.*
A pet form of *pihtsl.* See *pihtsl.*

pihtsl
Also spelled *pitsel.*
Small, tiny.

pih-tuhm
Also *pih-tom.**
Also spelled *pitom.*
The button-like protuberance on the *etrog* (citron) used on Sukkot.

pihz-mon
Also spelled *pizmon.*
A hymn.

pihz-mon-ihm
Also spelled *pizmonim.*
Hymns. Plural of *pihzmon.* Refers particularly to hymns sung on Saturday nights by Sephardim.

pi-ku-ach ne-fesh
1. Literally, "the saving of a soul."
2. The saving of an endangered life.

pilpul see *pihlpuhl*

pipik see *pupihk*

pirogen see *pihrogen*

piroshki see *pihrushki*

pisha paysha see *pihshe peishe*

pisher see *pihshr*

pishkeh see *pushke*

pisk see *pihsk*

pitom see *pihtuhm*

pitsel see *pihtsl*

pitsele see *pihtsele*

pi-yut
> Also spelled *piyyut.*
> 1. A liturgical Hebrew poem.
> 2. A poem.

pi-yut-ihm
> The plural of *piyut.* See above.

pizmon see *pihzmon*

plagn
> Also spelled *plagen.*
> Torment, harass, afflict.

plagn zihch
> Also spelled *plagen zich.*
> To torment oneself.

plapln
> Also spelled *plaplen.*
> To chatter, babble.

plat-ke
> To gossip.

plat-ke machr
> Also spelled *plotke macher.*
> A gossiper.

platz
> Also spelled *plotz.*
> 1. To burst open.
> 2. A place.

platzn
> Also spelled *platzen.*
> 1. To burst.
> 2. To split.

pla-va
> A Passover sponge cake in which ground almonds
> replaces flour.

pletzl
> Also spelled *pletzel.*
> A flat onion roll. *Pletzlach* is the plural form.

ploshr
> Also spelled *plosher.*

---

a as in father; aw as in law; ai as in aisle; ei as in neighbor; e as in bet; i as in vaccine; ih as in tin; o as in
solar; oi as in void; oo as in food; u as in put; uh as in but; ch as in chutzpa; zh as in Zhivago.

1. To chat.
2. To gossip.

plotz see *platz*

plotke-macher see *platke-macher*

poi-er
Also spelled *poyer*.
Peasant, farmer.

poik
A drum.

polke see *puhlke*

Poo-rihm
Also spelled *Purim*.
A holiday celebrated on Adar 14, marking the deliverance of the Jews of ancient Persia from Haman's plot to exterminate them, as recorded in the biblical Book (Scroll) of Esther.

Poo-rihm Shpiel
Also spelled *Purim Shpiel*.
A Purim masquerade play.

pootz see *puhtz*

por see *puhr*

porech see *puhrech*

poretz see *puhrihtz*

po-seik
Also *po-sek*.*
1. Literally, "one who decides."
2. A scholar who makes decisions on matters of Jewish law.

potchke see *patshke*

potsh see *patsh*

poyer see *poier*

prepln
Also spelled *preplen*.
To mutter, mumble.

pri-a*
Also *pri-aw*.

Also spelled *peria, periah.*
The uncovering of the glans penis at the time of circumcision.

prih-tse
Also spelled *pritzteh.*
1. Literally, "an aristocratic woman and a landowner's wife."
2. A proud woman, a prima donna. Feminine form of *puhrihtz.*

pritzteh see *prihtse*

prokes see *holishkes*

pruhst
Also spelled *prost.*
1. Common.
2. Vulgar.
3. Boorish.

pruhst-er
Also spelled *proster.*
1. A boor.
2. A vulgar person.

pruhst-ih-kait
Also spelled *prostikeit.*
Vulgarity.

p'shat
Also spelled *peshat.*
The plain meaning of the Torah text.

p'si-chuh
Also *pe-si-chaw, pe-ti-cha.**
1. Literally, "opening."
2. The honor given to a person who is designated to open the Holy Ark in the synagogue.

P'su- kei D'zihm-ruh
Also *P'su-kei D'zihm-ra.**
1. Literally, "verses of praise."
2. Psalms and other biblical passages of praise to God which form part of the introductory prayers of the morning service.

---

a as in father; aw as in law; ai as in aisle: ei as in neighbor; e as in bet; i as in vaccine; ih as in tin; o as in solar; oi as in void; oo as in food; u as in put; uh as in but; ch as in chutzpa; zh as in Zhivago.

p'tihl te-chei-let*
Also *pe-sihl t'chei-les.*
Also spelled *pesil t'cheiles.*
The blue thread of the *tsitsit* (no longer used except
by Bratzlaver *Chasidim).*

p'tsha
Also *pe-tshai.*
Also spelled *petsha, p'tcha.*
Jellied calf's or beef's feet, sometimes called *sulze.*

pu
An exclamation of disdain.

puhl-ke
Also *pul-ke.*
Also spelled *polke.*
The drumstick of a fowl.

puhl-kes
Also *pul-kes.*
Chicken legs.

puhr
Also spelled *por.*
A pair, couple.

puh-rech
Also spelled *porech.*
Dust.

puh-rihtz
Also spelled *poretz.*
1. An aristocrat.
2. A landowner.

puhtz
Also spelled *pootz, putz.*
1. To decorate.
2. A fool, a stupid person.
3. Penis (slang).

pul-ke see *puhlke.*

pul-ta-bul-tshas
Cinnamon buns.

punkt far-kert
1. The exact opposite.

---

a as in father: aw as in law; ai as in aisle; ei as in neighbor; e as in bet; i as in vaccine; ih as in tin; o as in
solar; oi as in void; oo as in food; u as in put; uh as in but; ch as in chutzpa: zh as in Zhivago.

    2. The reverse is true.

pu-pihk
>Also *pih-pihk.*
>Also spelled *pupik, pipik.*
>Navel, bellybutton.

Purim see *Poorhim*

push-ke
>Also *pihsh-ke.*
>Also spelled *pishke, pishkeh.*
>A charity box.

pust un pas
>Idle.

pust un pas-nihk
>A loafer, an idler.

putz see *puhtz*

R

rabbi
1. Literally, "my master."
2. My teacher.
3. An ordained Jewish clergyman.

ra-bo-sai n'vaw-reich
Also *ra-bo-tai ne-va-rech*.*
1. Literally, "Gentlemen, let us bless."
2. The call to say Grace After Meals when a quorum of three or more is present.

rach-muhn-es
Also *rach-ma-nut*.*
Also spelled *rachmones*.
1. Compassion.
2. Pity.
3. Mercy.

raich
Also spelled *reich*.
Rich, wealthy.

rain see *rein*

rainiken see *reinihken*

raisn
Also spelled *raisen, reissen*.
To rip, tear.

raisn di fleish
Also spelled *reissen di flaish*.
1. Literally, "to tear off the flesh."
2. Take someone apart.

raisn di hoit
Also spelled *reissen di hoit*.
1. Literally, "to tear off the skin."
2. Skin someone alive.

---

a as in father: aw as in law; ai as in aisle; ei as in neighbor: e as in bet: i as in vaccine: ih as in tin: o as in solar: oi as in void; oo as in food; u as in put; uh as in but; ch as in chutzpa: zh as in Zhivago.

rai-ze
   A trip, journey.

rasha see *rawshuh*

rav see *ruhv*

raw-le
   Also spelled *role*.
   1. A part in a play.
   2. A role.

raw-shuh
   Also *raw-shaw, ra-sha**.
   Also spelled *ruhshe*.
   1. A mean, evil, malicious person.
   2. A villain.

raw-zhihn-ke
   Also spelled *rozhinke*.
   Raisin.

raw-zhihn-kes miht mandln
   Also spelled *rozhinkes mit mandln, rozhinkes mit mandlen*.
   1. Literally, "raisins with almonds."
   2. The name of a folk lullaby adapted by Abraham Goldfaden in his operetta *Shulamis* (1880).

rayach see *reiach*

reb
   1. The equivalent of *rav,* meaning "mister."
   2. A short form of *rebi (rebbe).* See below. See also *ruhv.*

re-betzn
   Also *re-be-tsihn.*
   Also spelled *rebetsen, rebetsin, rebbetzen.*
   Rabbi's wife.

re-bi
   Also spelled *rebbe, rebbi.*
   1. Teacher.
   2. Title of a Chassidic leader.

re-chi-les
   Also *re-chi-lus, re-chi-lut**.

1. Gossip.
2. Slander.

redn
> Also spelled *reden.*
> To say, talk, speak, tell.

redn ihn der velt a-rain
> 1. Literally, "to talk into the world."
> 2. To speak nonsense.

redn re-chi-les
> Also spelled *reden rechiluhs.*
> 1. Literally, "to speak gossip."
> 2. To spread gossip.

redn tzoo der vant
> Also spelled *reden tzu der vant.*
> 1. Literally, "to talk to the wall."
> 2. To talk in vain.

redn uhn a maws
> Also spelled *reden un a moss.*
> 1. Literally, "to speak without a measure."
> 2. To be loquacious.
> 3. To chatter endlessly.

redn zihch ain *(a-rain)* a kreink
> Also spelled *reden zich ein a krenk.*
> 1. Literally, "to talk oneself into an illness."
> 2. Sickness by autosuggestion.
> 3. Hypochondria.

redn zihch ois daws hartz
> Also spelled *redn zich ois dos hartz.*
> 1. Literally, "talk one's heart out."
> 2. Get it off one's chest.

re-fu-e shlei-muh
> Also *re-fu-aw shlei-maw, re-fu-a shlei-ma.**
> Also spelled *refuah shlema.*
> 1. Literally, "a complete healing."
> 2. A wish for a full recovery.

refusenik see *refyuznihk*

re-fyuz-nihk
> Also spelled *refusenik.*

---

a as in father; aw as in law; ai as in aisle; ei as in neighbor; e as in bet; i as in vaccine; ih as in tin; o as in solar; oi as in void; oo as in food; u as in put; uh as in but; ch as in chutzpa; zh as in Zhivago.

In the late twentieth century, a Soviet Jew seeking to emigrate who meets with official refusal, harassment, and persecution.

regn
Also spelled *regen.*
Rain.

rei-ach
Also spelled *rayach.*
1. Odor, smell.
2. Flavor.

reich see *raich*

rein
Also spelled *rain.*
Clean, pure.

rei-nih-ken
Also spelled *rainiken.*
To clean up, purify, sanitize.

reisen di hoit see *raisn di hoit*

reish
Also spelled *resh.*
The twentieth letter of the Hebrew alphabet, corresponding in sound to the letter "r."

reissen see *raisn*

reitach see *rettach*

re-mez
1. A hint, a sign.
2. Hidden meaning in the text of the Torah.

resh see *reish*

re-shus
Also *re-shut.**
Permission.

Responsa
Answers by learned rabbis to questions submitted them on Jewish law. In Hebrew, *sh'ei-lot u-t'shu-vot.**

(es) ret zich a-zoi
1. Literally, "It speaks so."

---

a as in father; aw as in law; ai as in aisle; ei as in neighbor; e as in bet; i as in vaccine; ih as in tin; o as in solar; oi as in void; oo as in food; u as in put; uh as in but; ch as in chutzpa; zh as in Zhivago.

    2. This is what's said, but I don't believe it.
    3. It seems so.

rettach see *reitach*

Ri-bo-no Shel O-lawm
    Also *Ri-bo-no Shel O-lam**.
    1. Literally, "Master of the universe."
    2. God.

rihch-tihk
    Also *rihch-tihg*.
    Also spelled *richtig, richtik*.
    Correct, O.K., right.

rihch-tih-ker chei-fetz
    Also *richtiker chaifetz*.
    1. The right article.
    2. The real thing.

rihr-ev-dihk
    Also spelled *rirevdik*.
    Vivacious, lively, agile.

rihsl bawrsht see *ruhsl*

ri-mon
    Also spelled *rimmon*.
    1. Literally, "a pomegranate."
    2. A Torah crown that fits on one finial.

ri-mo-nihm
    Also spelled *rimmonim*.
    Plural of *rimon*. See above.

rirevdik see *rihrevdihk*

Roish Choidesh see *Rosh Chodesh*

roit
    Also spelled *royt*.
    Red.

role see *rawle*

roo see *ru*

Rosh Cho-desh*
    Also *Roish Choi-desh*.
    1. Literally, "the head of the month," the first day
    of each Hebrew month.

---

a as in father; aw as in law; ai as in aisle; ei as in neighbor; e as in bet; i as in vaccine; ih as in tin; o as in
solar; oi as in void; oo as in food; u as in put; uh as in but; ch as in chutzpa; zh as in Zhivago.

2. A semi-holiday marking the beginning of the Hebrew month.

Rosh Ha-shaw-naw
Also *Rosh Ha-sha-na**
Also spelled *Rosh Hashanah, Rosh Hashona.*
1. Literally, "the head (beginning) of the year."
2. The Jewish New Year, at the beginning of the month of Tishri (September-October), observed for two days by Orthodox and Conservative Jews, for one day by Reform Jews.

rov see *ruhv*

royt see *roit*

rozhinkes see *rawzhinkes*

ru
Also spelled *roo.*
1. Rest.
2. Calm.
3. Quiet.

ru-ach
Also spelled *ruah.*
1. Spirit.
2. Wind, breath.
3. Demon, evil spirit, ghost.

Ru-ach Ha-ko-desh
1. Literally, "The Holy Spirit."
2. God.

(a) ru-ach ihn dain ta-te's ta-ten a-rain
Also spelled *a ruach in dein tate's taten arein.*
1. Literally, "A demon (evil spirit) should enter your father's father!" (to which "Amen" is sometimes appended).
2. Go to the devil!

rufn *see also* Preface.
Also spelled *rufen.*
1. To call
2. To appeal.

---

ruhg-e-lach
Also spelled *rugelach, rugelah.*
A rolled-dough pastry filled with nuts and raisins.

ruhshe see *rawshuh*

ruhsl
Also spelled *ruhsel, russel.*
Fermented beet juice, also called beet sour, used to prepare borsht.

ruhsl fleish
Also spelled *russel flaish.*
Meat prepared with *ruhsl.* See *ruhsl.*

ruhv
Also *rav.**
Also spelled *rov* and *rawv.*
1. Rabbi.
2. Teacher.
3. The ordained leader of a Jewish congregation.

russel see *ruhsl*

S

Sabbateans
> Followers of seventeenth-century pseudo-messiah Sabbatai (Shabbetai Tzevi).

Sabbath see *Shabuhs*

sabra see *sabruh*

sab-ruh
> Also *sab-ra.**
> 1. Literally, "a cactus."
> 2. A native Israeli, reputed to be like a cactus, tough on the outside, sweet on the inside.

(a) sach
> A lot, many, much.

(a) sach tzoo redn
> Also spelled *(a) sach tzu reden.*
> Much to talk about.

(a) sach tzoo redn, vei-nihk tzoo her-en
> 1. Literally, "much to say, little to be heard."
> 2. Talk devoid of substance.

saftig see *zaftihg*

saichel see *seichl*

sa-ka-nat ne-fa-shot*
> Also *sa-kaw-nas ne-faw-shos.*
> Danger to life.

sa-kaw-ne
> Also *sa-kaw-naw, sa-ka-na.**
> Danger.

sa-lat
> 1. Lettuce.
> 2. Salad.

Samaritans see *Shomronihm*

sameiach b'chelko see *sawmeiach b'chelko*

---

sa-muhch
Also *sa-mech.**
The fifteenth letter of the Hebrew alphabet, corresponding in sound to the letter "s."

Sanctification of the Name see *kihdoosh ha-Shem*

san-dek*
Also *san-duhk.*
Also spelled *sandik, sondek.*
The godfather of a boy at the time of the infant's circumcision.

San-hed-rihn
Also spelled *Sanhedrin.*
1. The Jewish Supreme Court and legislative body in Palestine before 70 C.E.
2. A tractate of the Talmud.

Satan see *Sawtawn*

sawchawr veonesh see *s'char v'onesh*

saw-mei-ach b'chel-ko
Also *sa-mei-ach b'chel-ko.**
1. Literally, "happy with his portion."
2. A contented person.

Saw-tawn
Also *Sa-tan.**
1. The devil, Satan.
2. Adversary.
3. Evil inclination.

s'chach
Branches used to cover the roof of a *suka.*

schalet see *tschawlent*

s'char v'o-nesh*
Also *saw-chawr v'o-nesh.*
Reward and punishment.

scharf see *sharf*

schav see *shav*

schlemiel see *shlemiel*

schmaltz see *shmaltz*

schnaps see *shnaps*

---

a as in father: aw as in law; ai as in aisle: ei as in neighbor; e as in bet; i as in vaccine; ih as in tin: o as in solar; oi as in void; oo as in food; u as in put; uh as in but; ch as in chutzpa; zh as in Zhivago.

schnorrer see *shnawrer*

schochet see *shochuht*

s'choi-ruh
> Also *se-cho-ra,* se-cho-raw.*
> 1. Merchandise.
> 2. Goods, wares.
> 3. Commodity.

S'dom see *Sedom*

sechel see *seichl*

Se-da-rihm*
> Also *Se-daw-rihm.*
> Also spelled *Sedarim.*
> Plural of *Seidr.* See below.

Seder see *Seidr*

Se-dom
> Also spelled *S'dom, Sodom.*
> A biblical city destroyed, along with neighboring Gomorra, because of its sinfulness (Genesis 18-19).

sed-ruh
> Also *sihd-ra,* sihd-raw.*
> Also spelled *sidra.*
> 1. Literally, "order, arrangement."
> 2. One of the fifty-four sections into which the Pentateuch is divided for weekly sequential readings in the synagogue.

Se-far-dic
> Also *Se-far-di.**
> Also spelled *Sephardic, Sephardi.*
> 1. Literally, "Spanish."
> 2. Liturgical rites of the Spanish, Portuguese, and Oriental Jews.

Se-far-dihm
> Also spelled *Sefardim, Sephardim.*
> Iberian and Middle Eastern Jews and their descendants, so named because of their original residence in regions influenced by the hegemony or culture of Spain.

Sefer Torah see *Seifr Toruh*

---

a as in father; aw as in law; ai as in aisle; ei as in neighbor; e as in bet; i as in vaccine; ih as in tin; o as in solar; oi as in void; oo as in food; u as in put; uh as in but; ch as in chutzpa; zh as in Zhivago.

sefira see *s'firuh*

Se-fi-ras Haw-o-mer
Also *Se-fi-rat Ha-o-mer.**
1. Literally, "the counting of the *Omer.*
See also *s'firuh.*

seichel see *seichl*

seichl
Also spelled *seichel, saichel, sechel.*
1. Brains, common sense.
2. Good judgment.
3. Intelligence.
4. Reason.
5. Shrewdness, wits.

Seidr
Also *Se-der.**
1. Literally, "order, arrangement."
2. Passover service and banquet during which the
Haggadah, which recounts the exodus of the
Hebrew slaves from Egyptian bondage, is read.

seifr
Also *se-fer.**
1. Book.
2. A religious book from which one studies.

Seifr To-ruh
Also *Sei-fer To-raw, Sei-fer To-ra, Se-fer To-ra.**
Also spelled *Sefer Torah.*
The text of the Pentateuch, handwritten on a parch-
ment scroll by a scribe and read in the synagogue.

se-la*
Also *se-law.*
Also spelled *selah.*
A word of uncertain meaning, possibly an ancient
musical notation, appended to many Psalms and
liturgical selections.

selicha see *selichuh*

Se-li-chot*
Also *S'li-chuhs, S'li-chos.*
Penitential prayers. Plural of *Selicha.*

---

a as in father; aw as in law; ai as in aisle; ei as in neighbor; e as in bet; i as in vaccine; ih as in tin; o as in solar; oi as in void; oo as in food; u as in put; uh as in but; ch as in chutzpa; zh as in Zhivago.

se-li-chuh
Also *se-li-cha.**
Also spelled *selihah.*
1. Forgiveness.
2. (Modern Hebrew) Pardon me!
3. A penitential prayer.
Selichot is the plural form.

Semanada Buena
The Sephardic (Ladino) Saturday night greeting expressed on the departure of the Sabbath.

semicha see *smichuh*

Sephardi see *Sefardic*

Sephardic see *Sefardic*

Sephardim see *Sefardihm*

se-u-da*
Also *se-u-daw, su-duh, su-de.*
A festive meal.

Se-u-da She-li-shiht*
Also *Se-u-daw Shelishihs.*
The third meal of the Sabbath.

Se-u-dat Mihtz-va*
Also *Se-u-das Mihtz-vaw.*
Also spelled *Seudat Mitzvah.*
A feast in honor of the performance of a commandment *(mitzva).*

Sfardi see *sefardic*

Sfi-ruh
Also *Se-fi-ra.**
1. Literally, "counting."
2. A short form of *Sefirat Haomer,** meaning "counting the *Omer,*" the period of forty-nine days between the second day of Passover and the Shavuot festival.

sha
Be quiet! Shut up!

shaa see *shuh*

Shabat see *Shabuhs*

Sha-bat Ha-ga-dol*
>Also *Sha-baws Ha-gaw-dol.*
>1. Literally, "the Great Sabbath."
>2. The Sabbath before Passover.

Shabat Kodesh see *Shabuhs Koidesh*

Sha-bat Na-cha-moo*
>Also *Sha-buhs Nach-moo.*
>Also spelled *Shabbat Nachamu.*
>1. Literally, "Sabbath of Comfort," the Sabbath immediately following Tisha B'Av, when the *haftara* reading is from Isaiah 40, beginning with the words, *Nachamu, nachamu ami,* meaning "Comfort ye, comfort ye, my people."

Sha-bat Sha-lom*
>Also *Sha-baws Shaw-lom.*
>1. Literally, "Sabbath peace."
>2. A Sabbath greeting, the Yiddish equivalent of which is *Gut Shabes.*

Shabaws Hagawdol see *Shabat Hagadol*

Shabbat see *Shabuhs*

Shabbos see *Shabuhs*

Sha-bes goi
>Also *Sha-buhs goi.*
>Also spelled *Shabbos goy.*
>A non-Jew employed to perform minimum maintenance work (e.g., turning electricity on and off) prohibited to a traditional Jew on the Sabbath.

Sha-buhs
>Also *Sha-baws, Sha-bat.**
>Also spelled *Shabbos, Shabes, Shabbes.*
>1. Literally, "rest."
>2. The Sabbath day, a day of rest.

Sha-buhs Koi-desh
>Also *Sha-bat Ko-desh.**
>Holy Sabbath.

Sha-buhs tihsh
>Sabbath table.

---

sha-char
Dawn.

Sha-cha-riht*
Also *Sha-cha-rihs.*
Also spelled *Shaharit, Shachris.*
1. Dawn.
2. The morning prayer service.

Sha-dai*
Also spelled *Shaddai.*
Almighty God.

shadchn
Also *shad-chan,* shad-chawn, shad-chuhn.*
Also spelled *shadchen, shatchen.*
1. Matchmaker.
2. Marriage broker.

shaharit see *shachariht*

shaigetz see *sheiguhtz*

sh'ailos u'tshuvos see *she'eilos uteshuvos*

shain see *shein*

shaine kind see *sheine kihnd*

(a) shainem dank eich see *(a) sheinem dank aich*

(a) shainer gelechter see *(a) sheiner gelechter*

(a) shainer Yid see *(a) sheiner Yihd*

shainkeit see *sheinkait*

shaitel see *sheitl*

Shakuhl see *Shehakol*

Shalach Manot see *Shalachmuhnes*

shalet see *cholent*

sha-li-ach*
Also *shaw-li-ach.*
1. Emissary, messenger.
2. A representative dispatched by the State of Israel to Diaspora communities for public relations, fundraising, and educational purposes.

shaliach tsibur see *shliach tsibur*

---

a as in father; aw as in law; ai as in aisle; ei as in neighbor; e as in bet; i as in vaccine; ih as in tin; o as in solar; oi as in void; oo as in food; u as in put; uh as in but; ch as in chutzpa; zh as in Zhivago.

Shal-lach-muh-nes
Also *Shlach-maw-nes, Sha-lach Ma-not.**
Literally, "the sending of gifts," a tradition connected with the Purim holiday. The original form of the term as found in the Book of Esther is *mishloach manot.*

sha-lom*
Also *shaw-lom, shuh-lem.*
1. Literally, "peace."
2. Hello.
3. Goodbye.
4. Greetings!

shalom aleichem see *shawlom aleichem*

shalom bayit see *shuhlem bayihs*

shalosh regalihm see *shawlosh regawlihm*

sha-muhs
Also *sha-mes, sha-mash.**
Also spelled *shammes, shammos, shamus, shammus.*
1. Synagogue sexton or beadle.
2. The extra candle used to kindle the other tapers in the Chanukah *menorah.*

shana tova see *shuhnuh tovuh*

shan-de
Also *shan-der.*
A shame, a shameful situation, a disgrace.

(a) shan-de far di kihn-der
Also spelled *(a) shande far di kinder.*
1. Literally, "a disgrace for the children."
2. A terrible act.

(a) shan-de oon a char-pe
A shame and a disgrace.

shander see *shande*

shand-hoiz
1. Literally, "house of shame."
2. Brothel.

---

a as in father; **aw** as in law; **ai** as in aisle; **ei** as in neighbor; **e** as in bet; **i** as in vaccine; **ih** as in tin; **o** as in solar; **oi** as in void; **oo** as in food; **u** as in put; **uh** as in but; **ch** as in chutzpa; **zh** as in Zhivago.

sharf
>Also spelled *scharf.*
>1. Highly seasoned.
>2. Sharp.

shas
>Also spelled *shass.*
>An acronym from the two Hebrew words, *shisha sedarim,* "the six sections" of the Talmud.

shatchen see *shadchn*

shatn
>Also spelled *shaten.*
>1. Damage.
>2. Hurt.
>3. Harm

shat-nez
>Also spelled *shatnes.*
>The biblical prohibition against mixing certain materials (Deuteronomy 22:11). A fabric that is an animal product (silk or wool, for example) may not be mixed with a fabric that is a vegetable product (cotton, for example).

shav
>Also spelled *schav, s'shav.*
>1. Cold spinach soup.
>2. Sorrel (sour grass) soup.

sha-voo-a tov*
>Also *shaw-voo-a tov.*
>Also spelled *shavua tov.*
>1. Literally, "good week."
>2. A greeting used on Saturday night, after the Sabbath has ended.

shavua see *shawvoo-a*

Sha-vu-ot*
>Also *Shvoo-es, Shaw-voo-os.*
>Also spelled *Shevuos, Shvues, Shawvuos, Shavuoth.*
>1. Literally, "weeks." Plural of *sha-voo-a.*
>2. Pentecost, the Festival of Weeks, marking the receiving of the Torah by Moses on Mount Sinai.

---

shawliach see *shaliach*

shawliach tzibur see *shliach tsibur*

shawlom see *shalom*

shaw-lom a-lei-chem
Also *sha-lom a-lei-chem,* shuh-luhm a-lei-chem.*
Also spelled *shalom alaichem.*
1. Literally, "Peace be upon you!"
2. A salutation.
3. A pseudonym of the Yiddish writer Sholom Rabinowitz (1859-1916).

shawlom bayihs see *shuhlem bayihs*

shaw-losh re-gaw-lihm
Also *sha-losh re-ga-lihm.**
Also spelled *sholosh regolim.*
1. Literally, "three pilgrimage festivals."
2. Passover, Shavuot, and Sukkot. In Temple times these were festivals on which Jews visited the Temple in Jerusalem.

shawnaw tovaw see *shuhnuh tovuh*

shaw-voo-a
Also *sha-voo-a.**
Also spelled *shavua.*
Week.

Shawvuos see *Shavuot*

shaygetz see *sheiguhtz*

shayn see *shein*

shayner Yid see *sheiner Yihd*

shaytl see *sheitl*

Sh'chinah see *Shechinuh*

sh'chi-tuh
Also *she-chi-ta,* she-chi-taw.*
Also spelled *sh'chite.*
The slaughter of cattle and fowl according to Jewish law.

She-chi-nuh
Also *She-chi-naw, She-chi-na.**

---

a as in father; aw as in law; ai as in aisle; ei as in neighbor; e as in bet; i as in vaccine; ih as in tin; o as in solar; oi as in void; oo as in food; u as in put; uh as in but; ch as in chutzpa; zh as in Zhivago.

Also spelled *Sh'chinah, Shekhinah, Shechina, Shechinah.*
1. Literally, "indwelling."
2. The Divine Presence (God).
3. God's immanence.

shechita see *sh'chituh*

she'eila see *sheile*

she-ei-los u-te-shu-vos
Also *sh'ei-lot u'tshu-vot.**
Also spelled *sh'ailos u'tshuvos.*
1. Literally, "questions and answers."
2. Responsa, queries and responses on matters of Jewish law.

sheeny
A disparaging name for "Jew."

shefichat dam see *shfichas duhm*

She-ha-kol*
Also *Sha-kuhl.*
1. Literally, "for all."
2. The name of the blessing said over liquids, meats, and several other types of food.

She-he-che-yaw-nu
Also *She-he-che-ya-nu.**
1. Literally, "Who has kept us in life."
2. A prayer of gratitude and celebration, recited on the eve of a holiday and on other special occasions.

shei-guhtz
Also *shei-gihtz, she-ketz.**
Also spelled *shaigetz, shaggetz.*
1. A non-Jewish male.
2. Sometimes, a Jew ignorant of Judaism.
3. An unruly lad.
Shihkse is the feminine form.

sheim
Also *shem.**
Also spelled *shaym.*

---

a as in father; aw as in law; ai as in aisle; ei as in neighbor; e as in bet; i as in vaccine; ih as in tin; o as in solar; oi as in void; oo as in food; u as in put; uh as in but; ch as in chutzpa; zh as in Zhivago.

1. Literally, "name."
2. Shem, Noah's eldest son.

sheim tov
Also *shem tov.**
A good name.

shein
Also spelled *shain, shayn.*
Pretty, beautiful.

shein-e kihnd
Also spelled *shaine kind.*
Beautiful child.

(a) shein-em dank aich
Also spelled *(a) shainem dank eich.*
1. Literally, "a pretty thank you."
2. Thank you kindly.

(a) shein-em dank dihr ihn pupihk
Also spelled *(a) shainem dank dir in pupik.*
1. Literally, "a pretty thank-you in your bellybutton"
2. Thanks for nothing.

shein-e meidl
Also spelled *shaine maidel.*
Pretty girl.

(a) shein-e, rein-e ka-paw-re
Also spelled *(a) shaine, raine kapore.*
1. Literally, "a beautiful, pure sacrificial fowl."
2. Serves him (her) right!
3. To hell with it! It's doomed!

shei-ner-e leigt men ihn der erd (drerd)
1. Literally, "Prettier (more beautiful) ones than you are placed in the earth."
2. You are very ugly.

(a) shein-er ge-lech-ter
Also spelled *(a) shainer gelechter.*
1. Literally, "a pretty bit of laughter."
2. Some joke!
3. This is serious business.

(a) shein-er Yihd
Also spelled *shayner Yid, (a) shainer Yid.*
1. Literally, "a beautiful Jew."
2. A person of good character.

shein-kait
Also spelled *shainkeit.*
Beauty.

shein vi di le-vuh-ne
1. Literally, "as beautiful as the moon."
2. The title of a Yiddish song, the music of which
was popularized as the "Miami Beach Rumba."

shein vi di zih-ben velt-en
Also spelled *shain vi di zibben velten.*
1. As pretty as seven worlds.
2. Very beautiful.

sheitl
Also *shaitl.*
Also spelled *shaytl, sheitel, shaitel.*
Wig worn by married Orthodox Jewish women.

shekel see *shekl*

sheketz see *sheiguhtz*

Shekhinah see *Shechinuh*

shekl
Also *she-kel.**
1. An ancient unit of weight.
2. An ancient coin.
3. A unit of currency in modern Israel.

she-li-chihm
Also spelled *shlichim.*
Plural of *shaliach.*

shem see *sheim*

she-ma
Also spelled *sh'ma.*
1. Literally, "hear."
2. Short form of *Shema Yihsrael.* See below.

She-ma Yihs-ra-el*
Also *She-ma Yihs-raw-eil.*

---

a as in father; aw as in law; ai as in aisle: ei as in neighbor; e as in bet; i as in vaccine; ih as in tin; o as in solar; oi as in void; oo as in food; u as in put; uh as in but; ch as in chutzpa; zh as in Zhivago.

Also spelled *Shema Yisrael, Shema Yisroel, Sh'ma
Yisrael.*
1. Literally, "Hear, O Israel."
2. The basic declaration of Jewish faith, from Deuteronomy 6:4.

Shem Ha-me-fo-rash*
Also *Sheim Ha-me-fo-rawsh.*
1. Literally, "the explicit Name."
2. The name of God, pronounced only by the High
Priest in the Temple.

She-mi-ni A-tse-ret*
Also *She-mi-ni A-tse-res.*
Also spelled *Shmini Atzeres.*
1. Literally, "the eighth day of convocation."
2. The conclusion of the Sukkot festival, based on
Leviticus 23:36.

shemiras Shabbos see *shmiras Shabuhs*

shemita see *shmitaw*

shemn zihch
Also spelled *shemen zich.*
To be ashamed of oneself.

shemn zihch ihn dain vaitn haltz a-rain
1. Literally, "You should be ashamed down to the
bottom of your throat!"
2. Shame on you!

Shemoneh Esreh see *Shmone Esrei*

shem tov see *sheim tov*

shenadar see *shnuhdr*

She-ol
1. Literally, "to dig."
2. The biblical dwelling place of the dead in the
depths of the earth (Deuteronomy 32:22; Psalms
55:15, 86:13).
3. Hades.

shep a bihsl na-ches
Also spelled *shep a bissel nachas.*
1. To be proud.
2. Derive a bit of satisfaction.

---

a as in father; aw as in law; al as in aisle; ei as in neighbor; e as in bet; i as in vaccine; ih as in tin; o as in
solar; oi as in void; oo as in food; u as in put; uh as in but; ch as in chutzpa; zh as in Zhivago.

3. Enjoy, derive pleasure (especially from off-spring).

shepping naches
Deriving pleasure.

shepp naches
To derive joy.

shetar see *shtar*

shetar gerut see *shtar geirus*

Sheva Berachot see *Shevuh Brawches*

shevarim see *shevawrihm*

Shevat see *Shvat*

shevawrihm
Also *she-va-rihm.**
1. Literally, "broken."
2. *Shofar* blasts consisting of three staccato sounds.

She-vuh Brawch-es
Also *She-va Be-ra-chot.**
1. Literally, "seven blessings."
2. Prayers recited during the marriage ceremony.

Shevuos see *Shavuot*

shfi-chas duhm
Also *she-fi-chat dam.**
Bloodshed, including human contributory negligence leading to the death of innocents.

shihch
Shoes. Plural of *shuch.*

shih-duhch
Also *shi-dooch.**
Also spelled *shiduch.*
1. A match.
2. Engagement, betrothal.
3. An arranged marriage.

shihf
Also spelled *shif.*
A vessel, ship.

(a) shihf un a ruder
>   1. Literally, "a ship without a rudder."
>   2. Poor management.

shihk yihn-gel
>   Also spelled *shik yingel.*
>   Messenger boy, errand boy.

shihkn
>   Also spelled *shiken.*
>   To send.

shihkr
>   Also *shi-kor.**
>   Also spelled *shikur, shikker.*
>   1. Intoxicated.
>   2. Drunk.

shihk-tse
>   Also spelled *shikze, shiktsa, shiksa, shikza, shikse.*
>   A non-Jewish woman. The feminine form of
>   *sheigetz.*

shihn
>   Also spelled *shin.*
>   A letter of the Hebrew alphabet sounded like "sh."

Shihr Ha-ma-a-los
>   Also *Shihr Ha-ma-a-lot.**
>   Also spelled *Shir Hamaalos.*
>   1. Literally, "Song of Ascents," from the Book of
>   Psalms.
>   2. The prayer preceding the recital of Grace After
>   Meals.

Shihr Ha-shi-rihm
>   Also spelled *Shir Hashirim.*
>   The Song of Songs, one of the books of the Bible.

shihsr
>   Also spelled *shiser.*
>   Shooter, marksman.

shih-vuh
>   Also *shih-va,** *shihv-aw.*
>   Also spelled *shiva.*
>   1. Literally, "seven."

---

a as in father; aw as in law; ai as in aisle; ei as in neighbor; e as in bet; i as in vaccine; ih as in tin; o as in solar; oi as in void; oo as in food; u as in put; uh as in but; ch as in chutzpa; zh as in Zhivago.

2. The seven-day period of mourning for an immediate relative, beginning upon the return from interment.

shik yingel see *shihk yihngel*

shiken see *shihkn*

shikker see *shihkr*

shiksa see *shihktse*

Shim-shon ha-gi-bor
1. Literally, "Samson the strongman."
2. A designation for a very powerful person, derived from the biblical Samson, noted for his great strength.

shin see *shihn*

Shir Hamaalos see *Shihr Hamaalos*

Shir Ha-shi-rim see *Shihr Hashirihm*

shiser see *shihsr*

shiva see *shihvuh*

shkap-e
1. A mare.
2. A nag.
3. Worthless.

shlachmawnes see *shalachmuhnes*

shlafen see *shlawfn*

shlak
Also spelled *shlock*.
1. A stroke.
2. Shoddy merchandise.
3. Cheap, inferior, tacky, trashy.
4. A sloppy, ineffectual person.

shlang
1. Snake, serpent.
2. (Slang) penis.

shla-ten sha-mes
1. Community busybody.
2. Gossipmonger.

shlawfn
Also spelled *shlafen, shlofen.*
To sleep.

shlawgn
Also spelled *shlawgen, shlogen.*
To beat, hit, slug.

shlawgn kawp ihn vant
Also spelled *shlogen kop in vant.*
1. Literally, "hitting one's head against a wall."
2. Trying to do the impossible.
3. Wasting time.

shlawg zihch kawp ihn vant
Also spelled *shlog zich kop in vant.*
1. Literally, "beat one's head against the wall."
2. Attempt the impossible, but don't bother me!

shlawg zihch miht Gawt aroom
1. Literally, "Go fight with God!"
2. Fight a losing battle.

shlawsr
Also spelled *shlosser.*
Locksmith.

shlecht
Also spelled *shlehcht.*
Bad, wicked, mean, evil.

shlemazl see *shlihmazl*

shlemiel see *shlemil*

shle-mil
Also spelled *shlemiel.*
1. A clumsy, ineffectual, bungling person, often victimized.
2. A *klawtz.*
3. Synonymous with *shlimazl.*

(a) shlep
1. Literally, "drag."
2. A vacillator.
3. An ineffectual person.

shlepen see *shlepn*

a as in father; aw as in law; ai as in aisle; ei as in neighbor; e as in bet; i as in vaccine; ih as in tin; o as in solar; oi as in void; oo as in food; u as in put; uh as in but; ch as in chutzpa; zh as in Zhivago.

(a) shlep-er
  1. Literally, "one who drags."
  2. A vacillator, an uncertain person.
  3. One who expects something for nothing.

shlepn
  Also spelled *shlepen.*
  To drag, pull, tug, haul.

shli-ach tsi-bur*
  Also *shaw-li-ach tsi-bur, sha-li-ach tsi-bur.*
  1. Literally, "community emissary" or "messenger of the populace."
  2. Leader of a prayer service.
  3. A cantor.

shlichim see *shelichihm*

shlih-mazl
  Also spelled *shlimazl, shlimazel, shlemazl.*
  1. A luckless person.
  2. A misfit.
  Shlemil is a variant form.

shlihsh-kas
  Also spelled *shlishkas.*
  Potato noodles.

shlihsl
  Also spelled *shlisel.*
  A key.

shlimazel see *shlihmazl*

shlisel see *shlihsl*

shlock see *shlak*

shlofen see *shlawfn*

shlog see *shlawg*

shlogen see *shlawgn*

shlogen kop in vant see *shlawgn kawp ihn vant*

shloomp
  Also spelled *shlump.*
  1. A scatterbrain.
  2. Someone uncoordinated.

3. A dowdy, unkempt person.
4. A slob.

shlosh es-rei mi-dos
Also *sha-losh es-rei mi-dot.* *
Literally, "thirteen attributes (of God)."

shlo-shihm
Also spelled *shloshim, sheloshim.*
1. Literally "thirty."
2. The thirty-day mourning period for a close relative.

shlosser see *shlawsr*

shluhb see *zhluhb*

shluhmil see *shlemil*

shlump
1. An ineffectual person.
2. An unkempt person, a slob.

Sh'ma Yisroel see *Shema Yihsrael*

shmad
Apostasy from Judaism.

shmaichl see *shmeichl*

shmaisn
Also spelled *shmeisen.*
To hit, wallop, thrash.

shmaltz
1. Literally, "rendered fat," most often chicken fat.
2. Sweet-talk.
3. Superficiality.
4. Sentimentality.
5. Highly sentimental and banal music and literature.

shmant
Sweet cream.

shman-tzes
1. Trifles.
2. Nonsense.

shma-te
Also *shma-tuh.*

Also spelled *shmatteh.*
A rag.

shma-tes
1. Plural of *shmate.* See above.
2. Old clothes.

shmeer see *shmihr*

shme-ge-gi
1. A fool, jerk.
2. A buffoon.
3. An idiot.

shmeichl
Also *shmaichl.*
Also spelled *shmeichel.*
1. A smile.
2. To ingratiate oneself, fawn, dote.

shmei drei
Baloney, hot air.

shmeisen see *shmaisn*

shmek
1. Sniff.
2. Smell.

(a) shmek ta-bak
1. A pinch of tobacco.
2. Of little value, insignificant.

shmekn ta-bak
To take a sniff of tobacco.

shmen-drihk
Also spelled *shmendrik.*
1. An inept person, a nincompoop.
2. Hero of the satirical comedy *Shmendrik* (1877),
   by Abraham Goldfaden.

shmihr
Also spelled *shmir, shmeer.*
1. Smudge, smear.
2. A swath, an area.
3. A thing, a big thing, as in "the whole *shmihr.*"
4. Bribe.

---

a as in father; aw as in law; ai as in aisle· ei as in neighbor; e as in bet; i as in vaccine; ih as in tin; o as in solar; oi as in void; oo as in food; u as in put; uh as in but; ch as in chutzpa; zh as in Zhivago.

shmihrn
Also spelled *shmiren.*
To wipe. See also *shmihr.*

Shmini Atzeres see *Shemini Atseret*

shmi-ras Sha-buhs
Also *shmi-rat Sha-bat,* shmi-ras Sha-baws.*
Also spelled *shemiras Shabbos.*
Literally, "Sabbath observance."

shmirt zihch ois di shihch
1. Literally, "Wipe off your shoes!"
2. You're welcome in my home!

shmi-tuh
Also *shmi-ta,* shmi-taw.*
Also spelled *shemitah.*
1. Literally, "to abandon, forsake."
2. In the Bible, every seventh year is a Sabbatical
   year in which all debts are remitted and fields
   left fallow.

shmo
A foolish, stupid person.

shmok see *shmuhk*

Shmo-ne Es-rei*
Also *Shmo-naw Es-rei.*
Also spelled *Shemoneh Esreh.*
1. Literally, "eighteen."
2. The *Amida* prayer, which originally consisted of
   eighteen benedictions, recited at weekday services.

shmoosen see *shmusn*

shmooz
Also *shmus.*
To talk, converse idly, chat.

shmuhk
Also spelled *shmuk, shmuck, shmok.*
From the German meaning "ornament."
1. A contemptible person.
2. A foolish person.
3. (Slang) penis.

shmura matza see *matza shemura*

shmus see *shmooz*

shmusn
Also spelled *shmoosen.*
To chat, converse.

shmuts-ihk
Dirty, soiled.

shmutz
Dirt, filth.

shnaidr
Also spelled *shnaider, shneider.*
Tailor.

shnaps
Also spelled *shnapps, schnapps.*
Whiskey, liquor.

shnawr
Also spelled *shnor.*
Beg.

shnawr-en
Also spelled *shnorren.*
To beg, freeload.

shnawr-er
Also spelled *schnorrer, shnorrer.*
A beggar, mendicant.

shneider see *shnaidr*

shnei lu-chos ha-brihs
Also *shnei lu-chot ha-briht.**
1. Literally, "The two tablets of the Covenant."
2. The Decalogue, Ten Commandments.

shnekn
Also spelled *shneken.*
Fruit and nut coffee rolls.

shnel
1. Quick, fast.
2. Hurry up!

Shnihp-er-shawk
Also *Shnipishok.*

---

a as in father; aw as in law; ai as in aisle; ei as in neighbor; e as in bet; i as in vaccine; ih as in tin; o as in solar; oi as in void; oo as in food; u as in put; uh as in but; ch as in chutzpa; zh as in Zhivago.

A mythical European city used as the butt of jokes, much like the Chelm humor.

shnook see *shnuk*

shnoor see *shnur*

shnor see *shnawr*

shnorrer see *shnawrer*

shnuhdr
Also *she-naw-dar, she-na-dar.**
Also spelled *shnudder.*
1. Literally, "one who pledged."
2. A donation pledged at a synagogue service.

shnuk
Also spelled *shnook.*
1. A meek, naive, easygoing person.
2. A gullible person.

shnur
Also spelled *shnoor.*
Daughter-in-law.

sho-a*
Also spelled *shoah.*
1. Literally, "disaster, destruction, catastrophe."
2. The Holocaust, decimation of European Jewry under the Nazis from 1933 to 1945.

sho-chuht
Also *sho-cheit, sho-chet.**
A person certified to slaughter cattle and fowl in accordance with Jewish law.

shofar see *shofr*

shofr
Also *sho-fawr, sho-far.**
A ram's horn, sounded particularly on Rosh Hashanah at the synagogue service.
Shofrot* and *shofros* are plural forms.

shoin
Already, immediately.

shoin far-ges-en
1. Literally, "already forgotten."

2. Did you forget already?
3. Out of sight, out of mind.

shoin gei
Also spelled *shoin gai*.
Go already! Beat it! Also expressed in reverse: *gei shoin.*

shoin ge-nug
That's enough! Enough already!

shokel see *shuhkl*

sho-meir
Also *sho-mer.**
1. Guardian.
2. Watchman, security officer.

sho-meir Sha-baws
Also *sho-mer Sha-bat.**
Also spelled *shomeir Shabbat.*
1. A Sabbath observer.
2. A religiously observant Jew.

Sho-meir Yihs-raw-eil
Also *Sho-meir Yihs-ra-el.**
Also spelled *Shomer Yisrael.*
1. Literally, "Guardian of Israel."
2. God.

shomer Shabbat see *shomeir Shabaws*

shom-rihm
Also spelled *shomrim.*
Plural of *shomeir.*
1. Literally, "watchers, guardians."
2. Policemen.
3. Name of the New York society of Jewish police officers.
4. Armed Jewish guards in early agricultural settlements in pre-State Israel.

Shom-ro-nihm
Also spelled *Shomronim.*
1. Literally, "Samaritans."
2. In biblical times, residents of Shomron, the

northern part of Palestine where the Ten Tribes lived.
3. Today, a group of sectarians living on the West Bank of the Jordan who practice a primitive form of Judaism.

sho-teif
Also *sho-tef.**
1. Partner.
2. Associate.

shpai
Literally, "spit."

shpai ois
Literally, "spit out," said to children.

shpa-tsih-ren
Also spelled *shpatziren.*
To walk, stroll, hike.

shpet
Late.

shpetr
Also spelled *shpeter.*
Later.

shpihl-ke
Also spelled *shpilke.*
A pin, a needle.

shpihl-kes
Also spelled *shpilkes.*
1. Literally, "pins and needles."
2. Uneasiness, restlessness.
One who has *shpihlkes* is raring to go and can't sit still. Hyperactive children have *shpihlkes.*

shpihln
To play.

shpihln kawrt-en
To play cards.

shpih-tuhl
Also spelled *shpitol.*
Hospital.

---

a as in father; aw as in law; ai as in aisle; ei as in neighbor; e as in bet; i as in vaccine; ih as in tin; o as in solar; oi as in void; oo as in food; u as in put; uh as in but; ch as in chutzpa; zh as in Zhivago.

shpihtz
    Also spelled *shpitz.*
    1. Peak.
    2. Point.
    3. Tip, top.
shpihtz b'kih-tsur
    Also spelled *shpitz bekitzur.*
    1. Literally, "(Get to) the point briefly."
    2. Make it short and sweet.
shpihtz-fihn-ger
    Also spelled *shpitzfinger.*
    1. Toe.
    2. Fingertip.
shpil
    Also spelled *spiel.*
    A play.
shpilke see *shpihlke*
shpitol see *shpihtuhl*
shpitz see *shpihtz*
shprihch-vawrt
    Also spelled *shprichvort.*
    A proverb, a saying.
shpuh-gel nai
    Also spelled *shpogel nei.*
    1. Literally, "mirror new"
    2. Brand new.
shrai-en
    Also spelled *shreien.*
    To yell, cry out, shout.
shrek-lech
    1. Frightening.
    2. Terrible.
(a) shrek-le-che zach
    A frightening, terrible thing.
shtadln
    Also *shtad-lawn, shtad-lan,* shtad-len.*
    Also spelled *stadlan.*

---

a as in father; aw as in law; ai as in aisle ei as in neighbor; e as in bet; i as in vaccine; ih as in tin; o as in solar; oi as in void; oo as in food; u as in put; uh as in but; ch as in chutzpa; zh as in Zhivago.

In Europe in earlier centuries, a wealthy Jew who
was the spokesman of the Jewish community before heads of state.

shtain see *shtein*

shtait geshriben see *shteit geshrihbn*

shtar*
Also spelled *shetar.*
1. A contract.
2. A legal Jewish document.

shtarbn
Also spelled *shtarben.*
To die.

shtar gei-rus
Also *shtar gei-rut.**
Also spelled *shetar gerut.*
Certificate of conversion to Judaism.

shtark
Strong, brave.

shtar-ker
1. A strong person.
2. A tough guy, roughneck.
3. A bully.

shtayn see *shtein*

shtein
Also spelled *shtain, shtayn.*
Stone.

shtein raich
Also spelled *shtein reich.*
1. Literally, "stone rich."
2. Very rich.

shteit ge-shrihbn
Also spelled *shtait geshriben.*
1. Literally, "It is so written."
2. It is authoritative.

shtetl
Also spelled *shtetel.*

---

a as in father; aw as in law; ai as in aisle; ei as in neighbor; e as in bet; i as in vaccine; ih as in tin; o as in
solar; oi as in void; oo as in food; u as in put; uh as in but; ch as in chutzpa; zh as in Zhivago.

A small town, particularly in the Jewish communities of Eastern Europe.

shtihk
Also spelled *shtik*.
1. Literally, "a piece, a chunk."
2. A game, prank, caprice.
3. One's specialty.
4. A gimmick.
See also *shtihkl*.

shtihk hawltz
Also spelled *shtik holtz*.
1. Literally, "a piece of wood."
2. A dull, dumb person.

shtihkl
Also spelled *shtikel*.
1. A little piece.
2. A trick, prank.
See also *shtihk*.

shtihk-lach
1. Idiosyncracies.
2. Pranks.
See also *shtihk*.

shtihk na-ar
Also spelled *shtik nar*.
A bit of a fool.

shtihk na-ches
Also spelled *shtik naches*.
1. Literally "piece of pleasure."
2. Great satisfaction, pride, joy.

shtihl
Also spelled *shtil*.
Stillness, quiet.

shtihl-ihn-ker-heit
Also spelled *shtilinkerait*.
Quietly, unobtrusively.

shtik see *shtihk*

shtil see *shtihl*

---

a as in father; aw as in law; ai as in aisle; ei as in neighbor; e as in bet; i as in vaccine; ih as in tin; o as in solar; oi as in void; oo as in food; u as in put; uh as in but; ch as in chutzpa; zh as in Zhivago.

shtinkn
Also spelled *shtinken.*
To stink.

shtoltz see *shtuhltz*

shtoop see *shtup*

shtot see *shtuht*

shtraiml
Also spelled *shtreimel, streiml.*
Round, fur-trimmed hats worn by Chassidic Jews on Sabbaths and holidays and said to have originated with the Ba'al Shem Tov, founder of the Chassidic movement.

shtrawfn
Also spelled *shtrofen.*
1. Punish.
2. Upbraid.

shtreimel see *shtraiml*

shtrofen see *shtrawfn*

shtrudl
Also spelled *strudel, shtrudel.*
A pastry, sweet or savory, most often filled with fruit or cheese.

shtub
House.

shtuhltz
Also spelled *shtoltz.*
1. Proud.
2. An excessive amount of self-esteem.

shtuht
Also spelled *shtot.*
1. City.
2. A town.

shtunk
A stinker.

shtup
Also spelled *shtoop.*

---

a as in father; aw as in law; ai as in aisle; ei as in neighbor; e as in bet; i as in vaccine; ih as in tin; o as in solar; oi as in void; oo as in food; u as in put; uh as in but; ch as in chutzpa; zh as in Zhivago.

1. Push.
2. Aggression.

shtupn
Also spelled *shtupen.*
Push, shove, poke. See also *shtup.*

shtus
Also *shtut.**
Nonsense, foolishness.

shuch
Shoe.

shuh
Also *sha-a.**
1. An hour.
2. A moment in time.

shuhkl
Also spelled *shokel.*
1. Shake, sway.
2. Nod.

shuhkl mihtn kuhp
Also spelled *shokel mit dem kop.*
1. Literally, "to shake with the head."
2. To agree.

shuhlem see *shalom*

shuh-lem ba-yihs
Also *shaw-lom ba-yihs, sha-lom ba-yiht.**
Also spelled *shalom bayit.*
1. Literally, "household peace."
2. Family unity.

shuluhm aleichem see *shawlom aleichem*

shuh-nuh to-vuh
Also **shaw-na to-vaw, sha-na to-va.***
1. Literally, "good year."
2. Traditional Jewish New Year greeting.
3. New Year greeting card.

shul
1. Literally, "school."
2. Synagogue.

Shulchn Aw-ruch
Also *Shul-chan A-ruch.**
1. Literally, "prepared table."
2. The name of the code of Jewish law and custom compiled by Joseph Caro in 1565.

shu-le
School.

shura see *shure*

shu-re
Also *shu-raw, shu-ra.**
1. A line.
2. A row.

shush-ke
1. Whisper.
2. An aside.

shushkn
Also spelled *shushken.*
To whisper.

shustr
Also spelled *shuster.*
Shoemaker.

shvach
Weak, faint.

shvaig
Also spelled *shveig.*
Shut up!

shvaign
Also spelled *shveigen.*
To be still, silent.

shvartz
Black.

shvartz yawr
1. Literally, "a black year."
2. A miserable future.
3. An expression of disappointment and disgust.

shvartz-e
Also *shvartz-er.*

---

a as in father: aw as in law; ai as in aisle; ei as in neighbor; e as in bet; i as in vaccine: ih as in tin: o as in solar; oi as in void; oo as in food; u as in put; uh as in but; ch as in chutzpa: zh as in Zhivago.

A black person, a Negro.

Shvat*

Also spelled *Shevat.*

The eleventh month of the Jewish religious calendar, fifth of the Civil calendar, corresponding to January-February.

shvawgr

Also spelled *shvoger.*
Brother-in-law.

shve-be-le

1. Literally, "a sulphur match."
2. An excitable person.

shve-ge-rihn

Sister-in-law.

shveig see *shvaig*

shvein-ger

Also spelled *shvenger.*
To be pregnant.

shvein-ger-en

A variant form of *shveinger.* See above.

shven-kechtz

Mouthwash.

shver

1. Difficult, heavy, hard.
2. A father-in-law.

shver tzu ma-chen a le-ben

It's tough to make a living.

shvestr

Also spelled *shvester.*
Sister.

shvihgr

Also spelled *shviger.*
Mother-in-law.

shvihn-del-dihk

Also spelled *shvindeldik.*
Unsteady, dizzy.

---

a as in father; aw as in law; ai as in aisle; ei as in neighbor; e as in bet; i as in vaccine; ih as in tin; o as in solar; oi as in void; oo as in food; u as in put; uh as in but; ch as in chutzpa; zh as in Zhivago.

shvihndl
Also spelled *shvindel.*
1. Swindle.
2. Deception, trickery.
3. Fraud.
4. A hoax.

shvihndlt ihn di oign
Also spelled *shvindelt in di oigen.*
1. Literally, "dizzy in the eyes."
2. Staggering.

shvihtz
Also spelled *shvitz.*
Sweat, perspire.

shvihtz buhd
Also spelled *shvitz bod.*
1. Steambath, sauna.
2. Turkish bath.

shvihtz-er
Also spelled *shvitzer.*
1. Literally, "one who sweats (over nothing)."
2. A braggart.

shvindel see *shvihndl*

shvoger see *shvawgr*

Shvues see *Shavuot*

Siddur see *Sihdr*

Sidra see *Sedruh*

Sihdr
Also *Si-door.**
Also spelled *Siddur.*
1. Literally, "arrangement, order."
2. Prayerbook with the daily or Sabbath liturgies.

Sihf-rei To-raw
Also Sihf-rei To-ra.*
Plural of *Seifr Toruh.*

simcha see *sihmchuh*

sihm-cha shel mihts-va*
Also *sihm-chaw shel mihts-vaw.*

---

a as in father; aw as in law; ai as in aisle; ei as in neighbor; e as in bet; i as in vaccine; ih as in tin; o as in solar; oi as in void; oo as in food; u as in put; uh as in but; ch as in chutzpa; zh as in Zhivago.

Also spelled *simcha shel mitzva.*
The joy of performing a *mitzva.*

Sihm-chas To-ruh
Also *Sihm-chat To-ra,** Sihmchas Toraw.*
Also spelled *Simhat Torah, Simchat Torah.*
1. Literally, "Rejoicing in the Law."
2. The festival after Sukkot marking both the completion and beginning of the annual cycle of Torah readings in synagogue.

sihm-chuh
Also *sihm-chaw, sihm-cha.**
Also spelled *simcha, simha, simche.*
1. Joy, rejoicing.
2. A festive celebration.
3. A party.

sihm-chuhs
Also *sihm-chos, sihm-chot.**
Also spelled *simchos, simchot.*
Happy occasions. Plural of *sihmchuh.*

sihn
Also spelled *sin.*
A letter of the Hebrew alphabet sounded like "s."

simcha shel mitzva see *sihmcha shel mihtsva*

Simchat Torah see *Sihmchas Toruh*

simche see *sihmchuh*

simchos see *sihmchuhs*

sihtz-bawd
Also spelled *sitzbod, zihtzbawd.*
Literally, "a sit bath," that is, a hot tub.

sin see *sihn*

Si-van
The third month of the Jewish religious calendar, ninth of the Civil calendar, corresponding to May-June.

si-yum
1. Literally, "completion."
2. The celebration held upon the completion of the study of a tractate of the Talmud.

a as in father; aw as in law; ai as in aisle; ei as in neighbor; e as in bet; i as in vaccine; ih as in tin; o as in solar; oi as in void; oo as in food; u as in put; uh as in but; ch as in chutzpa; zh as in Zhivago.

skuhtzl kumt
  Also spelled *skotzel kumt.*
  1. Well, hello!
  2. Look who's here!
slihv-uh-vihtz
  Also spelled *slivovitz.*
  A plum brandy popular in Slavic countries.
sme-te-ne
  Sour cream.
smi-chuh
  Also *smi-cha* se-mi-cha.*
  1. Literally, "laying on of hands."
  2. Rabbinical ordination involving the laying on of
  hands by the rabbi performing the ceremony.
snoga
  Ladino for "synagogue."
Sodom see *Sedom*
sof see *suhf*
sofer see *soifr*
sof kol sof see *suhf kuhl suhf*
soifr
  Also *so-fer.**
  Also spelled *sofer.*
  A scribe, especially one who writes Torah Scrolls,
  mezuzot, and *tefilin.*
sondek see *sandek*
s'past niht see *past niht*
spiel see *shpil*
spuh-dek
  Also spelled *spodek.*
  A tall velvet or fur hat worn by Chassidic rabbis,
  particularly on weekdays.
s'ret zich azoi see *ret zich azoi*
s'shav see *shav*
stadlan see *shtadln*

---

staich
>Also spelled *steitsh*.
>1. What is the explanation?
>2. How is that possible?
>3. What do you mean?

steitsh see *staich*

s'toot mihr laid
>I'm sorry.

strashe mihr niht
>Also spelled *strashe mir nit*.
>Don't threaten me!

strashn
>Also spelled *strashen*.
>1. Intimidate, threaten.
>2. Tease.

strashn di genz
>1. Literally, "threaten the geese."
>2. Frighten.
>3. Tease.

strudel see *shtrudl*

succah see *suka*

Succoth see *Sukos*

sude see *seuda*

suhf
>Also spelled *sof*.
>1. The last letter of the Hebrew alphabet. Without a dot in it, it is sounded like an "s," with a dot, like a "t."
>2. The end, termination, conclusion.

(a) suhf! (a) suhf!
>Also spelled *a sof! a sof!*
>1. Enough!
>2. End it!

suhf kuhl suhf
>Also spelled *sof kol sof*.
>1. Finally.
>2. The end of the matter.

---

a as in father; aw as in law; ai as in aisle; ei as in neighbor; e as in bet; i as in vaccine; ih as in tin; o as in solar; oi as in void; oo as in food; u as in put; uh as in but; ch as in chutzpa; zh as in Zhivago.

su-ka*
Also *su-kaw, su-kuh.*
Also spelled *sukkah, succah.*
A booth covered with branches, constructed for the festival of Sukkot to commemorate booths lived in by Israelites during their wanderings after the exodus from Egypt.

Sukkot see *Sukos*

Su-kos
Also *Su-kot.**
Also spelled *Succoth, Sukkot.*
1. Literally, "booths."
2. The eight-day festival marking the fall harvest and the wandering of the Israelites in the wilderness of Sinai en route to the Promised Land following the Exodus from Egypt.

sukuh see *suka*

sulze see *p'tcha*

svi-von*
Also spelled *sevivon.*
1. A spinning top.
2. A *dreidl* used on Chanukah.

T

taam see *tam*

ta-am Sha-bat*
   Also *tam Sha-buhs.*
   The special taste of food on the Sabbath.

ta-a-nihs
   Also *ta-a-niht.**
   Also spelled *taanis, taanit.*
   A fast.

Ta-a-nihs Es-teir
   Also *Ta-a-niht Es-ter*.*
   Also spelled *Taanit Esther.*
   Literally, "the Fast of Esther," observed on the day
   preceding Purim, recalling Esther's intercession
   with her husband, King Ahasuerus, to nullify
   Haman's edict.

Taaniht Yartzait see *Tanihs Yawrtsait*

Tach-a-nun*
   Also *Tach-nun.*
   Pentitential prayers recited during the weekday
   service.

tachlihs
   Also *tach-liht.**
   Also spelled *tachlis, tachlit.*
   1. Purpose, object, practical result.
   2. The real thing, the bottom line.

tach-ri-chihm
   Also spelled *tachrichim.*
   Burial shrouds of white linen.

taf see *tuhf*

tag see *tawg*

tahara see *taharuh*

ta-ha-ras ha-mihsh-paw-chaw
   Also *ta-ha-rat ha-mihsh-pa-cha.**

---

a as in father; aw as in law; ai as in aisle: ei as in neighbor; e as in bet; i as in vaccine; ih as in tin; o as in solar; oi as in void; oo as in food; u as in put; uh as in but; ch as in chutzpa; zh as in Zhivago.

1. Literally, "family purity."
2. Immersion in a *mikva* by married women after menstruation.

ta-ha-ruh
Also *ta-ha-ra.**
1. Literally, "purification.
2. The ritual cleansing of a dead body by the *Chevruh Kadishuh.*

tai see *tei*

tai-er
Also spelled *teier.*
1. Expensive.
2. Valuable.
3. Costly.

tai-e-re kihnd
Also spelled *teiere kind.*
Dear child. Darling child..

tai-er-ihn-ker
Also spelled *teierinker.*
1. Sweetheart.
2. Dearest, darling.

taigechtz see *teigechtz*

taigel see *teigl*

taiglach see *teiglech*

taitsh
A Yiddish corruption of the German word *Deutsch* ("German").

taivl
Also *toivl.*
Also spelled *teivel, teuvel.*
1. Devil, demon.
2. Satan.

ta-ka-na*
Also *ta-kaw-naw, ta-kuh-nuh.*
Also spelled *takkana.*
1. Literally, "reform, regulation."
2. A regulation instituted by a community or congregation.

---

a as in father; **aw** as in law; **ai** as in aisle; **ei** as in neighbor; **e** as in bet; **i** as in vaccine; **ih** as in tin; **o** as in solar; **oi** as in void; **oo** as in food; **u** as in put; **uh** as in but; **ch** as in chutzpa; **zh** as in Zhivago.

3. A change in Jewish law instituted by scholars.

ta-ka-not*

Also *ta-kuh-nes, ta-kaw-nos.*
Plural of *takana.*

take see *takuh*

ta-ke a me-tsi-a

Also spelled *takeh a metzia.*
Really, a bargain!

takkana see *takana*

ta-kuh

Also *ta-ke.*
1. Really Is that so?
2. Indeed!
3. You don't say!
4. Are you putting me on?

takuhnes see *takanot*

takuhnuh see *takana*

tal

1. Literally, "dew."
2. The prayer for dew recited on Passover.

ta-lei-sihm

Also *ta-lei-tihm.**
Also spelled *taleisim, talaisim.*
The plural of *talit* in popular use, although *talitot**
is the correct form.

ta-lihs

Also *ta-liht.**
Also spelled *tallis, tallit, talith, talis, talit.*
A rectangular striped prayer shawl with fringes
(tzitziot) attached to the four corners.

ta-lihs kaw-tawn

Also *ta-liht ka-tan*.*
Also spelled *tallit katan.*
1. Literally, "a small *talit.*"
2. An undergarment with fringes *(tzitziot)* attached to its four corners.

talis see *talihs*

---

a as in father; aw as in law; ai as in aisle: ei as in neighbor; e as in bet; i as in vaccine; ih as in tin; o as in solar; oi as in void; oo as in food; u as in put; uh as in but; ch as in chutzpa; zh as in Zhivago.

talit see *talihs*

ta-li-tot see *taleisihm*

tal-mihd chaw-chuhm
> Also *tal-mihd chaw-chawm, tal-mihd cha-cham.**
> Also spelled *talmid chachem, talmid chacham.*
> 1. Literally, "disciple of the wise."
> 2. Scholar, learned person.

Tal-mud Bav-li
> The Babylonian Talmud.

Tal-mud To-raw
> Also *Tal-mud To-ra.**
> Also spelled *Talmud Torah.*
> 1. Literally, "Torah study."
> 2. An elementary Jewish religious school, sometimes called *cheder.*

Tal-mud Ye-ru-shal-mi
> The Jerusalem Talmud.

Tal-muhd
> Also *Tal-mud.**
> 1. Literally, "study, learning."
> 2. The compendium of discussions and interpretations of the biblical text by the scholars of Palestine and Babylonia from 500 B.C.E. to 500 C.E.

tam*
> Also *ta-am.*
> 1. Taste, flavor.
> 2. Good taste.
> 3. Zest.

tam me-vate
> Also spelled *tamevate.*
> 1. Literally, "a simpleton expressing himself."
> 2. A naive person.
> 3. A dope.

Tammuz see *Tamuz*

tam Shabuhs see *taam Shabat*

Ta-muz
> Also spelled *Tammuz.*
> The fourth month of the Jewish religious calendar,

---

a as in father; aw as in law; ai as in aisle; ei as in neighbor; e as in bet; i as in vaccine; ih as in tin; o as in solar; oi as in void; oo as in food; u as in put; uh as in but; ch as in chutzpa; zh as in Zhivago.

tenth of the Civil calendar, corresponding to June-July.

tana see *tanuh*

Ta-nach
Also spelled *Tanakh*.
1. The Hebrew Bible.
2. An acronym from the Hebrew initials of *Tora* (Pentateuch), *Nevi'im* (Prophets), *Ketuvim* (Writings).

ta-naw-ihm
Also *ta-na-ihm*.*
Also spelled *tanaim*.
Plural of *tanuh*. See below.

tan-det
Inferior, second-rate, cheap, bungled work.

Ta-nihs Yawr-tsait
Also *Ta-a-niht Yar-tzait*.*
Also spelled *Taanis Yahrzeit*.
A day of fasting to commemorate the anniversary of the passing of a relative.

tan-sen oif al-e cha-se-ṇes
1. Literally, "to dance at all weddings."
2. To be involved in everything (even where not invited).

tante see *tantuh*

tan-tuh
Also *tan-te*.
Aunt.

ta-nuh
Also *ta-naw, ta-na*.*
Any first or second-century scholar whose teachings on Jewish law and tradition are recorded in the Mishna, the first part of the Talmud.

ta-re-ram
Noise, fuss, hoopla.

Tar-gum
The Aramaic translation or paraphrase of the Hebrew Bible.

---

a as in father; aw as in law; ai as in aisle; ei as in neighbor; e as in bet; i as in vaccine; ih as in tin; o as in solar; oi as in void; oo as in food; u as in put; uh as in but; ch as in chutzpa; zh as in Zhivago.

Targum Onkelos
The Aramaic translation of the Pentateuch by Aquilas, the convert.

Tash-lihch
Also spelled *Tashlich.*
1. Literally, "You will cast out."
2. Ceremony, held on the first afternoon of Rosh Hashanah, of casting one's sins symbolically into a stream or river, usually by throwing crumbs into the water.
3. The prayer recited during the above ceremony.

Tat
A Persian dialect spoken by the "Mountain Jews" of the Caucasus.

ta-te
Also *ta-tuh.*
Also spelled *tata.*
Father, dad, papa.

ta-te-le
Also spelled *tateleh.*
An affectionate form of *tate.* See *tate.*

ta-te ma-me
1. Literally, "father-mother."
2. A cry of anguish and despair.

(a) ta-tens a kihnd
Also spelled *a tatens a kind.*
1. Literally, "a father's child."
2. Someone who takes after father.
3. Child of a good family.

ta-ten-yoo
Also spelled *tatenyu.*
1. Literally, "father dear."
2. An intimate manner of addressing God.

ta-ten-yoo fatr
Also spelled *tatenyoo fatr.*
1. Papa-father.
2. God.

---

a as in father; aw as in law; ai as in aisle; ei as in neighbor; e as in bet; i as in vaccine; ih as in tin; o as in solar; oi as in void; oo as in food; u as in put; uh as in but; ch as in chutzpa; zh as in Zhivago.

ta-tihn-ke
Also spelled *tatinke.*
An affectionate form of *tate.* See *Tate.*

tav see *tuhf*

taw-ches lekr
Also spelled *toches leker.*
1. Literally, ""buttocks-licker."
2. One who fawns over another person.

taw-ches oifn tihsh
Also spelled *toches oifn tish.*
1. Literally, "buttocks on the table."
2. Get down to business!
3. Put up or shut up!

tawchtr
Also spelled *tochter.*
Daughter.

tawg
Also spelled *tog, tag.*
Day.

tawg shu-le
Also spelled *tog shule.*
Day school.

tawg teg-lech
Also spelled *tog teglech.*
Day-to-day, daily.

tay see *tei*

t'chi-yas ha-meis-ihm
Also *te-chi-yat ha-mei-tihm.**
Also spelled *t'chias hameisim, techiat hametim.*
The resurrection of the dead, associated in
Orthodox Judaism with the coming of the Messiah.

tcholent see *tshawlent*

teba
The Sephardic word for *teva.* See *teva.*

Tebeth see *Teiveis*

tefila see *t'filuh*

---

a as in father; aw as in law; ai as in aisle· ei as in neighbor; e as in bet; i as in vaccine; ih as in tin; o as in
solar; oi as in void; oo as in food; u as in put; uh as in but; ch as in chutzpa; zh as in Zhivago.

tefilin see *t'filihn*
tehila see *t'hilaw*
Tehillim see *T'hihlihm*
tehi nihshmata see *t'hi nihshmawsaw*
tehi nihshmato see *t'hi nishmawso*
tei
>Also spelled *tai, tay.*
>Tea.

teier see *taier*
teiere kind see *taiere kihnd*
teierinker see *taierihnker*
tei-gechtz
>Also spelled *taigechtz.*
>A baked pudding made of rice, noodles, barley, or mashed potatoes.

teigl
>Also spelled *teigel, taigel.*
>A small cake filled with nuts and fruit and dipped in honey. A popular Rosh Hashanah delicacy.

teig-lech
>Also *teig-lach.*
>Also spelled *taiglech, taiglach.*
>Plural of *teigl. See above.*

Teitsh Chu-mesh
>Also spelled *Taitsh Chumash.*
>Yiddish translation of the Torah, read mostly by women who were not afforded a Hebrew education.

tei-va*
>Also *tei-vaw.*
>Also spelled *teva.*
>The *bima,* or platform, in the synagogue.

Tei-veis
>Also spelled *Tevet,* *Tebeth.*
>The tenth month of the Jewish religious calendar, fourth of the Civil calendar, corresponding to December-January.

---

a as in father; aw as in law; ai as in aisle; ei as in neighbor; e as in bet; i as in vaccine; ih as in tin; o as in solar; oi as in void; oo as in food; u as in put; uh as in but; ch as in chutzpa; zh as in Zhivago.

teivel see *taivl*

tekia see *tekiuh*

te-ki-uh
> Also *te-ki-a,** *te-ki-aw.*
> Also spelled *t'kiah, tekiah.*
> An unbroken *shofar* blast sounded in the synagogue on Rosh Hashanah.

tel-e-rel fun hihml
> Also spelled *telerel fun himmel.*
> 1. Literally, "saucers from heaven."
> 2. Something unattainable (the moon on a plate).

temp
> Dull, dense.

tenaim see *t'nawihm*

terefah see *treif*

te-roo-aw
> Also *te-roo-a.**
> Also spelled *teruah, t'ruah, terua.*
> A wavering *shofar* sound consisting of nine staccato notes.

te-roo-maw
> Also *te-roo-ma.**
> Also spelled *terumah, t'rumah.*
> 1. Offering.
> 2. Gift.
> 3. An offering of a product of the field, brought to the priests in the Temple in Jerusalem.

tes
> Also *tet.**
> The ninth letter of the Hebrew alphabet, corresponding in sound to "t."

te-shoo-vos
> Also *te-shoo-vot.**
> Also spelled *teshuvos, t'shuvot.*
> Plural of *teshoova (t'shoovuh).*

teshuva see *t'shoovuh*

tet see *tes*

---

a as in father; aw as in law; ai as in aisle: ei as in neighbor; e as in bet; i as in vaccine; ih as in tin; o as in solar; oi as in void; oo as in food; u as in put; uh as in but; ch as in chutzpa; zh as in Zhivago.

Tevet see *Teiveis*

t'fih-lihn*
Also *te-fi-lihn.*
Also spelled *t'filin, tefilin.*
Phylacteries, small boxes mounted on leather
straps, worn by male Jews during weekday morning prayers. One, worn on the arm, is called *t'filihn
shel yad;* the other, worn on the forehead, is called
t'filihn shel rosh. Verses from the Bible, handwritten on parchment, are enclosed in each box.

t'fila see *t'filuh*

T'fi-las Ha-de-rech
Also *Te-fi-lat Ha-de-rech.**
1. Literally, "prayer (for) the road."
2. A prayer recited before commencing a journey.

t'filaw see *t'filuh*

t'fi-luh
Also *t'fi-la,* t'fi-law.*
Also spelled *tefila, tefilaw, tefillah.*
1. Prayer.
2. In the Mishna the word refers to the *Amida*
prayer, also known as the *Shemone Esrei.*

t'hih-lihm
Also *te-hi-lihm.**
Also spelled *tehillim.*
1. Psalms.
2. The Book of Psalms.

t'hi-law
Also *te-hi-la,* te-hilaw.*
Also spelled *t'hila, tehilah.*
1. Psalm.
2. The singular of *t'hihlihm.*

tihk-vaw
Also *tihk-va.**
Also spelled *tikvaw, tikva.*
1. Hope.
2. "The Hope" *(Hatikva),* the Israeli national an-
them.

tihmtum
> Also spelled *timtum*.
> 1. A simple child, derived from the Hebrew *tam*.
> 2. A bisexual person.
> 3. An effeminate man.

tihsh
> Also spelled *tish*.
> Table.

Tihsh-aw B'Awv
> Also *Tihsh-a B'Av.**
> Also spelled *Tisha B'Av, Tisha B'ov,* and *Tisha Be'av.*
> 1. Literally, "the ninth of (the Hebrew month of) Av."
> 2. The name of a fast day marking the destruction of the First (586 B.C.E.) and Second (70 C.E.) Temples in Jerusalem.

Tihsh-ri
> Also *Tihsh-rei.**
> Also spelled *Tishri.*
> The seventh month of the Jewish religious calendar, first of the Civil calendar, corresponding to September-October. The first two days of Tihshri are the Jewish New Year. The tenth day is the Day of Atonement.

Ti-kun*
> Also spelled *Tikkun.*
> A devotional prayer service.

tikva see *tihkvaw*

timtum see *tihmtum*

tish see *tihsh*

Tisha B'Av see *Tihshaw B'Awv*

Tishri see *Tihshri*

t'kiah see *tekiuh*

t'naw-ihm
> Also *te-na-ihm.**
> Also spelled *tenaim.*
> 1. Literally, "conditions," referring particularly to

---

a as in father; aw as in law; ai as in aisle; ei as in neighbor; e as in bet; i as in vaccine; ih as in tin; o as in solar; oi as in void; oo as in food; u as in put; uh as in but; ch as in chutzpa; zh as in Zhivago.

the document spelling out the agreement for
marriage.
2. The betrothal ceremony.

toches see *tuhches*

toches leker see *tawches lekr*

toches oifn tish see *tawches oifn tihsh*

tochis see *tuhches*

to-cho k'va-ro
1. Literally, "His interior is as his exterior."
2. A sincere, open, and honest individual.

tochter see *tawchtr*

tog see *tawg*

togshule see *tawg shule*

tog teglech see *tawg teglech*

toign
Also spelled *toigen.*
Fit for, good for.

toign oif ka-paw-res
Also *toi-gen oif ka-po-res.*
1. Literally, "suitable for *kapores*," the atonement
fowl used before Yom Kippur to take away one's
sins and which is then slaughtered.
2. To be worthless.

Toi-ras luhkshn
Also spelled *Toras lukshen.*
1. Literally, "noodle Torah."
2. Learning of no consequence.
3. Faulty scholarship.

Toiruh see *Toruh*

Toi-ruh ihz di bes-te s'choi-re
Also spelled *Torah iz di beste s'chorah.*
Literally, "Torah is the best merchandise."

toit
Also *tot.*
Dead, deceased.

toit hun-ge-rihk
Also spelled *toit hungerik.*

---

a as in father; aw as in law; ai as in aisle; ei as in neighbor; e as in bet; i as in vaccine; ih as in tin; o as in
solar; oi as in void; oo as in food; u as in put; uh as in but; ch as in chutzpa; zh as in Zhivago.

1. Literally, "dead hungry."
2. Starved.

(a) toitn ban-kes
Also spelled *a toyten bankus.*
Literally, "(it will have as little avail as treating) a dead person with cupping."

toi-veh
Also *to-vaw, to-va,* toi-vuh.*
1. Good.
2. (To do) a favor.

too-be-ta-ka
Also spelled *tubetaka.*
A multicolored skullcap worn by Russian Jews.

too-en-vei
Also *tu-en vai.*
To hurt, pain.

toonkel see *tunkl*

(es) toot mihr laid
1. Literally, "It causes me pain."
2. I'm sorry.
Sometimes written as *s'toot mihr laid.*

(es) toot mihr vei
Literally, "It hurts me." Sometimes written as *s'toot mihr vei.*

(es) toot vei dem hartz
1. Literally, "The (my) heart hurts."
2. I'm heartbroken.
Sometimes written as *s'toot vei dos* (or *dem*) *hartz.*

Tora see *Toruh*

Torah see *Toruh*

Torah iz di beste s'chorah see *Toiruh ihz di beste s'choire*

To-ruh
Also *Toi-ruh, To-raw, Tora.**
Also spelled *Torah.*
1. Teaching.
2. The Law.

---

a as in father; aw as in law; ai as in aisle; ei as in neighbor; e as in bet; i as in vaccine; ih as in tin; o as in solar; oi as in void; oo as in food; u as in put; uh as in but; ch as in chutzpa; zh as in Zhivago.

3. Pentateuch
4. The totality of traditional Jewish wisdom, literature, culture.

To-ruh lih-shmaw
Also *To-ra lih-shma.**
Also spelled *Torah lishma.*
Literally, "(the study of) Torah for its own sake."

To-ruh mi-Si-nai
Also *To-ra mi-Si-nai,** *To-raw mi-Si-nai.*
Also spelled *Torah mi-Sinai.*
1. Literally, "Torah from (Mt.) Sinai."
2. Revelation.

To-ruh she-b'al pe
Also *To-raw she-b'al pe, To-ra she-b'al pe.**
Also spelled *Torah she-b'al pe.*
The unwritten Torah, the Oral Law as recorded in the Talmud.

To-ruh she-bihk-sav
Also *To-ra she-bihk-tav.**
1. Literally, "written Torah."
2. The Bible.

Tosafists
1. Literally, "supplementers, adders."
2. A group of scholars who added explanations to the Talmud. The earliest and more important ones were descendants of Rashi, living from the twelfth to fourteenth centuries.

To-sa-fot*
Also *Tos-fos.*
Notes and comments of the Tosafists. See above.

To-sef-taw
Also *To-sef-ta,** *To-sihf-ta.*
Also spelled *Tosifta.*
1. Literally, "supplement."
2. A collection of Jewish law similar to the Mishna but containing additional material. Its editors are believed to be the third-century scholars Oshaya and Rabbah.

tot see *toit*

---

a as in father: aw as in law; ai as in aisle; ei as in neighbor; e as in bet; i as in vaccine; ih as in tin; o as in solar; oi as in void; oo as in food; u as in put; uh as in but; ch as in chutzpa; zh as in Zhivago.

tova see *toiveh*

traibr see *treibr*

traif see *treif*

traife see *treif*

traifener bain see *treifener bein*

tran-te
1. Rag
2. Decrepit, worn out.

traw-ge-dihk
Also spelled *trogedik.*
1. Literally, "carrying."
2. Pregnant.

trawg ge-zunt-er-heit
Also spelled *trog gezunterhait.*
1. Literally, "Carry (wear) it in good health."

trawgn
Also spelled *trogen.*
1. To carry.
2. To bear.

trayf see *treif*

trefn
Also spelled *trefen.*
1. To meet.
2. To encounter, run across.
3. To guess right.

treibr
Also *traibr.*
Also spelled *treiber, traiber.*
To remove the sciatic nerve and certain other vessels and tendons from the hindquarter of an animal, rendering it kosher.

treif
Also *trei-fa,* trei-faw, treifuh.*
Also spelled *trayf, traif, traife, tref, trefa.*
1. Literally, "torn," a torn animal.
2. A nonkosher animal.
3. Nonkosher food.

---

a as in father; aw as in law; ai as in aisle; ei as in neighbor; e as in bet; i as in vaccine; ih as in tin; o as in solar; oi as in void; oo as in food; u as in put; uh as in but; ch as in chutzpa; zh as in Zhivago.

trei-fe-ne bihch-er
Also spelled *traifene bicher.*
1. Literally, "nonkosher books."
2. Forbidden literature.

trei-fe-ner bein
Also spelled *traifener bain.*
1. Literally, "nonkosher bone."
2. A nonobservant Jew.

treif puhsl
Also spelled *traif posel.*
1. Literally, "unfit and unqualified."
2. Defective.
3. Absolutely not kosher.

trihnkn
Also spelled *trinken.*
1. To drink.
2. To imbibe.

trogedik see *trawgedihk*

trogen see *trawgn*

trog gezunterhait see *trawg gezunterheit*

trombenik see *truhmbenihk*

t'ruah see *terooaw*

truhm-be-nihk
Also spelled *trombenik.*
1. A lazy person.
2. A ne'er-do-well.

t'rumah see *teroomaw*

tsa-ar ba-alei cha-yihm*
Also spelled *tza'ar ba'ale chayim.*
1. Literally, "the pain (suffering) of living things."
2. The concept of kindness to animals in Jewish tradition.
3. The Jewish aversion to and ban on hunting and on fishing with a hook.

tsa-ar gi-dul baw-nihm
Also *tza-ar gi-dul ba-nihm.**
Literally, "the pain (difficulty) of raising children."

---

a as in father; aw as in law; ai as in aisle; ei as in neighbor; e as in bet; i as in vaccine; ih as in tin; o as in solar; oi as in void; oo as in food; u as in put; uh as in but; ch as in chutzpa; zh as in Zhivago.

tsa-di*
Also *tsa-dihk, tsa-dei.*
Also spelled *tzadi.*
The eighteenth letter of the Hebrew alphabet, corresponding to "ts" in sound.

tsa-dihk
Also spelled *tzaddik, tzadik, zaddik.*
1. Literally, "a righteous person."
2. Pietist.
3. Saint.
4. A Chassidic rabbi or leader.
5. The popular pronunciation of the eighteenth letter of the Hebrew alphabet. See *tsa-di.*

tsait
Also spelled *tzeit.*
1. Time.
2. Era.

tsap mihr niht main blut
Also spelled *tzap mir nit mein blut.*
1. Literally, "Don't bleed me!"
2. Don't aggravate me!

tsarot see *tzuhruhs*

tsats-ke-le di ma-mes
Also spelled *tzatzkele di mames.*
Mama's pet.

tsatz-ke
Also spelled *tzatzke, tshatshke, chachke, chatshke.*
1. A bauble, plaything, trinket.
2. Something cute.
3. A doll.

tsa-vuh-uh
Also *tza-va-a,* *tzeva'a.*
Last will and testament.

tsawn
Also spelled *tzon.*
Tooth.

---

tsawres see *tzuhruhs*

tse-brech a fus
    1. Literally, "Break a foot!"
    2. Break a leg!

tsedaka see *tseduhkuh*

tse-dreit
    Also *tse-drait.*
    1. Literally, "turned, twisted, distorted."
    2. Mixed up, confused.
    3. Nutty, crazy.

tse-du-delt
    Mixed up.

tse-duh-kuh
    Also *tse-da-ka,* tse-daw-kaw.*
    Also spelled *tsedakah, tzedaka.*
    1. Philanthropy, charity, benevolence.
    2. Justice.

tse-geit zihch ihn moil
    Also spelled *tzegait zich in moil.*
    1. Literally, "It melts in the mouth."
    2. Delicious.

tsein
    Also spelled *tzain.*
    Teeth. The plural of *tsawn.*

tsein duhktr
    Also spelled *tzain dokter.*
    Literally, "tooth doctor," a dentist.

tse-kawcht
    Also spelled *tzekocht.*
    1. Literally, "overboiled."
    2. Excited, furious.

tse-lem
    Also spelled *tzelem.*
    1. An image.
    2. A crucifix.

tse-mihsh-e-nihsh
    Also spelled *tzemishenish.*
    Confusion.

---

a as in father: aw as in law; ai as in aisle; ei as in neighbor; e as in bet; i as in vaccine; ih as in tin; o as in solar; oi as in void; oo as in food; u as in put; uh as in but; ch as in chutzpa; zh as in Zhivago.

tse-mihsht
Also *tsu-mihsht.*
Also spelled *tsemisht, tzemisht.*
Mixed-up, confused, befuddled.

tse-rais ge-zunt-er-heit
Also spelled *tzereis gezunterhait.*
Literally, "Tear (it) in good health," addressed to
one who purchased a new garment.

tse-traw-gen
Also spelled *tzetrogen.*
Absent-minded.

tse-tu-melt
Also *tsu-tu-melt.*
Also spelled *tzetumelt.*
Mixed up, confused, befuddled.

tse -vihl-de-ter
Also spelled *tzevildeter.*
1. A wild person.
2. A misbehaving child.

tshai-nihk
Also spelled *tsheinik.*.
Teapot.

tshatshke see *tsatzke*

tshav see *shav*

tshaw-lent
Also spelled *tsholent, tcholent, cholent.*
A dish consisting of meat, potatoes, and legumes,
baked before sunset Friday and kept warm on Saturday to avoid cooking on the Sabbath. Also called
shalet and *sholet* by German-speaking Jews and
adafino and *chamin* by Sephardic Jews.

tsheinik see *tshainihk*

tshe-pe
Also spelled *tcheppeh.*
1. To pick on (someone).
2. To tease.
3. To annoy, bother, pester, irk, harass.

---

a as in father; aw as in law; ai as in aisle; ei as in neighbor; e as in bet; i as in vaccine; ih as in tin; o as in
solar; oi as in void; oo as in food; u as in put; uh as in but; ch as in chutzpa; zh as in Zhivago.

tshe-pe zihch niht tsu mihr
Also spelled *tzhepe zich nit tzu mir.*
Don't annoy me!

tshe-pe zihch uhp fun mihr
Also spelled *tzhepe zich op fun mir.*
1. Get away from me!
2. Leave me alone!

tshepn
Also *tze-pen.*
Also spelled *tzhepen.*
1. Annoy, harass.
2. Touch.

tsholent see *tshawlent*

t'shoo-vuh
Also *te-shoo-vaw, te-shoo-va.**
Also spelled *t'shuvuh, teshuvaw, teshuva.*
1. Literally, "a turning, returning."
2. Repentance.
3. An answer, retort.

tsi
Also *tsu.*
Also spelled *tzi.*
1. If.
2. Whether.

tsi bihst du me-shih-ge?
Also spelled *tzi bistu meshuge?*
(I wonder) are you crazy?

tsih-be-le
Also spelled *tzibele.*
Onion.

tsihkln zihch
Also spelled *tziklen zich.*
A cantor's falsetto repetition of a musical phrase.

tsih-mes
Also *tsih-muhs.*
Also spelled *tsimmes, tzimmes.*
1. A compote, usually of cooked fruit such as plums or prunes.

---

a as in father; aw as in law; ai as in aisle; ei as in neighbor; e as in bet; i as in vaccine; ih as in tin; o as in solar; oi as in void; oo as in food; u as in put; uh as in but; ch as in chutzpa; zh as in Zhivago.

2. A vegetable stew of carrots and sweet potatoes,
well spiced.
The word *tsihmes* may derive from the German
zum Essen, "to eat."

tsihmr
Also spelled *tzimmer.*
Room.

tsimmes see *tsihmes*

tsi-rung
Also spelled *tzirung.*
1. Jewelry.
2. Earrings.

tsi-tsiht*
Also *tsih-tshihs.*
Also spelled *tzitzit, tsitsit, tsitsis.*
Fringes attached to the four corners of the prayer
shawl.

tsitzel
Heavy rye bread with a thick crust, the bottom
coated with cornmeal. Also known as corn bread.

tsnies see *tsnius*

tsni-us
Also *tsni-es, tzni-ut.**
Modesty, humility.

tsnu-aw
Also *tse-nu-a.**
Also spelled *tzenuah.*
1. A chaste woman.
2. A modest woman.

tsouris see *tzuhruhs*

tsu see *tsi*

tsu fihl
Also *tzi fihl.*
Also spelled *tzu fil.*
1. Literally, "too much."
2. Too costly.

tsu-frih-den
Also spelled *tzufriden*.
Content, satisfied.

tsu ge-zunt
Also spelled *tzu gezunt*.
Literally, "to health," said when another sneezes.

tsu kumn oifn zihn-en
Also spelled *tzu kumen oifen zinen*.
1. Literally, "to come upon the senses."
2. To come to mind, to occur to someone.

tsukr
Also spelled *tzuker*.
Sugar.

tsu-lihb
Also spelled *tzulib*.
On account of, because of, for the sake of.

tsum glihk, tsum shlih-mazl
Also spelled *tzum glik, tzum shlimazel*.
For better, for worse.

tsumihsht see *tsemihsht*

tsuris see *tzuhruhs*

tsu shand un tsu shpuht
1. Literally, "to shame and to mock."
2. To be disgraced.

tsu tai-er
Also spelled *tzu teier*.
Too costly.

tsu-tshep-e-nihsh
Also spelled *tzutzhepenish*.
1. A nuisance, pest.
2. An unwanted person.
3. A hanger-on.

tsutumelt see *tsetumelt*

tsvi-bak
Also spelled *zweiback*.
A type of toast that has been baked twice.

tubetaka see *toobetaka*

---

a as in father; aw as in law; ai as in aisle; ei as in neighbor; e as in bet; i as in vaccine; ih as in tin; o as in solar; oi as in void; oo as in food; u as in put; uh as in but; ch as in chutzpa; zh as in Zhivago.

Tu Bi-Shvat
> Also spelled *Tu BiShevat.*
> The fifteenth day of the Hebrew month Shvat, also
> called "New Year for Trees" or "Arbor Day."

tuch
> 1. A kerchief.
> 2. A headcovering used by Orthodox Jewish mar-
> ried women.

tuchis see *tuhchuhs*

tuen see *tuhn*

tuen vai see *tooen vei*

tuh-chuhs
> Also spelled *toches, tochis, tuchis, tuches.*
> 1. Literally, "bottom."
> 2. The buttocks, the behind.

tuhf
> Also *taf, tav.*
> The twenty-second and final letter of the Hebrew
> alphabet, sounded like "s" or "t."

tuhn
> Also *tu-en.*
> Do, to do.

tumel see *tuml*

tu mihr a toi-ve
> Also spelled *tu mir a toyve.*
> Do me a favor.

tu mihr niht kain toi-ves
> Also spelled *tu mir nit kein toives.*
> Don't do me any favors.

tu mihr tzu-lihb
> Also spelled *tu mir tzulib.*
> 1. Do it for my sake.
> 2. Do me a favor.

tuml
> Also spelled *tumel.*
> Confusion, din, uproar, noise.

---

a as in father; aw as in law; ai as in aisle; ei as in neighbor; e as in bet; i as in vaccine; ih as in tin; o as in
solar; oi as in void; oo as in food; u as in put; uh as in but; ch as in chutzpa; zh as in Zhivago.

tun-ked
  Dipped, dunked.

tunkl
  Also spelled *toonkel.*
  1. Dark, shadowy, dim.
  2. Shady (affairs), sinister.

tza-ar ba'ale chayim see *tsaar baalei chayihm*

tza'ar gidul banihm see *tsaar gidul bawnihm*

tzadi see *tsadi*

tzaddik see *tsadihk*

tzain see *tsein*

tzain dokter see *tseinduhktr*

tzarot see *tzuhruhs*

tzatzke see *tsatzke*

tzedaka see *tseduhkuh*

tzegait zich in moil see *tsegeit zihch ihn moil*

tzeit see *tsait*

tzekocht see *tsekawcht*

tzelem see *tselem*

tzemisht see *tsemihsht*

tzenuah see *tsnuaw*

tzepen see *tshepn*

tzereis gezunterhait see *tserais gezunterheit*

tzetrogen see *tsetrawgen*

tzetumelt see *tsetumelt*

tzeva'a see *tsavuhuh*

tzevildeter see *tsevihldeter*

tzhepen see *tshepn*

tzhepe zich nit tzu mir see *tshepe zihch niht tsu mihr*

tzi see *tsi*

tzibbeles see *tsihbeles*
  Onions.

Tzi-duk Ha-Dihn
  Also spelled *Tzidduk Hadin.*

1. Literally, "Justification of the (Divine) Judgment."
2. A prayer recited at the Jewish burial service.

tzihtr
Also spelled *tziter*.
To tremble, to shake, to be nervous.

tziklen zich see *tsihkln zihch*

tzimmer see *tsihmr*

tzimmes see *tsihmes*

tzi-rung see *tsi-rung*

tziter see *tzihtr*

tzitzit see *tsitsiht*

Tzi-yon*
Also *Tzi-yoin*.
1. Zion.
2. Originally, a Canaanite fortress in Jerusalem captured by David.
3. The biblical city of David.

tzniut see *tsnius*

tznua see *tsnuan*

tzom
A fast.

Tzom Ge-dal-yuh
Also *Tzom Ge-dal-ya*.*
Also spelled *Tzom Gedaliah, Zom Gedalia*.
The Fast of Gedalia observed the day after Rosh Hashanah. On this day Gedaliah, the Babylonian-appointed governor of Judea, was murdered in 582 B.C.E.

tzon see *tsawn*

tzoo-tzoo klepn
To adhere to.

tzu
1. To.
2. Too, excessive.

tzu fil see *tsu fihl*

---

a as in father; aw as in law; ai as in aisle; ei as in neighbor; e as in bet; i as in vaccine; ih as in tin; o as in solar; oi as in void; oo as in food; u as in put; uh as in but; ch as in chutzpa; zh as in Zhivago.

tzufriden see *tsufrihden*

tzug
1. A draft of wind.
2. Pull.
3. Move.

tzu gezunt see *tsu gezunt*

tzuh-luh-ches
To make one angry. A distortion of two words: *tzoo* (Yiddish, "to") and *lehachihs* (Hebrew, "anger").

tzuh-ruhs
Also *tzaw-ros, tza-rot,** *tsaw-res.*
Also spelled *tzures, tsuris, tsouris.*
1. Troubles.
2. Aggravation.
3. Sufferings.
4. Distress.

tzuker see *tsukr*

tzu kumen oifen zinen see *tsu kumn oifn zihnen*

tzulib see *tsulihb*

tzum glik, tzum shlimazel see *tsum glihk, tsum shlihmazl*

tzung
Tongue.

tzures see *tzuhruhs*

tzu teier see *tsu taier*

tzutzhepenish see *tsutshepenihsh*

U

uh-ber
Also spelled *ober, uhbr.*
1. However.
2. But

uhch see *och*

uh-der
Also spelled *oder.*
1. Either.
2. Or.

uh-huh
Also spelled *oho.*
1. Yes.
2. Wow!

uhn
Also spelled *on.*
Without, sans.

uhn-ge-patsh-ket
Also spelled *ungepotchket.*
1. Cluttered, disordered, sloppy, littered, muddled,
    messed up.
2. Overdone, overdecorated.

uhn lang-e hak-daw-mes
Also spelled *on lange hakdomes.*
1. Literally, "without a long introduction."
2. Keep it short.
3. Get to the point.

uhvl
Also *aw-veil, a-vel.**
Also spelled *ovel.*
A mourner after the funeral.

ul-pan
1. Instruction, teaching.

---

2. In modern Israel, a school for the intensive study of Hebrew.

um-be-ru-fen
1. Uncalled for.
2. God forbid!

um-be-shri-en
1. God forbid!
2. May it not happen.!

um-ge-dul-dihk
Also spelled *umgeduldik.*
Petulant, impatient.

um-glihk
Also spelled *umglik.*
1. Literally, "without luck."
2. Misfortune.
3. Tragedy.

um-glihk-lihch-er mentsh
1. An unfortunate, unlucky person.
2. A born loser.

um-meg-lihch
Impossible.

u-mos haw-o-lawm
Also *u-mot ha-o-lam.**
1. Literally, "the peoples of the world."
2. Gentiles.

um-zihst
Also spelled *umzist.*
1. Free.
2. Useless.

un a zawrg
Without a worry.

ungepotchket see *uhngepatshket*

un-ter-fihr-er
Also spelled *unterfirer.*
Escort at a wedding.

un-ter-koi-fen
1. Literally, "to buy from under."

---

a as in father; aw as in law; ai as in aisle; ei as in neighbor; e as in bet; i as in vaccine; ih as in tin; o as in solar; oi as in void; oo as in food; u as in put; uh as in but; ch as in chutzpa; zh as in Zhivago.

2. To bribe.

un-ter-shmeich-len
>To cater to someone, curry favor, fawn upon.

un-ter-shte shu-re
>Also *un-ter-shte shuruh.*
>1. Literally, "the bottom line."
>2. The essence.

un-ter-velt mentsh
>1. Literally, "underworld man."
>2. Racketeer.

ush-pi-zihn
>Also spelled *ushpizin.*
>1. Guest.
>2. Prayers said to welcome the patriarchs into the
>   *suka.*

utsn
>Also spelled *utzen.*
>To goad, needle.

a as in father; aw as in law; ai as in aisle; ei as in neighbor; e as in bet; i as in vaccine; ih as in tin; o as in solar; oi as in void; oo as in food; u as in put; uh as in but; ch as in chutzpa; zh as in Zhivago.

V

V'Adar see *VeAdar*

vai see *vei*

vaib
> Also spelled *veib*.
> Wife.

vai-ber-nihk
> Also spelled *veibernik*.
> 1. Literally, "womanizer."
> 2. Lady-killer, debauchee.

vai iz mir see *vei ihz mihr*

vainen see *veinen*

vainik see *veinihk*

vainik vos see *veinihk vaws*

vais
> Also spelled *weiss, veis*.
> White

vais-e ze-ke-lach
> Also spelled *weisse zekelach*.
> Literally, "white stockings," worn by some *chasidim*.

vais ich vos? see *veis ihch vaws?*

vais-e ze-ke-lach
> Also spelled *weisse zekelach*.
> Literally, "white stockings," worn by some Chasidim.

vaist vos? see *veist vaws?*

vaist zihch mihr ois
> It seems to me.

vaitr
> Also spelled *veiter*.

---

a as in father; aw as in law; ai as in aisle; ei as in neighbor; e as in bet; i as in vaccine; ih as in tin; o as in solar; oi as in void; oo as in food; u as in put; uh as in but; ch as in chutzpa; zh as in Zhivago.

1. Further.
2. Next.

vaizn
Also spelled *veizen*.
1. To show, display.
2. To point to.

vaksn vi a tzih-be-le
Grow like an onion.

val-ge-ren
Also spelled *volgeren*.
To roam, wander.

val-ger-en zihch
1. Literally, "roll oneself around."
2. To roam around aimlessly.
3. To be homeless.

val-ger-er
1. One who wanders about.
2. A homeless person.

va-ne
Also spelled *vaneh*.
1. Bath.
2. Bathtub.

vant
Wall.

vantz
1. A bedbug.
2. A nobody.

va-re-nih-kes
Also spelled *varenikes*.
Dumplings filled with jelly, fruit, or cheese.

var-en-ya
Preserves.

varfn an oig
Also spelled *varfen an oig*.
1. Literally, "to cast an eye."
2. Watch out for, guard.
3. Attract.

---

a as in father; aw as in law; ai as in aisle; ei as in neighbor; e as in bet; i as in vaccine; ih as in tin; o as in solar; oi as in void; oo as in food; u as in put; uh as in but; ch as in chutzpa; zh as in Zhivago.

var-nihsh-kes
Also spelled *varnishkes.*
1. Stuffed potato cakes.
2. Kasha with noodles.

vart a mih-nut
Also spelled *vart a minut.*
1. Wait a minute!
2. Hold on!

vartn
Also spelled *varten.*
Await, wait for.

vas failt zai? see *vuhs feilt zei*

vash tsih-mer
Also spelled *vash tzimmer.*
Washroom, bathroom.

vasr
Also spelled *vasser.*
Water.

vater see *fawtr*

vav see *vuhv*

vawch
Also spelled *voch.*
Week.

vaws hert zihch
1. Literally, "What is heard?"
2. What's new?

vay see *vei*

Ve-A-dar*
Also *Ve-A-dawr.*
Also spelled *V'Adar.*
Literally, "and (plus) Adar," the second Adar, an extra month added to the calendar on leap years in order to reconcile the lunar and solar calendars.
Also called *Adar Sheni,* meaning Adar II.

vechtr
Also spelled *vechter.*
A watchman, guard.

---

a as in father: aw as in law; ai as in aisle; ei as in neighbor: e as in bet; i as in vaccine: ih as in tin: o as in solar: oi as in void; oo as in food; u as in put; uh as in but; ch as in chutzpa; zh as in Zhivago.

veg
    Way, path, road.
vei
    Also spelled *vai, vay.*
    Woe, alas.
veib see *vaib*
veibernik see *vaibernihk*
vei ihz mihr
    Also spelled *vai iz mir.*
    Woe is me.
vei-nen
    Also spelled *vainen.*
    To cry, weep.
vei-nihk
    Also *vei-nihg.*
    Also spelled *vainik.*
    1. Few.
    2. A little.
vei-nihk vaws
    Also spelled *vainik vos.*
    Not enough.
veis see *vais*
veis ihch vaws
    Also spelled *vais ich vos*
    1. Literally, "I know not what."
    2. I couldn't care less.
veis vi kalch see *vais vi kalch*
veist vaws?
    Also spelled *vaist vos?*
    1. Literally, "Do you know what?"
    2. Who says?
    3. Stuff and nonsense!
veiter see *vaitr*
vei-tig
    Also *vei-tihk, vei-tuhg.*
    Ache, pain, hurt.
veizen see *vaizn*

---

a as in father; aw as in law; ai as in aisle; ei as in neighbor; e as in bet; i as in vaccine; ih as in tin; o as in solar; oi as in void; oo as in food; u as in put; uh as in but; ch as in chutzpa; zh as in Zhivago.

vekn
> Also spelled *veken.*
> Awaken.

vekr
> Also spelled *veker.*
> 1. Literally, "awaker."
> 2. Alarm clock.

vek-zeigr
> Also spelled *vekzaiger.*
> Alarm clock.

velt
> World.

vemn
> Also spelled *vemen.*
> Whom.

vemn nar-stu?
> Also spelled *vemen narstu?*
> 1. Literally, "Whom are you fooling?"
> 2. Whom are you kidding?

ven
> When.

ven ihch es, huhb ihch zei a-le ihn drerd
> Also spelled *ven ich es, hob ich zai alle in drerd.*
> 1. Literally, "When I am eating, they can all go to hell!"
> 2. Don't bother me when I'm eating!

ver der-har-get
> 1. Literally, "Get killed!"
> 2. Drop dead!

ver-en a teil
> Also spelled *veren a tail.*
> To be ruined.

verenikes see *varenihkes*

ver far-bluhn-jet
> Also spelled *ver farblunzhet.*
> 1. Literally, "Get lost!"
> 2. Leave me alone!

ver-fe-nyihf-kiht
Dead drunk.

ver veis?
Also spelled *ver vais?*
Who knows?

ver vuhlt daws ge-gleibt?
Also spelled *ver volt dos geglaibt?*
Literally, "Who would have believed it?"

vi
1. How.
2. As.

vi a barg
As (large) as a mountain.

vi a lawch ihn kuhp
Also spelled *vi a loch in kop.*
1. Literally, "like a hole in the head."
2. Something unnecessary.

vi a loong oon leibr oifn nawz
Also spelled *vi a lung un leber oifn noz.*
1. Literally, "like a lung and liver on my nose."
2. Like a useless thing.
3. Something uncalled for.

vi a toitn ban-kes see *(a) toitn bankes*

vi a-zoi?
How so? How come?

vidder see *vihdr*

Vi-dui
Also spelled *Viddui.*
The confession of sins made to God on Yom Kippur
and on the deathbed.

vifil see *vihfihl*

vi geit duhs ge-sheft?
Also spelled *vi gait dos gesheft?*
1. Literally, "How's business?"
2. How are things?

vi geit es aich?
Also spelled *vi gait es eich?*

---

a as in father; aw as in law; ai as in aisle; ei as in neighbor; e as in bet; i as in vaccine; ih as in tin; o as in solar; oi as in void; oo as in food; u as in put; uh as in but; ch as in chutzpa; zh as in Zhivago.

1. Literally, "How goes it with you?"
2. How are you?

vihdr
Also spelled *vidder*.
Again.

vi heist du?
Also spelled *vi haistu?*
1. Literally, "How are you called?"
2. What's your name?

vi heist duhs?
Also spelled *vi haist dos?*
Literally, "What is this called?"

vihfihl
Also *vi-fihl, vifl.*
Also spelled *vifil.*
1. How much?
2. How many?

vihld
Also spelled *vild.*
Wild, savage.

vihl-de cha-ye
Also spelled *vilde chaya.*
Wild animal.

vihldr mensh
Also spelled *vilder mentsh.*
Wild person, savage person.

vihl-stu?
Do you want? Do you want to?

vihs-en-dihk
Also spelled *vissendik.*
With foreknowledge, knowingly.

vihsh-ni-ak
Also spelled *wishniak, vishnik.*
Cherry brandy.

vihsn
Also spelled *vissen.*
1. Know.
2. Learn.

a as in father; aw as in law; ai as in aisle; ei as in neighbor; e as in bet; i as in vaccine; ih as in tin; o as in solar; oi as in void; oo as in food; u as in put; uh as in but; ch as in chutzpa; zh as in Zhivago.

vihtz
> Also spelled *vitz.*
> A joke, wisecrack.

vi-ku-ach
> 1. Controversy.
> 2. Debate.

vild see *vihld*

vilde chaya see *vihlde chaye*

vilder mentsh see *vihldr mensh*

vishnik see *vihshniak*

vissen see *vihsn*

vissendik see *vihsendihk*

vitz see *vihtz*

voch see *vawch*

vo den see *vuh den*

voi-ler yung
> Mischievous youth, roughneck.

volgeren see *valgeren*

vortshpiel see *vuhrtshpil*

vos see *vuhs*

vu?
> Where? In what place?

vuh den?
> Also spelled *vo den.*
> What else?

vu hihn geist du?
> Also spelled *vuhin gaistu?*
> Literally, "Where are you going?"

vuhrt-shpil
> Also spelled *vortshpiel.*
> 1. Literally, "word play, play on words."
> 2. A pun.
> 3. A witticism.

vuhs?
> Also spelled *vos.*
> What?

a as in father; aw as in law; ai as in aisle; ei as in neighbor; e as in bet; i as in vaccine; ih as in tin; o as in solar; oi as in void; oo as in food; u as in put; uh as in but; ch as in chutzpa; zh as in Zhivago.

vuhs bai a nihch-te-ren oifn lung, ihz bai a shihk-er-en oifn tsung
Also spelled *vos bei a nichteren oifn lung, iz bei a shikkeren oifn tzung.*
Literally, "What a sober person has on the lung (mind), a drunk has on the tongue."

vuhs far a me-chutn bihn ihch dihr?
Also spelled *vos far a mechutan bin ich dir?*
1. Literally, "What kind of an in-law am I to you?"
2. What am I to you, anyway?

vuhs feilt zei
Also spelled *vas failt zai?*
1. What are they lacking?
2. What do they want?

vuhs gihchr als besr
Also spelled *vos gicher altz besser.*
Literally, "the quicker the better."

vuhs hakst du mihr ihn kuhp
Also spelled *vos hakst du mir in kop?*
1. Literally, "For what are you chopping my head off?"
2. Why are you talking me to death?

vuhs heist es?
Also spelled *vos haist es?*
What is it called? What's its name?

vuhs hert zihch?
Also spelled *vos hert zich?*
1. Literally, "What is heard?"
2. What's new?

vuhs hert zihch ep-es nai-es?
Also spelled *vos hert zich epes neies?*
1. Literally, "What of something new is heard?"
2. What's new?

vuhs huhb ihch duhs ge-darft?
Also spelled *vos hob ich dos gedarft?*
Literally, "For what did I need that?"

vuhs ihn der kuhrt
Also spelled *vos in der kort.*

1. Literally, "whatever is in the cards."
2. Whatever fate brings.

vuhs ihz?
Also spelled *vos iz?*
1. Literally, "What is?"
2. What's the matter?

vuhs ihz der chih-lek?
Also spelled *vos iz der chilek?*
Literally, "What's the difference?"

vuhs ihz der tach-lihs?
Also spelled *vos iz der tachlis?*
1. Literally, "What is the purpose?"
2. To what does it lead?
3. What's the end result?

vuhs ihz di chawch-me?
Also spelled *vos iz di chochma?*
1. What's the rationale (joke)?
2. What's the trick?
3. What's so clever?

vuhs ihz di un-ter-shte shu-re?
Also spelled *vos iz di untershte shure?*
1. Literally, "What is the bottom line?"
2. What's the point?
3. What's the end result?

vuhs ihz miht dihr?
Also spelled *vos iz mit dir?*
Literally, "What's wrong with you?"

vuhs ihz oifn kuhp ihz oifn tsung
Also spelled *vos iz oifen kop iz oifen tzung.*
1. Literally, "Whatever is on the head (mind) is on the tongue."
2. A talkative person.
3. An uninhibited person.
4. One who can't keep a thing to him/herself.

vuhs ihz oifn lung ihz oifn tsung
Also spelled *vos iz oifen lung iz oifen tzung.*
1. Literally, "Whatever is on the lung is on the tongue."
2. One who can't keep a thing to him/herself.

---

a as in father; aw as in law; ai as in aisle: ei as in neighbor; e as in bet; i as in vaccine; ih as in tin; o as in solar; oi as in void; oo as in food; u as in put; uh as in but; ch as in chutzpa; zh as in Zhivago.

vuhs kuhcht zihch ihn tepl?
Also spelled *vos kocht in teppel?*
1. Literally, "What's cooking in the pot?"
2. What's new?
3. What's happening?

vuhs macht duhs oif?
Also spelled *vos macht dos ois?*
What difference does it make?

vuhs macht duhs ois?
Also spelled *vos macht dos ois?*
What difference does it make?

vuhs macht ihr?
Also *vuhs machst du?*
1. How do you feel?
2. How do you do?

vuhs meint es?
Also spelled *vos maint es?*
What does it mean?

vuhs nawch?
Also spelled *vos noch?*
1. What else?
2. What then?
3. What further?

vuhs ret ihr e-pes?
Also spelled *vos ret ir epes?*
What are you talking about anyway?

vuhs rets du?
Also spelled *vos redstu?*
1. Literally, "What are you saying?"
2. What are you talking about?
3. No kidding?

vuhs tut zihch duh?
Also spelled *vos tut zich do?*
What's going on here?

vuhs vet zain?
Also spelled *vos vet zein?*
1. Literally, "What will be?"
2. What will happen?

---

a as in father: aw as in law; ai as in aisle; ei as in neighbor; e as in bet; i as in vaccine; ih as in tin; o as in solar; oi as in void; oo as in food; u as in put; uh as in but; ch as in chutzpa; zh as in Zhivago.

vuhs vet zain, vet zain
> Also spelled *vos vet zein, vet zein.*
> Literally, "What will be, will be."

vuhs zawgt ihr?
> Also spelled *vos zogt ir?*
> 1. Literally, "What are you saying?"
> 2. What do you mean?
> 3. You don't mean it!

vuhv
> Also *vav.**
> The sixth letter of the Hebrew alphabet, corresponding in sound to "v."

vund
> Wound

vursht
> Also spelled *wurst.*
> 1. Delicatessen.
> 2. Salami.
> 3. Sausage.

vu tut dihr vei?
> Also spelled *vu tut dir vai?*
> Where does it hurt you?

---

a as in father; aw as in law; ai as in aisle; ei as in neighbor; e as in bet; i as in vaccine; ih as in tin; o as in solar; oi as in void; oo as in food; u as in put; uh as in but; ch as in chutzpa; zh as in Zhivago.

W

weiss see *vais*
weisse zekelach see *vaise zekelach*
wishniak see *vihshniak*
wurst see *vursht*

Y

Ya-a-le V'ya-vo*

Also *Ya-a-le V'yaw-vo.*

1. Literally, "May our hopes and prayers go up (before God)."
2. A prayer inserted in the *Amidah* and in the Grace After Meals on holidays and New Moons.

yach-ne

Also *yach-na, yach-nuh.*

1. A strident, blabbermouth woman.
2. A gossip.

yach-sen

Also *yach-suhn, yach-san.**

1. A person of distinguished lineage.
2. Privileged character.

yad see *yawd*

Yad Va-shem*

Also *Yad Vaw-sheim.*

1. Literally, "a monument and a name" (Isaiah 56:5).
2. The State of Israel's Martyrs' and Heroes' Remembrance Authority.
3. A memorial museum of the Holocaust in Jerusalem.

yahrzeit see *yartsait*

yahrzeit licht see *yartsait lihcht*

Yahud

In the Koran, a name used contemptuously by Muhammed for Jews of his age.

Yahve

Also spelled *Yahwe, YHVH.*

The equivalent of Jehovah (God).

yam see *yuhm*

Yamin Noraim see *Yawmihm Norawihm*

---

a as in father; aw as in law; ai as in aisle; ei as in neighbor; e as in bet; i as in vaccine; ih as in tin; o as in solar; oi as in void; oo as in food; u as in put; uh as in but; ch as in chutzpa; zh as in Zhivago.

yar-muhl-ke
Also spelled *yamulke, yarmulka, yarmulke.*
A skullcap, worn by Orthodox and Conservative Jewish men at prayer, and at all times by observant Orthodox males.

yar-tsait
Also spelled *yahrtzeit, yohrtzeit, yortzeit, yartzeit, yahrzeit, jahrzeit.*
1. Literally, "year's time."
2. The anniversary of a death, observed by the lighting of a memorial lamp for twenty-four hours.

yar-tsait lihcht
Also spelled *yahrzeit licht.*
1. Literally, "annual light."
2. The memorial candle lit on the anniversary of a person's death and on the eve of the Day of Atonement.

yasher koi-ach
1. Literally, "May your strength increase!"
2. Congratulations!

ya-te-be-dam
1. A blusterer.
2. An intimidator.
3. A self-designated bigshot.

yatom see *yuhsuhm*

yawd
Also *yud, yad.**
Also spelled *yod.*
The tenth letter of the Hebrew alphabet, corresponding in sound to the letter "y."

yawgn
Also spelled *yogen.*
1. To hurry.
2. To chase.
3. To speed.

Yaw-mihm No-raw-ihm
Also *Ya-mihm No-ra-ihm.**

Also spelled *Yamim Noraim* and *Yomim Noraim.*
1. Literally, "Days of Awe."
2. The ten-day Jewish High Holy Day period, beginning with Rosh Hashanah and ending with
Yom Kippur.

yawr
Also spelled *jahr, yor.*
Year.

(a) yawr miht a miht-vawch
Also spelled *a yor mit a mitvoch.*
1. Literally, "a year plus a Wednesday."
2. A long, long time.

yawsom see *yuhsuhm*

ya-yihn ne-sech
Nonkosher wine.

y'dies see *yediuhs*

ye-der
Also *yeidr.*
Every, each.

yeder mentsh hot zein aigene meshugaas see *yeidr
mensh hawt zain eigene m'shugaas*

yediot see *yediuhs*

Ye-di-ot Ach-ro-not*
Also *Ye-di-os Ach-ro-nos.*
1. Literally, "last news."
2. The name of a daily afternoon Hebrew newspaper in Israel.

ye-di-uhs
Also *ye-di-ot,* y'di-es.*
1. News.
2. Announcements.

yefaifia see *y'feifiya*

Ye-hoo-di
Also spelled *Yehudi.*
1. A citizen of Judah in Bible days.
2. A Jew, a person born of a Jewish mother.
3. A person converted to Judaism.

---

a as in father; aw as in law; ai as in aisle ei as in neighbor; e as in bet; i as in vaccine; ih as in tin; o as in
solar; oi as in void; oo as in food; u as in put; uh as in but; ch as in chutzpa; zh as in Zhivago.

Yehudi see *Yehoodi*

yeidr see *yeder*

yeidr mensh hawt zain ei-ge-ne m'shu-ga-as
Also spelled *yeder mentsh hot zein aigene mesh-ugaas.*
Literally, "Every person has his own idiosyncrasies."

Yeishoo
Also spelled *Yeshu.*
Jesus.

yeitsr haw-raw
Also *yei-tser ha-ra*.*
Also spelled *yetzer hara.*
1. Literally, "evil inclination."
2. A negative impulse, a compulsion.

yeitsr tov
Also spelled *yetzer tov.*
The good inclination in man.

ye-ke
Also spelled *yekke.*
1. A Jew from Germany.
2. A "greenhorn" in Israel.

ye-nemz
1. Literally, "the other's."
2. Belonging to another person.

ye-ne velt
1. Literally, "the other world."
2. The world-to-come.

yenta see *yentuh*

yen-tuh
Also spelled *yenta, yente.*
A blabbermouth, a gossipy woman. A distortion of the Spanish name Juanita or, more likely, of the French name Gentille.

yentz
1. To fornicate, copulate.
2. To swindle, defraud.

---

a as in father; aw as in law; ai as in aisle; ei as in neighbor; e as in bet; i as in vaccine; ih as in tin; o as in solar; oi as in void; oo as in food; u as in put; uh as in but; ch as in chutzpa; zh as in Zhivago.

yentz-er
1. A promiscuous person.
2. A crook, swindler.

Ye-roo-shaw-la-yihm
Also *Ye-ru-sha-la-yihm.**
Also spelled *Y'rushawlayim.*
1. Literally, "city of peace."
2. Jerusalem.

Yerushalayihm see *Yerooshawlayihm*

ye-shihv-uh buhchr
Also spelled *yeshivah bawcher, yeshiva bocher.*
1. Literally "*yeshiva* youth."
2. A parochial school student.
3. A student at a Talmudic academy.

yeshiva see *y'shivuh*

yeshivot
Plural of *yeshiva.*

Yeshu see *Yeishoo*

ye-shuv-nihk
Also spelled *yeshuvnik.*
1. A farmer, a rustic.
2. An uncouth person.

yetzer hara see *yeitzr hawraw*

yetzer tov see *yeitsr tov*

yetzt see *ihtst*

y'fei-fi-ya*
Also *y'fei-fi-yaw.*
Also spelled *yefaifia.*
A beautiful woman, a belle.

yi-boom*
Also spelled *yibum.*
1. A Levirate marriage.
2. In the Bible, the obligation of a dead man's brother to marry the widow if there are no sons (Deuteronomy 25:5-10).

yiches see *yihchus*

---

a as in father; aw as in law; ai as in aisle: ei as in neighbor; e as in bet; i as in vaccine; ih as in tin; o as in solar; oi as in void; oo as in food; u as in put; uh as in but; ch as in chutzpa; zh as in Zhivago.

yi-chud*
Also spelled *yihud.*
1. Literally, "union."
2. The consumation of a marriage.
3. The mystical concept of Divine union.

yichus see *yihchuhs*

Yid see *Yihd*

Yidden see *Yidn*

Yiddene see *Yihdene*

Yiddish see *Yihdihsh*

Yidn
Also spelled *Yidden.*
Plural of *Yid.*

yigdal see *yihgdal*

yih-chuhs
Also *yi-chus.**
Also spelled *yiches.*
1. Lineage, pedigree, ancestry.
2. Status (achieved through scholarship, money or family).

Yihd
Also spelled *Yid.*
A male Jew.

Yihd-e-ne
Also spelled *Yiddene.*
A female Jew.

Yihd-ihsh
Also spelled *Yiddish.*
1. Literally, "Jewish."
2. The mother-tongue of Ashkenazic (East European) Jews and their descendants in other countries, derived from approximately 75 percent medieval High German and 25 percent Hebrew and written in Hebrew characters.

Yihg-dal
Also spelled *Yigdal.*
1. Literally, "May He be magnified."

---

a as in father; aw as in law; ai as in aisle; ei as in neighbor; e as in bet; i as in vaccine; ih as in tin; o as in solar; oi as in void; oo as in food; u as in put; uh as in but; ch as in chutzpa; zh as in Zhivago.

2. The title and opening words of a Hebrew hymn embodying Maimonides' Thirteen Articles of Faith. Attributed to Daniel ben Judah of early fourteenth-century Rome.

yihn-ge-le
Also spelled *yingele.*
A pet form of *yihngl.*

yihngl
Also spelled *yingel.*
Young boy.

yihr-as shaw-ma-yihm
Also *yihr-at sha-ma-yihm.**
Also spelled *yirat shamayim.*
1. Literally, "the fear of heaven."
2. Fear of God.
3. According to Psalm 111:10, the beginning of wisdom.

yihs-ga-dal v'yihs-ka-dash
Also *yiht-ga-dal v'yiht-ka-dash.**
Also spelled *yitgadal v'yitkadash.*
1. Literally, "May [God's great Name] be extolled and hallowed."
2. The opening words of the *Kaddish* prayer.

Yihs-raw-eil
Also *Yihs-ra-el.**
Also spelled *Yisroel, Yisrael*
1. Israel.
2. Another name for the biblical Jacob (Genesis 32:29)
3. A name for the Jewish people.
4. The state created in 1948.

yihud see *yichud*

Yihz-kuhr
Also *Yihz-kor.**
Also spelled *Yizkor.*
1. Literally, "May He remember."
2. The opening of the memorial prayer recited at the service for the dead held on Yom Kippur and

on the concluding days of Passover, Shavuot, and Sukkot.

yi-mach sh'mo
Literally, "May his name be erased." An epithet added when the name of an enemy of Jews is mentioned.

yingel see *yihngl*

yingele see *yihngele*

yirat shamayim see *yihras shawmayihm*

yi-shuv
1. Literally, "settlement."
2. The name of the Jewish community in Israel before the proclamation of the State in 1948.

yi-shuv ba-a-retz*
The religious obligation of residing in Israel.

yi-shuv-nihk
Also spelled *yishuvnik.*
One who lives on a *yishuv* in Israel.

Yisrael see *Yihsraweil*

yitgadal v'yitkadash see *yihsgadal v'yihskadash*

Yizkor see *Yihzkuhr*

yo see *yuh*

yod see *yawd*

yogen see *yawgn*

yohrtzeit see *yartsait*

yoich
Soup.

yoishr
Also *yo-sher.**
Also spelled *yoi-sher.*
Justice, fairness, integrity.

yoiveil see *yoveil*

yold see *yuhld*

yom
Day.

---

a as in father; aw as in law; ai as in aisle; ei as in neighbor; e as in bet; i as in vaccine; ih as in tin; o as in solar; oi as in void; oo as in food; u as in put; uh as in but; ch as in chutzpa; zh as in Zhivago.

Yom ha-Atz-ma-ut*
Also *Yom haw-Atz-maw-oos.*
Israel Independence Day, observed on the fifth day
of Iyar.

Yom ha-Dihn
Also spelled *Yom ha-Din.*
1. Literally, "judgment day."
2. Yom Kippur, the Day of Atonement.

Yom ha-Sho-a*
Also *Yom ha-Sho-aw.*
Literally, "Holocaust Day," observed on the twen-
ty-seventh day of Nisan as a memorial to the six
million Jews who perished during the Nazi era.

Yom ha-Zi-kaw-ron
Also *Yom ha-Zi-ka-ron.**
1. Literally, "day of remembrance."
2. Rosh Hashanah, the Jewish New Year.

Yomim Noraim see *Yawmihm Norawihm*

Yom Kihpr
Also *Yom Ki-poor.**
Also spelled *Yom Kippur.*
Literally, "Day of Atonement," observed on the
tenth day of Tishri as a day of fasting and prayer.

Yom Kippur see *Yom Kihpr*

Yom Te-roo-a*
Also *Yom Te-roo-aw.*
Also spelled *Yom Teruah.*
Literally, "a day of sounding the *shofar*," one of the
designations for Rosh Hashanah used in the litur-
gy.

yom tov*
1. Literally, "good day."
2. Synonym for Jewish holiday.

Yom Ye-ru-sha-la-yihm*
Also *Yom Ye-roo-shaw-law-yihm.*
Literally, "Jerusalem Day," observed on the twen-
ty-eighth of the month of Iyar in commemoration
of the unification of Jerusalem in 1967.

---

a as in father; aw as in law; ai as in aisle: ei as in neighbor; e as in bet; i as in vaccine; ih as in tin; o as in
solar; oi as in void; oo as in food; u as in put; uh as in but; ch as in chutzpa; zh as in Zhivago.

yontif see *yuhntihf*

yontifdik see *yuhntihfdihk*

yor see *yawr*

(a) yor mit a mitvoch see *(a) yawr miht a mihtvawch*

yortzeit see *yartsait*

yosher see *yoishr*

yo-tzeir
> Also *yo-tzer.**
> 1. Literally, "creation."
> 2. A prayer in the morning service lauding God as the Creator.
> *Yotzrot* is the plural form.

yo-veil*
> Also *yoi-veil, yoivl.*
> Also spelled *yovel.*
> 1. Literally, "jubilee."
> 2. Jubilation, gaiety, merriment.
> 3. In the Bible, a celebration every fiftieth year in which all lands were returned to the original owners.

Y'ru-shaw-la-yim see *Yerooshawlayihm*

y'shi-vuh
> Also *ye-shi-va,** *ye-shi-vaw.*
> Also spelled *yeshibah, yeshivah.*
> 1. Literally, "a sitting place."
> 2. An academy of Jewish learning for elementary, secondary, or higher learning.
> 3. A parochial school.

yud see *yawd*

yuh
> Also spelled *yo.*
> Yes, affirmative.

yuhkl
> Also *yu-kel.*
> A buffoon.

yuhld
> Also spelled *yold.*

---

a as in father; aw as in law; ai as in aisle; ei as in neighbor; e as in bet; i as in vaccine; ih as in tin; o as in solar; oi as in void; oo as in food; u as in put; uh as in but; ch as in chutzpa; zh as in Zhivago.

1. A dope.
2. A boor.
3. A chump.

yuhm
Also spelled *yam.**
Sea, ocean.

yuhn-tihf see *yom tov*

yuhn-tihf-dihk
Also spelled *yontifdik.*
1. In a holiday mood.
2. Jovial.

Yuhsh-ke
Jesus.

yuh-suhm
Also *yaw-som, ya-tom.**
Orphan.

yukel see *yuhkl*

yung
1. Young.
2. Youth.

yun-gatsh
1. A coarse person.
2. Street urchin, brat, young rogue.

yun-ger-man-tshihk
1. A young, vigorous lad.
2. A newlywed.

(a) yung miht beinr
Also spelled *(a) yung mit bainer.*
1. Literally, "a lad with (sturdy) bones."
2. A strongly-built person.

Z

zach
A thing.

zaddik see *tsadihk*

zaft
Juice.

zaf-tihk
Also *zaf-tihg*.
Also spelled *zaftik, zaftig, zoftik, zoftig, saftig*.
1. Literally, "juicy, succulent."
2. Shapely, full-bodied, referring to the female figure.

zai a-zoi gut
Also spelled *zei azoi gut*.
1. Literally, "Be so good (as to . . .)!"
2. Please!

zaicher see *zeicher*

zaide see *zeiduh*

zaier see *zeir*

zaiger see *zeigr*

zai ge-zunt
Also spelled *zei gezunt*.
1. Literally, "Be well!"
2. Sometimes said in place of goodbye.

zai mihr frei-lach
Also spelled *zei mir frailech*.
Be happy!

zai mihr ge-zunt
Also spelled *zei mir gezunt*.
Literally, "Be healthy!" with the implication "and leave me alone!"

---

a as in father; aw as in law; ai as in aisle; ei as in neighbor; e as in bet; i as in vaccine; ih as in tin; o as in solar; oi as in void; oo as in food; u as in put; uh as in but; ch as in chutzpa; zh as in Zhivago.

zai mihr moichl
> Also spelled *zei mir moichel.*
> Pardon me. Excuse me.

zain
> To be.

zai niht a nar
> Also spelled *zei nit a nar.*
> Don't be a fool!

zai niht a vai-zaw-suh
> Also spelled *zei nit a vayzoso.*
> 1. Literally, "Don't be a Vaizata!" Vaizata is Haman's youngest son in the story of Purim.
> 2. Don't be an idiot!

zai niht kein goi-lem
> Also spelled *zei nit kain golem.*
> 1. Literally, "Don't be a robot!"
> 2. Don't be a dummy!

zai zihch mat-ri-ach . . .
> Also spelled *zei zich matriach . . .*
> 1. Take the trouble to. . .
> 2. Be so kind as to . . .

zak
> A sack, a bag.

zakain see *zawkein*

zalaven see *zhalevn*

zaltz
> Salt.

zawgn
> Also spelled *zogen.*
> 1. To say.
> 2. To tell.

zawgn a lihgn
> Also spelled *zogen a ligen.*
> To tell a lie.

zawgn a pawr ver-ter
> Also spelled *zogen a por verter.*
> 1. To say a few words.
> 2. To make a brief speech.

---

a as in father; aw as in law; ai as in aisle; ei as in neighbor; e as in bet; i as in vaccine; ih as in tin; o as in solar; oi as in void; oo as in food; u as in put; uh as in but; ch as in chutzpa; zh as in Zhivago.

zaw-guhr-ke
Also spelled *zogerke*.
1. Literally, "a female communicator."
2. The woman who led prayers in the section of Orthodox synagogues reserved for ladies, particularly in pre-World War II Eastern Europe.

zaw-kein
Also *za-kein, za-ken.**
Also spelled *zakain*.
Old man.

zawl
Also spelled *zol*.
1. Should.
2. May.
3. Let.

zawl dihch chapn baim boich
Also spelled *zol dich chapen beim boich*.
You should get a stomach cramp!

zawl dihr grih-men ihn boich
May you get a cramp in your stomach!

zawl dihr klapn ihn kuhp
Also spelled *zol dir klappen in kop*.
It should bang in your head (that which is annoying me)!

zawl er tsu-brechn a fus
Also spelled *zol er tsebrechen a fus*.
May he break a leg!

zawl es bren-en
Also spelled *zol es brenen*.
1. Let it burn!
2. The hell with it!

zawl Gawt mihr helfn
Also spelled *zol Gott mir helfen*.
May God help me!

zawl Gawt uhp-hihtn
Also spelled *zol Gott ophiten*.
May God prevent (it)!

---

a as in father; aw as in law; ai as in aisle; ei as in neighbor; e as in bet; i as in vaccine; ih as in tin; o as in solar; oi as in void; oo as in food; u as in put; uh as in but; ch as in chutzpa; zh as in Zhivago.

zawl ihch a-zol vihsn fun tsuh-res
Also spelled *zol ich azoi vissen fun tsores.*
1. Literally, "I should so know from trouble (as I know about this matter)."
2. I haven't the faintest idea.

zawlst du a-zoi leibn
Also spelled *zolstu azoi leben.*
Literally, "You should live so (long)!"

zawlst ge-shvawln ve-ren vi a barg
Also spelled *zolst geshvollen veren vi a barg.*
Literally, "May you swell up (as big) as a mountain!"

zawlst leibn oon zain ge-zunt
Also spelled *zolst leben un zein gezunt.*
Literally, "May you live and be well!"

zawlst lihgn ihn der erd
Also spelled *zolst ligen in drerd.*
1. Literally, "You should lay in the earth!"
2. Drop dead!

zawlst niht vihsn fun kein shlechtz
Also spelled *zolst nit vissen fun kain shlechts.*
Literally, "You shouldn't know from anything bad!"

zawl vaksn tsih-be-les fun pu-pihk
Also spelled *zol vaksen tzibeles fun pupik.*
Literally, "May onions sprout from your navel."

zawl zain
Also spelled *zol zein*
1. Literally, "Let it be!"
2. That's it!

zawl zain a-zoi
Also spelled *zol zein azoi.*
1. Literally, "Let it be so!"
2. O.K.

zawl zain ge-zunt
Also spelled *zol zein gezunt.*
Let everything (everyone) be well!

---

a as in father; aw as in law; ai as in aisle; ei as in neighbor; e as in bet; i as in vaccine; ih as in tin; o as in solar; oi as in void; oo as in food; u as in put; uh as in but; ch as in chutzpa; zh as in Zhivago.

zawl zain miht glihk
Also spelled *zol zein mit glik.*
1. Literally, "Let it be with luck."
2. May you have luck!
3. May your new venture be successful!

zawl zain sha
1. Literally, "Let there be silence!"
2. Keep quiet!

zawl zain shtihl
1. Literally, "Let there be quiet!"
2. Keep still!

zawrgn
Also spelled *zorgen.*
To worry, be concerned, care about.

zawrg zihch niht
Also spelled *zorg zich nit.*
Don't worry!

zayde see *zeiduh*

za-yihn
Also spelled *zayin.*
The seventh letter of the Hebrew alphabet, corresponding in sound to "z."

z'chus aw-vos
Also *ze-chut a-vot.* *
Literally, "merit of the fathers." According to tradition, the good deeds of the patriarchs—Abraham, Isaac, and Jacob—win favor for their descendants.

zecher see *zeicher*

ze-chus
Also *ze-chut,* * *z'chus.*
Merit.

zechut avot see *z'chus awvos*

zeh nor see *zei nawr*

zei azoi gut see *zai azoi gut*

zei-cher li-tsi-as Mihtz-ra-yihm
Also *ze-cher li-ye-tzi-at Mihtz-ra-yihm.* *
Also spelled *zaicher litzias Mitzraim.*

---

a as in father; **aw** as in law; **ai** as in aisle; **ei** as in neighbor; **e** as in bet; **i** as in vaccine; **ih** as in tin; **o** as in solar; **oi** as in void; **oo** as in food; **u** as in put; **uh** as in but; **ch** as in chutzpa; **zh** as in Zhivago.

Literally, "in remembrance of the Exodus from Egypt," a phrase that is part of the *Kiddush* recited on the Sabbath and holidays.

zei-chr tza-dihk lihv-raw-chaw
Also *zeicher tzadihk livracha.**
Also spelled *zecher tzaddik livrachah.*
Literally, "The memory of the righteous is a blessing!"

zeide see *zeiduh*

zei-duh
Also spelled *zaide, zeide, zayde.*
Grandfather.

zeien see *zein*

zeigel see *zeigl*

zei-ge-lach
1. Teeth.
2. Serrated edges.

zei gezunt see *zai gezunt*

zeigr
Also spelled *zeiger, zaiger.*
1. A watch.
2. A clock.

zei-lihg
Also spelled *zelig.*
A contraction of *zichrono livracha,* "May his memory be blessed."

zei mir see *zai mihr*

zein
Also *zei-en.*
1. To look.
2. To see.

zei nawr
Also spelled *zeh nor.*
1. Literally, "Just see!"
2. Look here!
3. Well! Well!

zei nit see *zai niht*

---

a as in father; aw as in law; ai as in aisle; ei as in neighbor; e as in bet; i as in vaccine; ih as in tin; o as in solar; oi as in void; oo as in food; u as in put; uh as in but; ch as in chutzpa; zh as in Zhivago.

zeir
> Also spelled *zaier*.
> 1. Very.
> 2. Much too much.

zeir gut
> Also spelled *zaier gut*.
> 1. Literally, "very good."
> 2. O.K.

zeir shein ge-zuhgt
> Also spelled *zaier shain gezogt*.
> 1. Literally, "very beautifully stated."
> 2. Well said!

zei zich matriach see *zai zihch matriach*

zek
> Plural of *zak*. See above.

zekeinaw see *z'keine*

zelig see *zeilihg*

zel-ten-kait
> Also spelled *zeltenkeit*.
> Exception, rarity.

zeman matan Torateinu see *z'man matan Toraw-seinu*

zemel see *zeml*

ze-mer
> The singular of *zemirot*. See below.

zemirot see *zmiruhs*

zeml
> Also spelled *zemel, zemmel*.
> A crusty roll, soft on the inside.

ze-ro-a*
> Also *z'ro-a*.
> 1. The wing or neck of fowl.
> 2. The shankbone placed on the *Seder* tray.

zetst zihch a-vek
> Also spelled *zetzt zich avek*.
> Please be seated.

---

a as in father: aw as in law; ai as in aisle; ei as in neighbor; e as in bet; i as in vaccine; ih as in tin; o as in solar; oi as in void; oo as in food; u as in put; uh as in but; ch as in chutzpa; zh as in Zhivago.

zetz
> Punch, bang, hit, slam.

zetzen see *zetzn*

(a) zetz in erd
> Also *a zetz in drerd.*
> 1. Literally, "a knock in the ground."
> 2. A useless action.
> 3. A futile motion.

zetzn
> Also spelled *zetzen.*
> 1. To hit.
> 2. To place, to seat.
> 3. Sexual intercourse.

zetzt zich avek see *zetst zihch avek*

zha-levn
> Also *zal-a-ven.*
> Also spelled *zhaleven.*
> 1. Sparing.
> 2. Miserly.

zhluhb
> Also spelled *zhlob, shluhb, zhlawb.*
> 1. A coarse person.
> 2. A slob.

zhu-lihk
> Also spelled *zhulik.*
> Faker, scoundrel.

zhu-met mihr ihn kup
> A buzzing in one's head.

zhu-pe-tze
> A robe worn by *Chasidim.*

zi
> She.

zihch-ro-nos
> Also *zihch-ro-not.* *
> Also spelled *zichronot.*
> 1. Literally, "memories."
> 2. A portion of the Rosh Hashanah *musaf* service.

---

a as in father; aw as in law; ai as in aisle; ei as in neighbor; e as in bet; i as in vaccine; ih as in tin; o as in solar; oi as in void; oo as in food; u as in put; uh as in but; ch as in chutzpa; zh as in Zhivago.

zihn-dihk niht
Also spelled *zindik nit.*
1. Don't sin.
2. Don't complain.
3. Don't tempt fate.

zihn-en
Also spelled *zinnen.*
1. Mind.
2. Senses.

zihs
Also spelled *zis.*
Sweet.

zih-se ne-shuh-me
Also spelled *zisse neshama.*
1. Literally, "sweet soul."
2. A sweet person.
3. A saintly person.

zihs-kait
Also spelled *ziskeit.*
1. Sweetness.
2. A sweet thing.
3. A term of endearment, especially for a child.

zihts-fleish
Also spelled *zitsflaish.*
1. Literally, "sitting flesh."
2. Patience.

zihtzen oif shpihl-kes
Also spelled *zitzen oif shpilkes.*
1. To sit on pins and needles.
2. To be nervous about a situation.

zihtzn shih-vuh
Also spelled *zitzen shiva.*
1. Literally, "to sit seven," to stay in one's home for seven days of mourning following the death of an immediate relative.
2. To mourn.

zindik nit see *zihndihk niht*

---

a as in father; aw as in law; ai as in aisle; ei as in neighbor; e as in bet; i as in vaccine; ih as in tin; o as in solar; oi as in void; oo as in food; u as in put; uh as in but; ch as in chutzpa; zh as in Zhivago.

zingn
>Also spelled *zingen.*
>To sing.

zinnen see *zihnen*

Zion see *Tziyon*

zis see *zihs*

ziskeit see *zihskait*

zisse see *zihse neshuhme*

zitzen oif shiplkes see *zihtzn oif shpihlkes*

zizit see *tzihtzit*

z'kein-e
>Also *ze-kei-naw, ze-kei-na.**
>Old woman.

z'man ma-tan To-raw-sei-nu
>Also *ze-man ma-tan To-ra-tei-nu.**
>1. Literally, "the season of the giving of our Torah."
>2. The festival of Shavuot.

z'mirot see *zmiruhs*

zmi-ruhs
>Also *zmi-ros, ze-mi-rot, z'mi-rot.**
>1. Literally, "melodies."
>2. Sabbath table songs.

zoftig see *zaftihk*

zogen see *zawgn*

zogerke see *zawguhrke*

Zo-har
>1. Literally, "brightness."
>2. A commentary on the Pentateuch, the principal source of Jewish mysticism.

zoier zaltz
>1. Sour salt.
>2. Citric acid.

zoi-nuh
>Also *zo-naw, zo-na.**
>A prostitute.

---

a as in father; aw as in law; ai as in aisle: ei as in neighbor; e as in bet; i as in vaccine; ih as in tin; o as in solar; oi as in void; oo as in food; u as in put; uh as in but; ch as in chutzpa; zh as in Zhivago.

zol see *zawl*
zolst see *zawlst*
Zom Gedalia see *Tzom Gedalyuh*
zona see *zoinuh*
zorg zich nit see *zawrg zihch niht*
zorgen see *zawrgn*
z'roa see *zeroa*
zun
  1. The sun.
  2. A son.
zun-ihn-ke
  Also spelled *zuninke.*
  Little son, darling son.
zuz
  The singular of *zuzim.* See below.
zuzim
  Babylonian coins referred to in the Passover song *Chad Gadya,* "One Only Kid."
zweiback see *tsvibak*